RAW GENERALS AND GREEN SOLDIERS

Catholic Armies in Ireland 1641–1643

Pádraig Lenihan

'This is the Century of the Soldier', Fulvio Testi, Poet, 1641

HELION & COMPANY

Helion & Company Limited
Unit 8 Amherst Business Centre
Budbrooke Road
Warwick
CV34 5WE
England
Tel. 01926 499 619
Email: info@helion.co.uk
Website: www.helion.co.uk
Twitter: @helionbooks
Visit our blog http://blog.helion.co.uk/

Published by Helion & Company 2023
Designed and typeset by Mary Woolley, Battlefield Design (www.battlefield-design.co.uk)
Cover designed by Paul Hewitt, Battlefield Design (www.battlefield-design.co.uk)

Text © Pádraig Lenihan 2023
Illustrations and maps as individually credited
Colour artwork by Seán Ó Brógain © Helion & Company 2023

Every reasonable effort has been made to trace copyright holders and to obtain their permission for the use of copyright material. The author and publisher apologize for any errors or omissions in this work and would be grateful if notified of any corrections that should be incorporated in future reprints or editions of this book.

ISBN 978-1-804511-94-7

British Library Cataloguing-in-Publication Data.
A catalogue record for this book is available from the British Library.

All rights reserved. No part of this publication may be reproduced, stored in a retrieval system, or transmitted, in any form, or by any means, electronic, mechanical, photocopying, recording or otherwise, without the express written consent of Helion & Company Limited.

For details of other military history titles published by Helion & Company Limited contact the above address or visit our website: http://www.helion.co.uk.

We always welcome receiving book proposals from prospective authors.

Contents

Acknowledgements ... iv
Glossary of Terms ... v
Author's Note ... vii
Introduction ... ix

1 Winter 1641–1642 ... 15
2 Summer and Autumn 1642 ... 56
3 Winter 1642–1643 ... 96
4 Summer 1643 ... 123
Conclusion ... 147

Colour Plate Commentaries ... 152
Bibliography ... 155

Acknowledgements

There are so many people I want to thank. Charles Singleton of Helion & Company encouraged me to revisit 1640s Ireland. The staff of the Bodleian Libraries, Oxford, and Marie Boran, Margaret Hughes, Kieran Hoare and Geraldine Curtin of the Hardiman Library, University of Galway, were all very helpful. Thanks to The National Archives, United Kingdom, to the Rijksmuseum, Amsterdam, and to the *Bibliothèque nationale de France* for providing digital images. Not to forget my children and their spouses, Donncha, Megan, Manus, Deirdre, Cora and Síle. Then there is Tomás Ó Brógáin, TV & Media at Oireas; Kevin Glynn of Big Idea Films; Brendan Scott; William Linhart; Micheál Ó Siochrú; Nicholas Canny; Mark Empey; Conor Lenihan; Bríd McGrath; Annaleigh Margey; Marie-Louise Coolahan; Evan Bourke; John Cronin and Harman Murtagh of the Irish Military History Society. I owe special thanks to Patrick McCarthy of the Irish Military History Society for reading the draft twice and helping me with perceptive suggestions. The errors are my own. Caitriona, I could not have done it without you. *Go raibh maith agaibh go léir.* The Commissioning Editor would like to thank Seán Ó Brógain for his help with this project

Glossary of Terms

Irish Words

Hiberno-English	Irish	Meaning[1]
A, In	*an*	The
Ballagh	*Bealach*	'… a road, way, path …'
Beg	*Beag*	'… small, tiny, few …'
Bog	*Bogach*	'… a swamp, quagmire …'
Boo	*Bua*	'… victory, conquest, success …'
Boreen	*Bóthairín*	Lane or track
Cassey	*Ceasach*	'… a causeway made of wattles'
Keen	*Caoineadh*	'… an elegy …'
Clan	*Clann*	'… race, children; sept …'
Creaghts	*Coruighechta*	Herds and herders
–	*Dearbhfhine*	Male descendants of a common great-grandfather
Ditch	–	Embankment and fosse
Drumlin	*Droimnín*	'… glacial mound, any small hill …'
Garrough, Garve	*Garbh*	'rough, rugged, coarse …'
–	*Gairm Slua*	'Call to Arms'
Knock	*Cnoc*	Hill
–	*Rath*	Ringfort
Maghery	*Machaire*	'a plain, a flat or low-lying country …'
Meddog	*Meadóg*	Pocket knife
More	*Mór*	Big or great
–	*Oireacht*	Country or territory

---

1 Quotes are from Patrick S. Dinneen (ed.), *Foclóir Gaedhilge agus Béarla. An Irish-English Dictionary, Being a Thesaurus of the Words, Phrases and Idioms of the Modern Irish Language, with Explanations in English* (Dublin: Irish Texts Society, 1904).

Reagh	*Riabhach*	'… roan, swarthy …'
Roe	*Rua*	'… red, reddish, brown …'
Skeane, Skine	*Scian*	'a knife, a dagger …'
Slew, Slow	*Slua*	'… a host, legion or army …'
Suggane	*Súgán*	'a hay or straw rope …'
Togher	*Tóchar*	'a causeway, a raised way or embankment …'
Totane	*na dTóiteán*	Genitive: '… a fire, a conflagration …'

Place Names

Seventeenth Century	Modern
Annasamry	Summer Island
Ballymacpatrick	Careysville
Carriganedy	Castlehyde
Drumrusk	Carrick-on-Shannon
Fort Falkland	Banagher
Kinard	Caledon
Lisnegarvy	Lisburn
Lynch's Knock	Summerhill
Maryborough	Portlaoise
Parsonstown	Birr
Philipstown	Daingean
Rachra	Shannonbridge
King's County	Offaly
Queen's County	Laois
Clonodfoy	Castle Oliver

Author's Note

I generally use the most common modern form of first names and surnames in English while retaining the 'O' or 'Mac' where, as is usually the case, the old and present surname forms are recognisably the same: 'O'Neill' or 'MacCarthy' for instance. I retain the older 'O'Cahan' rather than 'O'Kane' because the O'Cahan form remains so widely used by historians. 'Roger Moore' is reincarnated as 'Rory O'More', 'Daniel' becomes 'MacDonnell', but 'Fox' does not become 'Mac an tSionnaigh'. 'Miles O'Reilly' is rendered as 'Maolmhuire O'Reilly', and 'Betagh' is 'Beatty'. The correct modern spelling of Irish language nicknames is usually used rather than their phonetic equivalents: 'Rua' rather than 'Roe' and so on. To demonstrate how all this works in practice, the Ulster general signed himself as 'Don Eugenio O Neill' in Spanish language documents and 'Owen O'Neill' in English; he was 'Eoghan' to his wife, 'Eoghan Ua Néill' in the pages of O'Mellan's diary and was generally known as 'Owen Roe' or 'McArt'. Here, he appears as 'Eoghan Rua O'Neill'.

Introduction

Straw-Rope Soldiers: Catholic Armies in Ireland 1641–1643

Thirty years ago, when I wrote *Confederate Catholics at War*, I was certain that class was the key to unlocking the meaning of the 1641 rising. All things being equal, nobles were less likely to revolt than gentry, and top-ranking nobles least of all. Today, I would give more weight to recent experience of official expropriation and to religion, a bitter grievance in itself and a badge of convenience for other issues.[1] It is appropriate, then, to call the 12 years of conflict that engulfed Ireland (1641–1653) the 'Wars of Religion'. These 12 years fall into three acts, so to speak, of a bitter and blood-soaked drama. Each act drew Ireland into progressively closer alignment with conflicts in the other two Stuart kingdoms, Scotland and England.

Act One, the shortest but 'most vicious', began in October 1641 with a rising in Ulster and shuddered to a halt in September 1643 when the insurgents, now organised as the 'Confederate Catholics', agreed a ceasefire with James Butler, Earl of Ormond and Charles I's representative in Ireland.[2] This cessation, as it was called, was more than just a ceasefire. The Confederate Catholics paid a hefty annual tribute to their King, sent an army to Scotland to fight his enemies and made it their political priority to reach a definitive agreement with him.

Dialogue dominated Act Two. Irish Catholics pleaded for religious toleration or demanded freedom of religion, either of which necessitated some sort of regal union in which an autonomous Ireland maintained an arm's-

---

1   Eamon Darcy, *The Irish Rebellion of 1641 and the Wars of the Three Kingdoms* (Woodbridge: Boydell & Brewer, 2013), p.7; John Morrill, 'The Rule of Saints and Soldiers: The Wars of Religion in Britain and Ireland, 1638-1660', in J. Wormald (ed.), *Short Oxford History of the British Isles: The Seventeenth Century* (Oxford: Oxford University Press, 2008), pp.83–115 and 'Three Kingdoms and One Commonwealth? The Enigma of Mid-Seventeenth Century Britain and Ireland', in A. Grant and K. Stringer (eds), *Uniting the Kingdom? The Making of British History* (London: Routledge, 1995), p.190.
2   Inga Jones, '"Holy War"? Religion, Ethnicity and Massacre during the Irish Rebellion 1641-2', in E. Darcy, A. Margey, and E. Murphy (eds), *The 1641 Depositions and the Irish Rebellion* (London: Pickering & Chatto, 2014), p.129.

length relationship with the monarch's two Protestant kingdoms, sharing with them only the diminished person of a common monarch. Charles grew increasingly desperate for an Irish army to act as a counterweight in England to the Covenanter army supporting the English Parliament, but his man in Dublin stalled on offering the religious concessions that would have given Charles an army in time to make a difference.[3] The war in England wound down in favour of the Scots Covenanters and their English Parliamentary allies, and, in 1647, Ormond sold Dublin to the winners, choosing to 'give up those places under his command rather to the English rebels than the Irish rebels'.[4] After annihilating the Leinster and Munster Catholic armies, the roundheads looked set to crush the Confederate Catholics until a plot twist brought the curtains down on Act Two.

Parliament beheaded Charles for treason, at which Confederate Catholics, Covenanters and even many Parliamentary supporters in Ireland recoiled in horror. Ormond shepherded them all into an improbable pan-Royalist alliance. A smooth intriguer rather than a gifted soldier, Ormond did little to obstruct Oliver Cromwell from eviscerating the Catholic and Royalist heartland of south Leinster and east Munster in 1649–1650. Defeat at Worcester and the surrender of Limerick in September and October 1651 dashed hopes of Royalist victory. By then, Charles II had disavowed Irish Catholics as the price of Scottish Covenanter support. The Irish struggled on for another year and a half to avoid unconditional surrender and a vengeful peace. They failed on both counts.

This study confines itself to Act One. Even though this episode was mercifully brief, a stand-alone study is justified for reasons of scope and scale. Not a single county in Ireland was unscathed by war in 1642, and, in summer of that year, there were more men under arms than there ever had been or would be again. Moreover, it was a singularly nasty episode.[5] Insurgent slaughter of Protestant settlers in the winter of 1641–1642 quickly gained canonical status while English and Scots armies routinely massacred so many natives in the springtime and summer that followed that 'it is very far from clear on which side the balance of cruelty rests'.[6] Because it was more distinct from events in Britain, Act One is open ended – the stakes would never be higher and the range of outcomes wider. Distinct but never entirely detached, the rising generated rumours of the King's complicity, prevented Charles from proroguing the English Parliament and so led to the English Civil War.

---

3 John Lowe, 'Charles I and the Confederation of Kilkenny, 1643-9', *Irish Historical Studies*, 14:53 (1964), p.2.

4 David Scott, *Politics and War in the Three Stuart Kingdoms, 1637-49* (London: Palgrave Macmillan, 2003), p.78; Mícheál Ó Siochrú, *Confederate Ireland, 1642-1649: A Constitutional and Political Analysis* (Dublin: Four Courts Press, 1999), p.147.

5 Inga Jones, 'A Sea of Blood? Massacres during the Wars of the Three Kingdoms, 1641-53', in P. Dwyer and L. Ryan (eds), *Theatres of Violence: Massacre, Mass Killing and Atrocity throughout History* (New York: Berghahn, 2012), p.64.

6 W. E. H. Lecky, *A History of England in the Eighteenth Century* (London: Longmans, Green and Co., 1878), vol. II, p.155.

INTRODUCTION

The narrative backbone of this study of the Catholic armies in those two years between October 1641 and September 1643 does not recount everything they did but only what I believe really mattered. Otherwise, the reader would struggle to comprehend what was, like the war in England, 'a disjointed series of battles, sieges and skirmishes' that seem 'devoid of form or pattern'.[7] The narrative should disclose, not impose, a pattern. It will focus in and out, from the strategic (Why was the war being fought in the first place?) through the operational (which might deal with a campaign or a long operation like a siege) down to the tactical and what happened in a particular place (a literal battlefield) on a given day.

It is mostly a story of sieges. In the British Isles, we are told that 'battles predominated' and less than a third of all actions in England were sieges.[8] But can one calculate a battle and a siege as equal? A battle is an event lasting no longer than the daylight hours of a summer's day, whereas a siege is a process that usually takes time. Measured by the drumbeat of war, the siege dominated in Ireland in 1641–1643. No fewer than 19 Protestant castles were beleaguered across County Limerick in spring and summer 1642, and the average duration of those we can count was, on average, 10 weeks. Of battles, there were none in the county. Outside of Ulster, practically all battles and skirmishes were incidental to sieges.

---

7 Alfred H. Burne and Peter Young, *The Great Civil War: A Military History of the First Civil War, 1642-1646* (London: Eyre and Spottiswoode, 1959), p.xi.
8 Charles Carlton, *Going to the Wars: The Experience of the British Civil Wars, 1638–1651* (London: Routledge, 1992), p.155; Anke Fischer-Kattner, 'Colchester's Plight in European Perspective: Printed Representations of Seventeenth-Century Siege Warfare', in A. Fischer-Kattner and J. Ostwald (eds), *The World of the Siege: Representations of Early Modern Positional Warfare* (Leiden: Brill, 2019), p.45.

Sieges in County Limerick, 1642

Name	Number of Weeks
Askeaton[9]	
Aughinish	
Ballynoe[10]	A 'long time'
Callow[11]	4
Cappagh[12]	
Castletown (Kenry)[13]	6
Castle Matrix[14]	16
Cloghnarold[15]	24
Croom[16]	22
Hospital[17]	5
Kilfinny[18]	24
Knockmonihy[19]	
Limerick Castle[20]	6
Lough Gur[21]	23
Mahoonagh[22]	3
Newcastle (Connello)[23]	13
Newcastlewest[24]	28
Pallas[25]	6
Rathkeale	

9 Thomas J. Westropp, 'The Principal Ancient Castles of the County Limerick', *Journal of the Royal Society of Antiquaries of Ireland*, 5th series, 37:2 (1907), p.159.
10 Trinity College Dublin Library (TCDL) 1641 Depositions, MS 829 (County Limerick), fol. 142v: Deposition of Samuell Wishlade.
11 Callow was 'close besieged' on 8 July and for some time before. It capitulated before mid-September. Westropp, 'Ancient Castles', p.161; John Begley, *The Diocese of Limerick in the Sixteenth and Seventeenth Centuries* (Dublin: Browne and Nolan, 1927), p.129; TCDL: 1641 Depositions, MS 829 (County Limerick), fol. 268r: Deposition of Thomas Southwell.
12 Westropp, 'Ancient Castles', p.160.
13 Parish of Ardcanny. TCDL: 1641 Depositions, MS 829 (County Limerick), fol. 284r: Deposition of Sir Hardress Waller.
14 TCDL: 1641 Depositions, MS 829 (County Limerick), fols 190v: Deposition of Bushopp Planke and Ann Reynes, 265v: Deposition of John Mayes, 268r: Deposition of Thomas Southwell.
15 Westropp, 'Ancient Castles', p.161; TCDL: 1641 Depositions, MS 829 (County Limerick), fol. 344v: Deposition of ffrances Jarman and Henry ffoord.
16 TCDL: 1641 Depositions, MS 829 (County Limerick), fol. 154r: Deposition of John Howell.
17 Westropp, 'Ancient Castles', p.161.
18 TCDL: 1641 Depositions, MS 829 (County Limerick), fol. 138r: Deposition of Elizabeth Dowdall.
19 Westropp, 'Ancient Castles', p.161.
20 TCDL: 1641 Depositions, MS 829 (County Limerick), fol. 132v: Deposition of John Lilles.
21 TCDL: 1641 Depositions, MS 829 (County Limerick), fol. 217v: Deposition of Thomas Ally.
22 Mahoonagh was taken on 17 February 1642. Westropp, 'Ancient Castles', p.161; TCDL: 1641 Depositions, MS 829 (County Limerick), fol. 142v: Deposition of Samuell Wishlade.
23 Westropp, 'Ancient Castles', p.161.
24 TCDL: 1641 Depositions, MS 829 (County Limerick), fols 136v: Deposition of Richard Lacky, 142v: Deposition of Samuell Wishlade, 145r: Deposition of Richard Turnor, 183v: Deposition of Jane Meriett, 327r: Depositions of Walter James & Thomas Atkins.
25 TCDL: 1641 Depositions, MS 829 (County Limerick), fols 158r: Deposition of Edmond Pierce, 194v: Deposition of John Potter, 342v, 343v: Deposition of Roger Williams.

INTRODUCTION

I am an academic historian and would like nothing better than to invite the reader to peer under the bonnet of the car, so to speak, and, were this a strictly academic study, I would dutifully weigh the probabilities of conflicting evidence, sternly warn about the limitations of partial, biased or mendacious sources and carefully set out the opposing viewpoints in long-running controversies before pronouncing a judiciously worded compromise. Instead, I have mostly ironed out the historiographical creases. To take just one example, I employ the terms 'Catholic', 'Irish' and 'native' interchangeably while also recognising that many individuals defied rigid categorization, that varieties of 'Irishness' existed, that some insurgents were not Irish and that some loyalists were not English. The author of 'Tuireamh na hÉireann' sniffed that, in Munster in the summer of 1647, the Irish army was led by a 'Gall' or foreigner (the Anglo-Welsh Catholic Earl of Glamorgan) and that Baron Inchiquin Morrogh O'Brien, a 'geinearál Gaeulach' (Gaelic general), led the Munster Protestants or 'armáil Gallda' (English army).[26] Cattle rustlers justified attacking a member of one long-established Old English family: 'though he was an Irishman, yet he was a Protestant'.[27] Religion was 'at the root of all the problems that led to the 1641 rebellion', and, when put to it, most English Catholics in Ireland or Catholics of recent English descent 'chose religion' over national solidarity. When they picked a side, men like Oliver Stephenson of County Limerick proved exceptionally committed. Littlest but not least, comes the diminutive James Tuchet, 3rd Earl of Castlehaven, who was that rare bird, a lucky Confederate Catholic general.[28]

I drew heavily on five Irish primary sources. Richard Bellings enjoyed a seat beside the coachman. He was son-in-law to Viscount Mountgarret Richard Butler, president of the Supreme Council of the Confederate Catholics and secretary to that council. Bellings penned his manuscript history two decades after the events that he described, when it was clear that those like him who had been aligned to the Butlers had got their estates back, whereas the majority of his landowning countrymen had been irretrievably ruined by the Cromwellian confiscations.

Castlehaven wrote his *Memoirs* in a 'plain and simple' style and insisted they were unblemished by 'lie or mistake', but, like Bellings, he was knitted by marriage into the Butler axis and exhibited the same gushing admiration for

---

26 Michelle O'Riordan, *Poetics and Polemics: Reading Seventeenth-Century Irish Political Verse* (Cork: Cork University Press, 2021), p.401; Cecile O'Rahilly (ed.), *Five Seventeenth-Century Political Poems* (Dublin: Dublin Institute for Advanced Studies, 1952), p.75.
27 Brian Mac Cuarta, 'Religious Violence against Settlers in South Ulster, 1641-2', in D. Edwards, C. Tait, and P. Lenihan (eds), *Age of Atrocity: Violence and Political Conflict in Early Modern Ireland* (Dublin: Four Courts Press, 2007), p.155.
28 Michael Perceval-Maxwell, *The Outbreak of the Irish Rebellion of 1641* (Dublin: Gill and Macmillan, 1994), p.251; Donal F. Cregan, 'The Confederate Catholics of Ireland: The Personnel of the Confederation, 1642–9', *Irish Historical Studies*, 29:116 (1995), p.494; David Edwards, 'A Haven of Popery: English Catholic Migration to Ireland in the Age of Plantations', A. Ford and J. McCafferty (eds), *The Origins of Sectarianism in Early Modern Ireland* (Cambridge: Cambridge University Press, 2005), p.126; Edmund Hogan (ed.), *The History of the Warr of Ireland from 1641 to 1653. By a British Officer, of the Regiment of Sir John Clottworthy* (Dublin: McGlashan and Gill, 1873), pp.94, 99.

Butlers in general and Ormond in particular. Yet his account must be central because he was active as a general in all four provinces, commanding armies ranging in size from the hundreds to thousands.

We can infer from internal evidence that 'P. S.', the author of the manuscript 'Aphorismical Discovery of Treasonable Faction', was a Leinsterman, probably hailing from or near the Mac Geoghegan Country of south-east County Westmeath. His hatred of 'factionists' like Bellings for betraying the common cause, as he saw it, makes for intrusive bias. Yet P. S. had an eye for the colourful story, the telling detail and the gritty texture of wartime experience.[29]

Friar O'Mellan of Brantry Friary in Tyrone kept a laconic war diary in Irish, which stops abruptly in 1647, meaning he did not get to see how it all turned out. His focus was on Ulster and especially the doings of Phelim Rua O'Neill, who cuts a more considerable figure in the pages of his diary than Eoghan Rua O'Neill.

Henry Mc Tuoll O'Neill was an officer in Eoghan Rua's army, and his *Impartial Relation* dutifully narrates the wanderings and doings of that host in the plodding style of an official history.

---

29 John Dorney, '"Deceived as Hereafter to the Destruction of Both" – Stories from the 1641 Rebellion', *Irish History Online* (2015), <https://www.theirishstory.com/2015/12/03/deceived-as-hereafter-to-the-destruction-of-both-stories-from-the-1641-rebellion/#.ZF0xjXbMJD8>, accessed 23 Jan. 2021.

1

Winter 1641–1642

Native Irish discontent had long flowed through subterranean courses before it broke out in a cascade on the evening of 22 October 1641. The biggest source of that discontent was the unrelenting acquisition of land by Protestant newcomers from Catholic natives, whether as a result of outright confiscation through plantation, by legal loopholes or through indebtedness and mortgage.[1] The proportion of land owned by Catholics stood at around 60 percent by 1640. If the Ulster Plantation had been a big-bang event that had happened back in 1609, then it could not convincingly explain the rising 30 years later. But it was a process, not an event, in which, for instance, the displacement of native occupiers accelerated when immigration from Britain picked up over subsequent decades.

While not all natives suffered expropriation, all were excluded from office by their creed and reduced to a minority in a packed Parliament. Added to systemic religious discrimination, the apparently imminent threat of outright persecution upset the 'uneasy equilibrium' between 'the various religious and ethnic communities' and transformed a regional uprising into a national one.[2]

The threat of persecution and the destabilizing 'billiard-ball effect' across the three kingdoms began with the Scots' refusal to adopt a state-sanctioned prayer book.[3] This refusal forced Charles to call the English Parliament, which, in turn, supplied an institutional focus for anti-Catholic hysteria such that, by summer 1641, it looked as if the opposition in the Commons would be in a position, insurgents would later complain, to 'raze the name of Catholic and Irish out of the whole Kingdom'.[4] Lord Deputy Wentworth had raised a largely Irish Catholic army to put down the Scots Covenanters, but the army was being disbanded even though several would-be colonels had first been granted license to recruit the de-mobbed soldiers for the killing fields of the

---

1 Nicholas Canny, *Making Ireland British, 1580–1650* (Oxford: Oxford University Press, 2001), p.325.
2 Darcy, *Irish Rebellion*, p.7.
3 Conrad Russell, *The Causes of the English Civil War* (Oxford: Clarendon Press, 1990), p.199.
4 Quoted in Conrad Russell, *The Fall of the British Monarchies, 1637-1642* (Oxford: Clarendon Press, 1990), p.379.

Thirty Years' War. Some of these colonels, together with some leaders of the Pale (the old bridgehead of Crown authority in Ireland), plotted to seize Dublin Castle, the seat of government and the main storehouse of arms and ammunition.[5] Nothing came of this plot except that a second Ulster ring of conspirators borrowed the plan to seize the castle and claim royal sanction.

The five ringleaders who met on 5 October 1641 at Lough Ross, County Armagh, to put the finishing touches to the plans for Ulster embody different threads of conspiracy. Heber Mac Mahon, Bishop-elect of Down and Connor, personified the priestly interest; Conor Baron Maguire and Sir Phelim O'Neill of south-east County Tyrone personified the precariously propertied. The latter pair sprung from loyalist branches of Gaelic families that had been fobbed off with what they considered paltry plantation grants, and both had been politically active in the recent tumultuous meetings of the Irish Parliament. Phelim might have thought himself 'the most considerable person of his name left in Ulster' and sported 'bright clothes' to set off his 'fiery red hair', but he was 'living on borrowed time' and borrowed money.[6] The propertyless youngest son of a youngest son, Brian Mac Hugh O'Neill was a captain in the regiment of Eoghan Rua O'Neill, who had come home, ostensibly, to raise recruits.[7] The fifth man was Rory O'More or Roger Moore, whose names reflect his mutability. He was 'the first that laid the foundation of the rebellion' and was '… well-spoken in English and Irish, affable and courteous, & one of the most handsome, comely, and proper persons of his time'.[8] Grandson of a Crown-backed contender for the O'More chieftaincy, landowner in County Kildare and lessee of a plantation estate in south County Armagh, he lived in Dundalk on the blurry margins of Ulster and the Pale.[9] His marriage connections within the Pale included the Flemings of Slane, Sarsfields of Lucan (Patrick Sarsfield, the hero of the Jacobite War, would be his grandson) and Barnewalls of Donabate.[10]

These first-tier conspirators organised the rising in their own counties: Rory Maguire on behalf of his brother Conor in Fermanagh, Phelim in

---

5   Perceval-Maxwell, *Outbreak of the Irish Rebellion*, pp.200–07, 223–24, 421–30; Aidan Clarke, 'The Genesis of the Ulster Rising of 1641', in P. Roebuck (ed.), *Plantation to Partition: Essays in Ulster History in Honour of J. L. McCracken* (Belfast: Blackstaff Press, 1981), pp.32–40.

6   Gerard Farrell, *The 'Mere Irish' and the Colonisation of Ulster, 1570-1641* (London: Palgrave Macmillan, 2017), pp.247–48; O'Rahilly (ed.), *Five Seventeenth-Century Political Poems*, p.23; John T. Gilbert (ed.), *A Contemporary History of Affairs in Ireland from 1641 to 1652. Now for the First Time Published. With an Appendix of Original Letters and Documents* (Dublin: Irish Archaeological and Celtic Society, 1879–1880), vol. III, p.197.

7   Tomás Ó Fiaich, 'The O'Neills of the Fews', *Seanchas Ard Mhacha: Journal of the Armagh Diocesan Historical Society*, 7:1 (1973), pp.1–64; Perceval-Maxwell, *Outbreak of the Irish Rebellion*, pp.206, 209.

8   The National Archives (TNA) *A Treatise or Account of the War and Rebellion in Ireland since the Year 1641* (London: Publisher unknown, n.d.) and *HMC 2nd Report* (London: HMC, 1871), p.230.

9   Séamus P. Ó Mórdha, 'Heber Mac Mahon, Soldier-Bishop of the Confederation of Kilkenny', *Clogher Record*, 3 (1975), p.47.

10 John T. Gilbert (ed.), *History of the Irish Confederation and the War in Ireland 1641-1649* (Dublin: M. H. Gill and Son, 1879–1880), vol. I, pp.13–14.

Tyrone and Armagh and so on.[11] The key to the whole operation was Dublin Castle were eight 'old and weak' warders and 40 halberdiers were all that stood between the plotters and the seat of government, armoury and well-stocked munitions store.[12] Conor Maguire was to infiltrate the walled city with a band of 30 to 40 followers armed with skeanes and swords and to attack the main gate on the tolling of the castle clock at ten o'clock on the morning of Saturday, 23 October. Rory O'More's band was to seize the stable gate of the castle from outside the city walls at the same time as Maguire. The plan was betrayed, and Lords Justices Parsons and Borlase secured the castle and lifted Maguire together with most of his followers.[13] If they had not scotched the plot, it is 'difficult to imagine' how the Lords Justices could have kept control of any part of Ireland.[14]

Happily unaware, the other ringleaders rose and overran a swath of south Ulster.[15] For decades, the standing army of 2,300 foot and 1,000 horse had been scattered in penny packets, most heavily in planted regions. While dispersal had smothered the constant sparks of local unrest, it left thinly manned outposts vulnerable in the event of a bigger revolt.[16] On days one to three of the revolt, the ringleaders overran seven outposts – Charlemont, Mountjoy, Newry, Monaghan, Augher, Cavan and Dundalk – effectively reducing Dublin Castle's paper strength of foot soldiers by one-tenth. Meanwhile, the common people plundered Protestant settlers and sometimes murdered them, especially if they were clergymen.[17] This popular violence was sometimes in collusion and at other times in collision with strategically purposeful military actions carried out by bands or companies of more than 50 armed men under the command of named captains.[18] The latter is what interests us.

Phelim Rua turned west to the Clogher Valley, and Rory Maguire thrust east in the second week of November. The two met at Augher, where they

---

11 Terry Clavin, 'Maguire, Rory (Roger)', *Dictionary of Irish Biography* (2009), <https://www.dib.ie/biography/maguire-rory-roger-a5364>, accessed 24 Jan. 2020.
12 Thomas Carte, *An History of the Life of James Duke of Ormonde* (London: J. J. and P. Knapton, 1736), vol. I, p.169.
13 Canny, *Making Ireland British*, pp.469, 471; Gilbert (ed.), *Irish Confederation*, vol. I., p.7; Brendan Fitzpatrick, *Seventeenth-Century Ireland: The War of Religions* (Dublin: Gill and Macmillan, 1988), pp.141–42.
14 Darcy, *Irish Rebellion*, p.77.
15 Tadhg Ó Donnchadha, 'Cín lae Uí Mheallláin', *Analecta Hibernica*, 3 (1931), p.6; Trinity College Dublin Library (TCDL) 1641 Depositions, MS 835 (County Fermanagh), fol. 252v: Deposition of Brian Mc Guire; Raymond Gillespie, 'The Murder of Arthur Champion and the 1641 Rising in Fermanagh', *Clogher Record*, 14:3 (1993), pp.52–66.
16 Mark C. Fissel, *English Warfare, 1511–1642* (London: Routledge, 2001), p.253; Gilbert (ed.), *Irish Confederation*, vol. I, p.14; Ian Ryder, *An English Army for Ireland* (Leigh-on-Sea: Partizan Press, 1987), p.8; The National Archives (TNA) SP 63/237, fol. 36: 'List of Officers, General and Provincial Constables and Warders'; Malcolm Wanklyn, *The Army of Occupation in Ireland 1603-42: Defending the Protestant Hegemony* (Warwick: Helion & Company, 2022), pp.186–87, 240–46.
17 David Finnegan, 'What Do the Depositions Say about the Outbreak of the 1641 Rising', in E. Darcy, A. Margey, and E. Murphy (eds), *The 1641 Depositions and the Irish Rebellion* (London: Pickering & Chatto, 2014), p.29; Darcy, *Irish Rebellion*, p.53; Perceval-Maxwell, *Outbreak of the Irish Rebellion*, p.227.
18 Perceval-Maxwell, *Outbreak of the Irish Rebellion*, p.227.

burnt the town and laid siege to the castle, a substantial three-storey building enclosed by a bawn with four 'flankers', behind which 1,000 men, women and children huddled. The insurgents 'shot continually' with a captured field gun. The gun punched a hole in the roof: the gunner must have overshot by accident, or he realised that it was a waste of time firing so light a shot against walls. Maguire retired west, assaulting Aughentaine Castle on his way home, and Phelim marched off in the opposite direction, but not before his followers perpetrated one of the first, if not the first, Catholic-on-Protestant massacre of, in this case, Protestant civilian soldiers.[19] Meanwhile Sir William Stewart sent 500 foot and 100 horse from Newtownstewart to relieve Augher and Aughentaine and attacked a Maguire castle at Rossbeg: '… we fired some outhouses, in the smoke whereof we approached the gate, set it on fire, entered the castle, put the men to the sword'.[20] Rory Maguire responded by mopping up all the settler outposts in County Fermanagh except for Enniskillen. On 23 December, his followers burned Lisgoole House, near Enniskillen, and killed those sheltering within. The next day, Tully Castle, on the southern shore of Lower Lough Erne, surrendered to Maguire on condition of safe conduct for the Hume family and the settlers who had sought refuge within the walls. Instead, Maguire's men locked everyone in the vaults, and, the next day, they massacred men, women and children, sparing only the Hume family.[21]

Red Phelim next joined with Con Magennis of County Down in setting out on the snow-covered highway to Carrickfergus Castle. Arthur Viscount Chichester's troop of cavalry had been spooked by 'a great noise of people' and fled Dromore one night in early November, followed by the garrison's irregular soldiery.[22] That left only the outpost of Lisburn, 16 miles from Carrickfergus.[23] After attending mass on Sunday, 28 November, O'Neill and Magennis beat their drums and drew their troops 'in battalia' near Lisburn. The town's streets formed a triangle with the River Lagan as its base, Bridge Street and High Street the sides and the marketplace the apex. It should have been a walkover, like Dundalk or Armagh: Lisburn was unwalled, the bridge was still standing, and the Irish had the advantage in numbers, along with two artillery pieces and gunpowder taken from Newry Castle. Holed up in the church, market house and castle were upwards of 500 demoralised and poorly armed refugees. Even in the six officially planted counties, the proportion of settlers mustering with a firearm was small and diminishing: where one settler in eight owned a firearm in 1619, only one in 33 did so

---

19 Trinity College Dublin Library (TCDL) 1641 Depositions, MS 839 (County Tyrone), fol. 21v: Deposition of Roger Markham and MS 836 (County Tyrone), fol. 128v: Examination of Michaell Harrison; Perceval-Maxwell, *Outbreak of the Irish Rebellion*, p.229.
20 Éamon Ó Doibhlin, 'Domhnach Mór: Part IV: The Insurrection of 1641 and Its Background', *Seanchas Ard Mhacha: Journal of the Armagh Diocesan Historical Society*, 3:2 (1959), p.420.
21 Donald M. Schlegel, 'A Clogher Chronology: October, 1641 to July, 1642', *Clogher Record*, 16:1 (1997), p.82; Michael Perceval-Maxwell, 'The Ulster Rising of 1641, and the Depositions', *Irish Historical Studies*, 21:82 (1978), p.152.
22 The National Archives (TNA) *HMC Report on the Manuscripts of the Earl of Egmont* (London: Mackie & Co., 1905–1909), vol. I, pp.145–46, 'John Galbraith to Sir Philip Percival, Lisburn, 10 November'.
23 Perceval-Maxwell, *Outbreak of the Irish Rebellion*, pp.213–14.

in 1630.²⁴ Protestant civilians east of the Bann were no more likely to own a musket or caliver. More formidable were the regular cavalrymen, 120 of them armoured 'back and breast', who waited in the marketplace. O'Neill sent one battalion of 600 men up Bridge Street and another up Castle Street to converge on the place, but the advance was not simultaneous, and the cavalry drove back first one battalion and then the other 'at the sword's point after a discharge of pistols'. Waiting until nightfall, Phelim's followers set houses ablaze and launched a 'fierce assault', taking advantage of the 'confusion and heat of the fire', but they were met by reinforcements of regular horse and foot. As darkness fell, the attackers darted forwards in the shadows cast by flames, but the horsemen materialised like 'fairies or such like' supernatural beings and 'hewed them down'. It was touch and go for four of five hours until Phelim's men withdrew to their rendezvous at a nearby mansion, burned it to the ground and pulled back closer to the Bann.²⁵

While a charge canalised down narrow streets could certainly produce shock and awe, in general, horsemen did not perform best in urban combat. O'Neill should have packed both streets with pikemen, presenting an impenetrable hedge, pausing, checking their alignment, and pressing on steadily while towing one of the field guns along with them. Such guns may have lacked the punch to knock a hole in the market house or church, but a shot would have ripped a tightly packed troop of horse apart. That kind of coordinated action was best done in daylight, and the piecemeal actions of darkness suited the defenders rather than the attackers. A general had to strike the right balance between 'come-on' and 'go-on' and intuitively know when he should demonstratively take risks and when prudence was the better part of valour.²⁶ Phelim Rua chose prudence. Through that whole day and night, he waited outside the town, when he really should have gone forwards, at least once. The other first-tier conspirators did not choose Phelim as commander-in-chief to replace the imprisoned Baron Maguire for his military prowess but rather for his political skills and glibly persuasive tongue.²⁷ Phelim was a 'raw general', but he did not learn on the job from this and later mistakes, 'not being bred anything of a soldier'.²⁸

In some ways, the Ulster rising looked like the mobilisation of the ghost of the O'Neill clan. An O'Neill was in charge, though one who could not claim membership of the derbfine or kin-group of men who were eligible

---

24　Rolf Loeber and Geoffrey Parker, 'The Military Revolution in Seventeenth-Century Ireland' in J. Ohlmeyer (ed.), *Independence to Occupation: Ireland 1641–1660* (Cambridge: Cambridge University Press, 1995), p.73.
25　The National Archives (TNA) SP 63/277, fol. 121: 'Account of an Attack by the Irish Insurrectionary Forces Upon Lisnegarvy, 28 Nov 1641'; Hogan (ed.), *History of the Warr of Ireland*, pp.12–13, 17, 21; Ó Donnchadha, 'Cín lae', p.7; Lennon Wylie (LW) Anon., 'A brief Relation of the miraculous Victory gained there that day over the first formed Army of the Irish, soon after their Rebellion, which broke out the 23rd October, 1641', in *Historical Account of the Town of Lisburn*; TCDL: 1641 Depositions, MS 839 (County Tyrone), fol. 12r: Deposition of John Kerdiff.
26　Richard Holmes, *Firing Line* (Harmondsworth: Penguin, 1986), p.343.
27　Farrell, 'Mere Irish', p.256.
28　My thanks to Patrick McCarthy for bringing this quotation to my attention. Hogan (ed.), *History of the Warr of Ireland*, pp.17, 148.

to be chosen as chieftain because they shared descent from a common great-grandfather. Turlough Mac Art óg, grandson of Turlough Luineach (d. 1595), who raised seven companies in west Tyrone, would have been a more eligible candidate by blood.[29] Moreover, nearly all the one-time O'Neill underkings (except for the O'Cahans in County Derry) were out, and their old O'Donnell allies in the final war against Tudor conquest were represented by Manus O'Donnell, son of Niall Garbh (d. 1626).[30] To capture Charlemont, County Armagh, and Glaslough, County Monaghan, Phelim trusted his brother Turlough, half-brother Alexander Hovenden, his fosterers the Ó hAodha (anglicised as 'Hughes') and Turlough's fosterers the Mac Quaids.[31] Traditionally, families of importance committed their offspring to be fostered by clients of lower status, which forged a bond 'stronger than blood'.[32] Other bands in east County Tyrone, the nucleus of the old O'Neill lordship, answered to Phelim directly and were led by members of the one-time O'Neill *luchttighe* or demesne families, including Mac Donnell, O'Donnelly, O'Quinn and O'Hagan.

The rising spread 'like a brush fire' south, and, by the end of November, an impressive roll call of O'Farrells of County Longford was laying siege to Castleforbes.[33] At the same time, sparks thrown off by the wildfire leaped over the firebreak of the Pale to erupt in other regions that had been subjected to plantation, including east Wicklow, north Wexford, the 'plague sore of rebellion' that was the O'Dunne patrimony in Laois, the Mac Coghlan country of west Offaly and Idough in north Kilkenny, where '… all the sept of the Brenans' overran Castlecomer, armed with 'guns, pikes, pitchforks, swords, darts, and skeanes'.[34] On the seaward side of the Wicklow massif, Fiach O'Toole of Castlekevin had hung on as a lessee on part of the O'Toole patrimony and was the 'colonel' of the County Wicklow forces, leading the

---

29   Ó Doibhlin, 'Domhnach Mór', p.422.
30   TCDL: 1641 Depositions, MS 839, (County Donegal), fol. 131r: Deposition of James Kenedy.
31   Trinity College Dublin Library (TCDL) 1641 Depositions, MS 834 (County Monaghan), fol. 109r: Deposition of Alexander Creichton; TCDL: 1641 Depositions, MS 836 (County Armagh), fols 108v, 167r: Examination of Sir Phelim O'Neill, 171: Examination of William Skelton.
32   John Davies, 'A Discovery of the True Causes Why Ireland Was Never Entirely Subdued nor Brought under Obedience of the Crown of England until the Beginning of His Majesty's Happy Reign', in H. Morley (ed.), *Ireland under Elizabeth and James the First* (London: George Routledge and Sons, 1890), p.296; Gilbert (ed.), *Irish Confederation*, vol. I, p.8.
33   Trinity College Dublin Library (TCDL) 1641 Depositions, MS 816 (County Meath), fol. 223: Examination of Captain William Cadogan and MS 817 (County Longford), fols 187v: Deposition of Dame Jane Forbes, 199r: Deposition of William Smyth; Matthew Kelly (ed.), *Cambrensis Eversus. The History of Ancient Ireland Vindicated : The Religion, Laws and Civilization of Her People Exhibited in the Lives and Actions of Her Kings, Princes, Saints, Bishops, Bards, and Other Learned Men …* (Dublin: Celtic Society, 1848–1852), vol. I, p.13; Ó Siochrú, *Confederate Ireland*, p.37; Gilbert (ed.), *Irish Confederation*, vol. I, p.226; Perceval-Maxwell, *Outbreak of the Irish Rebellion*, pp.254, 258.
34   Trinity College Dublin Library (TCDL) 1641 Depositions, MS 812 (County Kilkenny), fol. 190r: Deposition of William Parkinson and MS 814 (County Offaly), fols 205v: Deposition of Chidley Coote, 230r: Deposition of Thomas Le Strange, 230v: Deposition of Thomas Le Strange, 238r: Deposition of Hugh Roberts; Canny, *Making Ireland British*, p.176.

capture of Knockrath and the attacks on the Black Castle of Wicklow town from mid-November.[35]

Son of one of the four most favoured natives in Wexford's plantation, Dermot Mac Dowling Kavanagh was nonetheless a 'ringleader, author and producer of the war', who reinforced disgruntled locals attacking English settlements in Idough in north County Kilkenny.[36] The son of another Kavanagh plantation grantee, Sir Morgan of Clonmullen, also rose in north Wexford and in the adjacent part of County Carlow where Walter Bagnall, governor of Leighlin Fort, a bridge on the River Barrow, defected.[37] The unplanted middle of the county was somewhat slower to rise and was ultimately led by Piers Butler of Clogh and Kayer, a large landowner who was swept up in the later tide of Butler defections.[38]

The main front of the wildfire would pause north of the Boyne for almost the whole month of November. Puzzled that Phelim O'Neill was not bearing down on them, the authorities in Dublin assumed he had a plan '… to quiet themselves behind and then to unite all their forces for besieging this city and castle'.[39] The insurgents took Dundalk on the last day of October, but, before they marched farther south, Sir Henry Tichborne quickly recruited 1,000 men in Dublin, the first batch of reinforcements for the Drogheda garrison.[40] Hugh O'Byrne shadowed a second column of reinforcements, 600 strong, all the way from Dublin. On the morning of 29 November, he sent a groom ahead to rouse the O'Reilly contingent at Slane to attack the English column: '… it so fell out as they were ready to give Fire, one of the Officers commanded a Counter-March, in which they being compelled to take a Ditch were disordered, and the Enemy judging it a Flight gave such a Shout that frighted them into a further Confusion, and so presently charging them were routed'.[41]

'Counter-March' probably signified 'firing by two ranks advanced', whereby the front two ranks of musketeers would march forwards 10 or 20

---

35 Emmet O'Byrne, 'O'Toole, Fiach (Luke)', *Dictionary of Irish Biography* (2009), <https://www.dib.ie/biography/otoole-fiach-luke-a7091>, accessed 9 March 2021 and 'O'Byrne, Aodh', *Dictionary of Irish Biography* (2009), <https://www.dib.ie/biography/obyrne-aodh-a6527>, accessed 13 April 2021; Trinity College Dublin Library (TCDL) 1641 Depositions, MS 811 (County Wicklow), fols 29r: Deposition of Richard Bretner, 34r: Deposition of Richard Carpenter, 40r: Deposition of Edward Deane.

36 Trinity College Dublin Library (TCDL) 1641 Depositions, MS 818 (County Wexford), fols 21r: Examination of William Stafford, 38r: Examination of Richard Greene, 59r: Deposition of Richard Cleybrooke; Jason McHugh, 'The North Wexford Gentry and the Rebellion of 1641', *The Past: The Organ of the Uí Cinsealaigh Historical Society*, 24 (2003), pp.18, 31, 34; Canny, *Making Ireland British*, p.508.

37 TCDL: 1641 Depositions, MS 812 (County Carlow), fol. 27r: Deposition of Robert Wadding.

38 TCDL: 1641 Depositions, MS 818 (County Wexford), fol. 64r: Deposition of Edward Harris.

39 The National Archives (TNA) SP 63/260, fol. 160: 'The Lords Justices and Council to Secretary Vane, Dublin, 13 Nov 1641'.

40 TCDL: 1641 Depositions, MS 834 (County Louth), fols 9r: Deposition of William Vesey, 28r: Examination of Christopher Barnwall; Ó Fiaich, 'O'Neills of the Fews', pp.1–64.

41 Nicholas Bernard, *The whole proceedings of the siege of Drogheda in Ireland, vvith a thankfull remembrance for its wonderfull delivery. Raised with Gods speciall assistance by the prayers, and sole valour of the besieged, with a relation of such memorable passages as have falne out there, and in the parts neer adjoyning since this late rebellion* (London: VVilliam Bladen, 1642), p.16.

paces. The front rank would then fire, turn around and march back to reload. The second rank did so in turn. Then the third and fourth ranks began to march forwards to where the first two had halted to fire (or a little farther if they were advancing) and then fired in their turn.[42] This fire system produced relatively few shots flying through the air because of the time wasted marching forwards and backwards. The manoeuvre would have been too complex for raw troops to execute at the last moment, and clambering over a 'ditch' (which in Ireland meant the fosse, the embankment created by the excavated spoil and the hedge planted on top of the bank) had to have disordered the musketeers. Worst of all, as suggested by Julianstown and later encounters, was the fact that the musketeers turned their backs on the enemy.[43]

O'Byrne, a veteran of Spanish service, noticed the confusion, and his men set up a 'shout'. This battle cry should be distinguished from the 'word' that was designed for mutual recognition in the heat of battle: the current 'word' was 'Clan Phádraig' [Klon-faw-rick] or 'Patrick's children'.[44] This battle cry may have sounded like that 'hubbub' that Spenser's *View* describes as an onomatopoeia for the 'terrible yell … which their kern use at their first encounter' and that ended in the words '*a bua*' [aboo] (to victory).[45] Or the cry may have sounded something like the 'Rebel yell', a falsetto whoop repeated over and over. The Irish were agreeably surprised that the yell paralysed the English, who did not fire their muskets even once.[46]

The battle cry proved even more unnerving at an encounter near Killyleagh, County Down. Old-timer James Hamilton, Viscount Clandeboye, held on to his coastal stronghold, and, on Christmas Day 1641, he felt confident enough to send out one Major Barclay and Captain Inglis with 240 men, 140 of them musketeers and the rest pikemen:

> They met with a party of the rebels, whose custom is to fall one with a great shout or cry, whereupon the most part of the soldiers that were with Barclay and Inglis fled before ever the rebels charged them; so as these two or three gentlemen, with the most part of all the men, together with their arms were lost.[47]

---

42 Anon., *The Military discipline wherein is martially showne the order for driling the musket and pike : set forth in postures with ye words of comand and brief instructions for the right use of the same* (London: Tho. Jenner, 1642), p.4; William Barriffe, *Military Discipline: or, the yong artillery man …* (London: Thomas Harper, 1635), p.184; Richard Elton, *The Compleat Body of the Art Military: Exactly Compiled, and Gradually Composed for the Foot, in the Best Refined Manner, According to the Practice of the Modern Times …* (London: Robert Leybourne, 1650), pp.192–93.

43 Keith Roberts, *Pike and Shot Tactics 1590-1660* (Oxford: Osprey, 2010), pp.39–40; David J. Blackmore, *'Destructive and Formidable': British Infantry Firepower, 1642-1765.* 2012. Nottingham Trent University, PhD, p.34.

44 Irish Manuscripts Commission (IMC) Stanislaus Kavanagh (ed.), *Commentarius Rinuccinianus, de sedis apostolicae legatione ad foederatos Hiberniae Catholicos per annos 1645–1649* (Dublin: Publisher unknown, 1944), vol. I, p.277.

45 John Dryden, *The Works of that Famous English Poet, Mr. Edmond Spenser* (London: Henry Hills, 1679), p.219.

46 Trinity College Dublin Library (TCDL) 1641 Depositions, MS 833 (County Cavan), fol. 232r: Deposition of George Creighton.

47 George Hill (ed.), *The Montgomery Manuscripts: (1603–1706)* (Belfast: James Cleeland and Thomas Dargan, 1869), pp.309–10, 'Viscount Montgomery, Mountalexander, 31 December 1641, to Alexander Montgomerie, 6th Earl of Eglinton'.

This charge was not a Celtic revenant. Tyrone and his allies had converted their kern into arquebusiers during the Nine Years' War (1594–1603), and their grandsons naturally envisaged pike-and-shot warfare. Nonetheless, those grandsons suffered from an acute shortage of gunpowder, so their tactics can best be seen as a response to that shortage. The trick was to shadow the enemy, keep out of range of his shot until he fell into disorder and then race across the musket killing zone to close with blade weapons. Easier to describe than to do. The charge might depend on happy chance (e.g., the mist that descended on English troops at Redmond's Hall on the Hook Peninsula in County Wexford) and worked best against raw troops who were either fearful or foolishly overconfident. Accounts of Julianstown (November 1641), Killyleagh (December 1641) and Bendooragh or the Laney (February 1642) convey the opportunistic nature of the Irish attack in which so much depended on the leader's 'eye', that ability to pick out the stirrings of disorder or hesitancy in enemy ranks and pounce.[48] The charge was comparable to the Swedish *Gå–På* or the French *á prest* attack. When the Duke of Buckingham's troops landed in July 1627 on a beach at the eastern extremity of the Isle of Ré, French infantry advanced 'within a Pike and a half of our Men before they discharged; and the Leader of the Foot (being a brave and goody Gentleman) took off his hat, whereupon all their Foot discharged their Muskets, and after they fell to it with Swords and push of Pike'.[49]

In County Louth, 'all the freeholders and gentlemen' met on a hill just north of Drogheda in early November and joined the Ulstermen.[50] Otherwise, the nobles and gentry of the north Pale held back or partook by proxy through 'their cousins or brothers, who have little to lose'. The rout at Julianstown nudged them into rebellion.[51] Viscount Gormanston Nicholas Preston, governor of County Meath, had ordered the sheriff to issue a summons to the nobles and gentry to 'confer' on Crufty Hill, south of Drogheda, some days later.[52] When Rory O'More and other leading insurgents appeared with a guard of musketeers, Gormanston demanded of them, 'for what reason they came so with arms into the Pale'. O'More memorably replied that Palesman and Gael should stand together from now on to defend 'a part of the earth which our ancestors for so many hundred years did inhabit', and he insisted that his followers acted for 'the freedom & liberty of their consciences the maintenance of his Maiestie's Prerogative'.[53] This was not just the usual bluster commonly deployed by rebels: the Palesmen actually believed that they could be good Catholics and good subjects. Gormanston, Baron Slane

---

48 Bernard, *The whole proceedings of the siege of Drogheda*, p.22; Maighréad Ní Mhurchadha, 'War in Winter: The 1641 Rising in the Balbriggan Area', *Dublin Historical Record*, 68:2 (2015), p.166.
49 Anon., *A continued iournall of all the proceedings of the Duke of Buckingham his Grace, in the Isle of Ree, since the last of Iuly ...* (London: Augustine Mathewes, 1627), p.7.
50 TCDL: 1641 Depositions, MS 834 (County Louth), fol. 20r: Deposition of Christopher Barnewell.
51 Perceval-Maxwell, *Outbreak of the Irish Rebellion*, p.242.
52 Bríd McGrath, 'Mount Taragh's Triumph: Commitment and Organisation in the Early Stages of the 1641 Rebellion in Meath', in E. Darcy, A. Margey, and E. Murphy (eds), *The 1641 Depositions and the Irish Rebellion* (London: Pickering & Chatto, 2014), p.53.
53 TCDL: 1641 Depositions, MS 816 (County Meath), fol. 45v: Examination of Edward Dowdall.

William Fleming ('the two best peers of Leinster, for wit and loyalty'), Earl of Fingall Christopher Plunkett (Gormanston's brother-in-law) and other peers led the Palesmen to ally with the Ulstermen in beleaguering Drogheda.[54] On 4 December, Luke – a younger son of Viscount Netterville, who had attended the Crufty hosting – summoned a general meeting at Swords for 8 December to organise the insurgency in Fingal.[55]

The leading lords and gentry parcelled out the baronies of County Meath into spheres of responsibility and undertook to nominate captains for infantry companies of 100 men, to bring eight of the 'ablest men' out of each ploughland to a rendezvous and to provision them near Drogheda for as long as it took.[56] To take one example, Gormanston personally took charge of Duleek barony. The link between peacetime status and wartime military leadership was replicated, which made it easier for heads of gentry and aristocratic households to press servants, tenants and other dependants into the ranks. Three of Gormanston's captains (Bath, Aylmer and Caddle) were among the larger proprietors in the barony while the fourth was the son of the largest of them all, Nicholas Darcy of Platin. In a noteworthy example of social continuity, those very surnames, with Gormanston preeminent, come first in a list assigning the number of soldiers to be raised from the barony for a hosting on the Hill of Tara 60 years earlier.

Fingal took charge of the cavalry and proclaimed that named nobles and gentry were to send one or two horsemen, mounted and armed 'as every one was esteemed able', to the Tara muster.[57] The miniscule proportion of horsemen, less than 6 percent of the whole, fell far short of the one-third considered necessary for campaigning in open countryside.[58] But this was not to be a field campaign.

Drogheda was to be taken first, then 'we would quickly have Dublin'.[59] The plan was feasible because Drogheda sat 'in a plain open Country, no Bogs or Marsh-land near it, encompassed with an old Stone Wall, without Bulwarks, or any kind of Rampiers, or other Fortifications, but an ordinary Ditch'.[60] Yet the first of three assaults was hurled in vain against St John's Gate on 20 December 1641.[61] The besiegers reverted to blockade until 12 January 1642 when relief ships smashed through the boom.[62] Later that night,

---

54 Gilbert (ed.), *Contemporary History*, vol. I, p.53.
55 Maighréad Ní Mhurchadha, *Fingal, 1603–60: Contending Neighbours in North Dublin* (Dublin: Four Courts Press, 2005), pp.260–61, 268–69.
56 TCDL: 1641 Depositions, MS 816 (County Meath), fols 44r–44v, 47r: Examination of Edward Dowdall, 78r: Examination of Garratt Aylmer.
57 TCDL: 1641 Depositions, MS 816 (County Meath), fols 3r: Examination of John Talbott, 46r: Examination of Edward Dowdall, 77r: Examination of Garratt Aylmer.
58 John Heath (ed.), *Observations upon military & political affairs written by the Most Honourable George, Duke of Albemarle* (London: R. White, 1796), p.21; Brendan Scott and Kenneth Nicholls, 'The Landowners of the Late Elizabethan Pale: "The Generall Hosting Appointed to Meet at Ye Hill of Tarrah on the 24 of September 1593"', *Analecta Hibernica*, 43 (2012), pp.4–9.
59 TCDL: 1641 Depositions, MS 834 (County Louth), fol. 6v: Deposition of Luce Spell.
60 British History Online (BHO) John Rushworth, 'Historical Collections: Passages relating to Ireland 1642-43', in *Historical Collections of Private Passages of State: Volume 5, 1642-45* (London: D. Browne, 1721), pp.504–59.
61 Carte, *History of the Life of James Duke of Ormonde*, vol. I, p.286.
62 TCDL: 1641 Depositions, MS 816 (County Meath), fol. 77r: Examination of Garratt Aylmer.

sympathetic townsmen broke open a hole in the wall, and several besiegers slipped through, but, rather than open the gate, they set up a battle cry, which roused the English, most of them 'dead with drink and sleep'.[63] The next day, everyone agreed that Phelim O'Neill should be put in command of the siege after he vowed to bring guns 'to batter Drogheda in four places'.[64] The guns never came, and the blockade resumed.

Troops Besieging Drogheda[65]

Commander	County	Foot	Horse
Christopher Barnwall	Louth	1,000	
Gormanston	Meath	2,000	120
Philip O'Reilly	Cavan	1,700	
Colla Mac Mahon	Monaghan	1,900	
Brian MacHugh Buí O'Neill	Armagh	400	
	Total	7,000	120

The Ulstermen's numbers peaked at about 4,000 in December before some had to be pulled back: Philip O'Reilly, for example, withdrew 1,000.[66] Gormanston beseeched the loyalist Earl of Westmeath to send him 1,000 reinforcements, and it was too late by the time a more tractable Nugent was elected insurgent governor of the county.[67] The Irish were too few and spread too thinly around a circuit of some 18 miles straddling both sides of the River Boyne, with the nearest crossing point to Drogheda being at Oldbridge, over three miles upstream. Consequently, the 2,000 defenders enjoyed the advantage of 'interior lines', in that they could switch forces quickly from one

---

63 Trinity College Dublin Library (TCDL) 1641 Depositions, MS 840 (County Dublin), fol. 7r: Letter from Philip Bysse to his brother.
64 Trinity College Dublin Library (TCDL) 1641 Depositions, MS 832 (County Cavan), fol. 216r: Deposition of Thomas Crant.
65 TCDL: 1641 Depositions, MS 816 (County Meath), fols 69r: Examination of Nicholas Dowdall, 75: Examination of Garret Aylmer, 207r Deposition of Henry Smith, MS 834 (County Louth), fols 28r–29v: Examination of Christopher Barnwell, and MS 834 (County Monaghan), fols 100v: Deposition of Mathew Brown, 132r–35r: Deposition of John Mountgomery; Brendan Scott (ed.), *Dr Henry Jones' Account of the 1641 Rising: Plantation and War in County Cavan* (Newtownards: Ulster Historical Foundation, 2021), p.51.
66 Ulick Burke, *The Memoirs and Letters of Ulick, Marquis of Clanricarde, and Earl of Saint Albans …* (London: J. Hughs, 1757), p.104, 'Fingal, Gormanstown, Netterville and Trimlestown, camp near Drogheda, 23 February 1642, to Ulick Burke Earl of Clanricard'; Trinity College Dublin Library (TCDL) 1641 Depositions, MS 810 (County Dublin), fol. 196v: Examination of Teige Kelly; Ó Donnchadha, 'Cín lae', p.7.
67 TCDL: 1641 Depositions, MS 817 (County Westmeath), fols 20r: Deposition of John Stroughan, 37r–40v: Deposition of Thomas Fleetwood, 61v: Examination of Ralph Turner; Micheál Ó Siochrú, 'Nugent, Sir Richard', *Dictionary of Irish Biography* (2009), <https://www.dib.ie/biography/nugent-sir-richard-a6258>, accessed 18 Nov. 2020.

side of the Boyne to the other and could achieve local superiority of numbers. Agricultural societies typically could not afford to withdraw more than about 3 percent of their population from food production without precipitating famine, but that constraint did not apply in deepest winter when the crops were harvested, grain threshed, cows dried up and there was little work to do. The ceiling of the possible was not a shortage of men, as such, but of food to feed them. The countryside was hard put to supply a beef and half a barrel of corn a day for every company, and so the besiegers endured 'cold, want & misery'.[68]

That said, on 12 January, the besiegers had come within a hair's breadth of taking Drogheda. Determinism is best avoided in military history. *Because* it happened like that does not mean it *had* to happen like that.

Kildare, the final county of the Pale, joined the revolt right after Crufty. In deciding when the revolt actually began, the activities of robber bands, like that of Gilbert Talbot of Carton, County Kildare, have been ignored: Talbot insisted that he was a follower of Charles' Catholic consort, Henrietta Maria.[69] In contrast to County Meath, companies armed by Dublin Castle held on to their weapons. Encouraged by news of Julianstown and by that 'Hellhound' O'More, the company garrisoned in Naas joined a band of insurgents who had entered the town. Piers Mac Thomas Fitzgerald garrisoned Casteldermot in the south of the county for the government until soldiers overpowered the owner 'with their swords and skeines drawn' and the watchword 'Sancta Maria' on their lips.[70] Edward Mac Thomas Fitzgerald (not one of those made captain by the Crown) seized Maynooth Castle on 14 January, claiming that he was the 'real' Earl of Kildare of that line that Henry VIII had cut short on the chopping block in the 1530s.

Captain's commission. (The National Archives)

68 TCDL: 1641 Depositions, MS 834 (County Monaghan), fol. 134r: 'Deposition of John Mountgomery'.
69 Trinity College Dublin Library (TCDL) 1641 Depositions, MS 813 (County Kildare), fol. 250r: Deposition of Patrick Gosson.
70 TCDL: 1641 Depositions, MS 813 (County Kildare), fols 1r: Information of William Pilsworth, 306r: Deposition of John Walsh.

Insurgents might hanker for an imagined native past, but they followed contemporary English and Spanish models of military organization. Their companies were nearly always 100 strong, and they aspired to equip them 'with pikes, muskets and swords'.[71] The insurgents followed the English practice of embodying regiments comprising about 10 companies rather than the larger Spanish tercio. A surviving captain's commission from Red Phelim recites the formal words of authority in English, the written language of command and administration (e.g., musters, payrolls and orders).[72] Officers mostly spoke English amongst themselves but code-switched to Irish when ordering the common soldiery about, and it is was thought remarkable that Castlehaven could not speak or even understand Irish.[73]

To the south of Kildare lay Kilkenny, home of James Butler Earl of Ormond, commander of the army in Ireland, and head of the senior branch of the Butlers. Ormond's conversion to Protestantism and alliance with the execrated Wentworth meant that his grand-uncle, the 63-year-old Richard Butler, Viscount Mountgarret, was now looked up to as the 'real leader' of the Butler affinity.[74] Mountgarret had not forgotten the 'undue and sinister means' that forced him to hand over tracts of Idough in north County Kilkenny. He also shared the common fear that the 'English and Scots' would 'come into Ireland with the bible in one hand, the Sword in the other ... to raze the name of Catholic and Irish out of the whole kingdom'.[75] Forty years ago Mountgarret had been Tyrone's son-in-law and ally and he rightly suspected that, whatever he did, Dublin Castle would fix blame on an 'old rebel' like him. His defection brought with him Counties Kilkenny and Tipperary, the territorial core of the future Confederate Catholic regime. By 13 December, Tipperary rose under the heads of three Butler cadet houses, Viscount Ikerrin and Barons Dunboyne and Cahir, together with Tibbott Purcell of Loughmoe, whose family had been, by tradition, the captains of Ormond's kern.[76] Richard Butler, son of Viscount Ikerrin, took a leading role, no doubt because of his military

---

71 TCDL: 1641 Depositions, MS 813 (County Kildare), fols 8v: Examination of Edmond English, 148r: The Examination of Hannagh Ffarrell, 279r: Deposition of George Elkin and MS 818 (County Wexford), fol. 247r: Examination of James Clandalke.
72 The National Archives (TNA) SP 63/260, fol. 210: 'Commission of Sir Phelim O'Neall to Hugh Murray O'Devin', 28 Jan 1642'; TCDL: 1641 Depositions, MS 818 (County Wexford), fol. 57r: Deposition of George Charlton.
73 P. Lynch (ed.), *The Earl of Castlehaven's Memoirs Or, His Review of the Civil Wars in Ireland* (Dublin: Espy and Cross, 1815), p.134; Canny, *Making Ireland British*, pp.452–55.
74 David Edwards, '"The Poisoned Chalice": The Ormond Inheritance, Sectarian Division and the Emergence of James Butler, 1614-1642', in T. C. Barnard and J. Fenlon (eds), *The Dukes of Ormonde, 1610-1745* (Woodbridge: Boydell & Brewer, 2000), p.78.
75 Cited in Aidan Clarke, *The Old English in Ireland, 1625-42* (London: MacGibbon and Kee, 1966), pp.109, 196; Sean Kelsey, 'Butler, Richard, Third Viscount Mountgarret (1578–1651)', *Oxford Dictionary of National Biography* (2004), <https://doi.org/10.1093/ref:odnb/4202>, accessed 13 May 2023; Canny, *Making Ireland British*, p.271; Darcy, *Irish Rebellion*, pp.28, 61; Gilbert (ed.), *Contemporary History*, vol. I, p.360.
76 Trinity College Dublin Library (TCDL) 1641 Depositions, MS 830 (County Galway), fols 30r, 30v, 31r: Deposition of Samuell Pullein; W. J. Smyth, 'Property, Patronage and Population – Reconstructing the Human Geography of Mid Seventeenth-Century County Tipperary', in W. Nolan and T. G. McGrath (eds), *Tipperary: History and Society* (Dublin: Geography Publications, 1985), p.113; The National Archives (TNA) SP 63/260, fol. 190: 'Earl of Ormond to Charles I, Dublin, 12 Dec 1641'.

experience with the forces of the Polish–Lithuanian Commonwealth at the relief of Smolensk in 1633.[77] Ormond's brother, Richard Butler of Kilcash, carried the rebellion into County Waterford, though it would be March before the officer commanding the citadel defected and forced the city to join the Catholic cause.[78]

In both the Pale and the Butler domain, social hierarchy may be imagined as a pyramid with a broad base and thin apex in which baronial and aristocratic revolt could unfold smoothly: Dunboyne, for instance, took command of the Middlethird barony, 'in respect of the merits of his predecessors'.[79] Other regions, like south County Wexford, had a squat pyramid with more gentry, smaller landowners and many middling tenants shading imperceptibly from 'husbandman' up to 'yeoman'. Here, the gentry took the lead. William Browne, second largest landowner in the barony of Bargy, began by recruiting household servants and undertenants. His lieutenant and neighbour John Cheevers, together with the latter's two brothers, represented another important familial and economic network. Browne chose the son of a landowner from the adjoining parish of Kilmore as his ensign. We have the names and occupations of 14 private soldiers in Browne's company, and, in descending order of class, six were gentlemen rankers, two were farmers and one each a yeoman, a farrier and a copyholder. Three were servants.[80]

Revolt in Connacht began sluggishly except in south County Leitrim where Eoghan and Con O'Rourke must have been party to the Ulster plot as followers of Rory Maguire. Fatefully, they did not, or could not, take on the garrisons of regular soldiers in Carrick-on-Shann and Jamestown.[81] Lough Allen cuts off north Leitrim, which was overwhelmingly in settler ownership and looked to County Sligo for effective native leadership against Manorhamilton's forays. It is likely that the Sligo gentry acted before the Palesmen's defection. Tadgh O'Connor Sligo, the chosen 'Colonel of the County', had lost his patrimony in 1635 when a client of Wentworth's

---

77 Máire Ní Cheallacháin, *Filíocht Phádraigín Haicéad* (Dublin: An Clóchomhar, 2003), p.54; Michał Paradowski, 'Aston, Butler and Murray – British Officers in the Service of Polish Vasa Kings 1621-1634', in S. Jones (ed.), *Britain Turned Germany: The Thirty Years' War and Its Impact on the British Isles 1638-1660* (Warwick: Helion & Company, 2019), p.65.

78 Gilbert (ed.), *Irish Confederation*, vol. II, p.21, 'Mrs Briver's Account of Proceedings in Waterford, 1642'.

79 Trinity College Dublin Library (TCDL) 1641 Depositions, MS 821 (County Tipperary), fols 19r: Deposition of Robert Hamilton, 56v: Deposition of Thomas Grove, 231r: Examination of David Powell, 231v: Examination of David Powell; Bodleian Library (BoL) Carte MS 64, fols 458r, 460r: Kearney of Fethard, 'Memorials of the War'.

80 TCDL: 1641 Depositions, MS 818 (County Wexford), fols 240v: Examination of John O Murrow, 293: Examination of Marcus Power, 326r: Examination of Robert Browne; Trinity College Dublin Library (TCDL) 1641 Depositions, MS 819 (County Wexford), fols 37r: Examination of Nicholas Staples, 37v: Examination of Phillip O Cassey, 79: Deposition of Ursula Rowe, 85r: Examination of Marcus Power, 85v: Depisition of John Cheevers, 121r: Examination of John Whitty, 122r: Examination of Edward Sinnot, 291r–91v: Examination of Robert Browne, 292r, 294r, 294v: Examination of John O Murrow.

81 Trinity College Dublin Library (TCDL) 1641 Depositions, MS 831 (County Leitrim), fols 17r: Deposition of John Winder, 21r: Deposition of Anthony Milles, 28r: Deposition of Gilbert Corbin, 48r: Deposition of James Stevenson.

had snapped it up at a fire-sale price after threats that it would otherwise be confiscated.[82] A more important leader was Sir Lucas Taaffe, who, in the absence of his nephew 2nd Viscount Theobald, one of the would-be recruiting colonels, mobilised kin and dependents of this servitor family that had been extravagantly rewarded after the Nine Years' War. Viscount Taaffe was but one of several Protestant heads of overwhelmingly Catholic familial networks that were co-opted, typically, by insurgent brothers, uncles or grand-uncles. West of the Shannon, such disconnected heads included Taaffe's cousin Tibbot Viscount Dillon of Costello-Gallen, Earl of Thomond Barnabas O'Brien, and Viscount Mayo Myles Burke.

Amongst the earliest rebels in County Sligo were Philip O'Dowd and a dozen followers near Moyne Abbey in the west of the county, who were all that was left of a company that Taaffe had enlisted from Wentworth's disbanded soldiers and kept in readiness to take ship for Spain.[83] By forbidding Wentworth's army from embarking, the English Parliament left hundreds, maybe even thousands, of trained soldiers to be recruited by the insurgents while the order, counterorder and disorder of demobilisation and recruitment had given plausible cover for men to congregate in public spaces, ostensibly to enlist. It was such a dangerous thing to do that many wondered then and since if Pym's junto was deliberately fomenting violence in Ireland.[84]

In mid-December, Viscount Mayo took six companies of soldiers to put down troublemakers in the western baronies of the county, but a priest suborned them. Mayo's brother Richard of Partry took Carra Castle by bringing a supposed prisoner and escort to be examined by the owner and local justice of the peace, the castle 'being very strong & not to be taken or forced but by ordinance, famine, or fraud'.[85] Later, Sir Henry Bingham surrendered his stronghold at Castlebar to Mayo, who would soon convert to Catholicism.

Catholic clergymen showed 'feverish activity' in Connacht, not only inciting but even organising military action.[86] Archbishop of Tuam Malachy O'Queally travelled all over the ecclesiastical province of Tuam (more or less coterminous with Connacht) as one of 'the most active incendiaries' among the clergy and maintained two standing companies of foot at his own

---

82 TCDL: 1641 Depositions, MS 831 (County Sligo), fols 81r: Examination of Oliver Albanagh, 118r: Examination of John Crean; Perceval-Maxwell, *Outbreak of the Irish Rebellion*, pp.249–50; Canny, *Making Ireland British*, p.496.

83 TCDL: 1641 Depositions, MS 831 (County Sligo), fols 79r–80v: Examination of Patrick Dowd.

84 Keith Roberts, *Cromwell's War Machine: The New Model Army 1645-1660* (Barnsley: Pen and Sword, 2005), p.21; James S. Wheeler, *The Irish and British Wars, 1637–1654: Triumph, Tragedy, and Failure* (London: Routledge, 2002), p.45; Trinity College Dublin Library (TCDL) 1641 Depositions, MS 838 (County Derry), fol. 38r: Examination of Neile oge ó Quin; Wanklyn, *Army of Occupation*, pp. 176-178

85 TCDL: 1641 Depositions, MS 831 (County Mayo), fols 177r: Deposition of Andrew Adair, 202v, 202r: Deposition of J. Bringhurst.

86 Aoife Duignan, '"All in a Confused Opposition to Each Other": Politics and War in Connacht, 1641-9: PhD. Thesis, University College Dublin, 2005', *Irish Economic and Social History*, 33:1 (2006), pp.72–73.

expense.[87] On Christmas Day, a brother of Sir Robert Lynch seized Clonboo Castle and within weeks, Lynch's fellow lawyers and brothers-in-law Patrick Darcy and Richard Martin ' moved the town of Galway to rebellion'.[88] The townsmen planted guns on their ramparts and blockaded the fort, built as a citadel on a nearby hill to overawe the citizens. One of these guns burst when fired against an English pinnace and killed the amateur gunner and member of the municipal 'Council of Eight'.[89]

Ulick Burke, Earl of Clanricarde, a Catholic and the dominant noble in the county, raised an army of 900 men, most of whom he posted in his castles at Claregalway, Terryland and Oranmore, while his cavalry scoured the plains and choked off supplies coming from the east of the county to the besiegers.[90] Clanricarde had put a stop to the rising in County Galway for the moment. His singular and persistent loyalty to Dublin Castle is best explained by the fact that in February 1639, Charles had specifically exempted his estates from any future plantation.

The rising in County Roscommon begun in earnest on Christmas Eve, when O'Rourke and O'Farrell contingents from neighbouring Leitrim and Longford joined local 'loose and Idle Rogues' to burn Roscommon Abbey.[91] Among the incendiaries present was Hugh O'Conor Don, son of Charles of Ballintober, the lineal descendant of Ireland's last High King. In an echo of what was happening in County Sligo, an O'Conor proved an ineffectual leader while a Catholic of loyalist stock, Sir Lucas Dillon of Loughglynn, replaced him and incited the Catholic gentry of the county to rise because 'the Puritan Parliament of England would otherwise destroy them'.[92]

Bellings spoke of common soldiers being recruited by 'the chief of the sept', as if the Gaelic clan still represented a collective entity, and English sources do the same when they speak of a surname like 'O'Kelly' as being a

---

87 TCDL: 1641 Depositions, MS 830 (County Galway), fols 134v: Deposition of William Hammond, 259r: Examination of Joseph Hampton and MS 831 (County Mayo), fols 170r, 170v: Examination of Walter Bourke, 201r: Deposition of J. Bringhurst; Charles P. Meehan (ed.), *The Rise and Fall of the Irish Franciscan Monasteries, and Memoirs of the Irish Hierarchy, in the Seventeenth Century. With Appendices Containing Documents from the Rinuccini Manuscripts, Public Records, and Archives of the Franciscan Convent, Dublin* (Dublin: James Duffy and Sons, 1872), p.303, 'Edmund O'Dwyer, La Rochelle, 16 October 1642'; Micheál Ó Siochrú, 'Martin, Richard', *Dictionary of Irish Biography* (2009), <https://www.dib.ie/biography/martin-richard-a5486>, accessed 18 Nov. 2020; Edward MacLysaght and H. F. Berry, 'Report on Documents Relating to the Wardenship of Galway', *Analecta Hibernica*, 14 (1944), p.22, 'O'Queally to unk, 31 October and 17 December 1637'.

88 TCDL: 1641 Depositions, MS 830 (County Galway), fols 138r–39v: Deposition of Joseph Hampton.

89 TCDL: 1641 Depositions, MS 830 (County Galway), fols 148v: Deposition of Thomas Bagworth, 229r: Examination of John Morgan, 286v: Examination of Martin Lynch.

90 Burke, *Memoirs and Letters of Ulick*, pp.68, 358; Demetri D. Debe, 'The Fifth Earl of Clanricarde and the Founding of the Confederate Catholic Government 1641-3', *Irish Historical Studies*, 36:143 (2009), pp.316, 328.

91 TCDL: 1641 Depositions, MS 830 (County Roscommon), fol. 15v: Deposition of John Ridge and MS 831 (County Roscommon), fols 198r: Deposition of Richard Chapman, 216r: Deposition of Ismah Darby.

92 TCDL: 1641 Depositions, MS 830 (County Roscommon), fols 9r, 9v: Examination of Hugh ô Connor.

'nation' and of some notable insurgent as the 'chief man of that name'.[93] They may be right. In Ulster, Connacht and the Midlands, at any rate, residual clan affiliation seems to have been more important than elsewhere in smoothing collective military action. Redmond O'Fallon, son and heir to the erstwhile 'chief of his name', took Grange Castle, County Roscommon, which had been out of O'Fallon hands for 60 years.[94] Nine of the dozen named men who helped Redmond were O'Fallons. In the western half of Laois and Offaly, leading representatives of the pre-conquest Mac Coghlans, Foxes, O'Molloys, O'Carrolls, O'Dunnes and Fitzpatricks took charge. For instance, the 'colonel' of the old O'Molloy country of Ferceall was Art O'Molloy of Rathlihen, a grandson of Calbhach, the last chieftain.[95] In contrast, the O'Mores, O'Lalors, Mac Evoys and other septs of east Laois and Offaly (except for the loyalist O'Dempseys) had been scattered.

Shockwaves from the epicentre in south Ulster reverberated south, but the rising stalled on the northern edge of the old O'Neill *oireacht* (country or territory) for two whole months.[96] Twenty-four years previously, the authorities had uncovered a plot to seize planter settlements in north Ulster and executed 25 conspirators: the decapitation of the malcontents may have dissuaded others in 1641. For whatever reason, O'Cahans and Mac Donnells had not been in on the original plot and initially sided with the planters. A native and a Scots Highlander company formed part of a largely Lowland Scots regiment quartered near the ford of Portnaw on the Bann to block the spread of the rising into County Antrim. The Highlanders were led by Alasdair Mac Colla Ciotach, already regarded as the best warrior amongst the Mac Donalds. He stood half a head taller than most men and had the sinews and shoulders of a swordsman, the best in Ireland by his own reckoning. Two hours before dawn, on 2 January 1642, the two companies fell on their sleeping comrades. They may have wanted to pre-empt what happened 12 days before and less than 30 miles away when the natives in one predominantly settler company had been disarmed and sent home.[97] That night, the lieutenant of the company, with 80 soldiers, fell on the village of Templepatrick, and 'with their swords & pikes' killed 26 of the disarmed

---

93 Gilbert (ed.), *Irish Confederation*, vol. I, p.80; Anon., *A true relation of the manner of our Colonell Sir Frederick Hammiltons return from London-Derry in Ireland* (London: Publisher unknown, 1645), pp.17, 23, 25; TCDL: 1641 Depositions, MS 830 (County Roscommon), fols 30r, 30v: Deposition of John Dodwill.

94 Kenneth Nicholls (ed.), *The Irish Fiants of the Tudor Sovereigns: During the Reigns of Henry VIII, Edward VI, Philip & Mary, and Elizabeth I* (Dublin: Éamonn de Búrca, 1994), vol. II, p.515 and vol. III, p.123; TCDL: 1641 Depositions, MS 830 (County Roscommon), fols 30r–31v: Deposition of John Dodwill.

95 Gilbert (ed.), *Contemporary History*, vol. I, p.16; TCDL: 1641 Depositions, MS 814 (County Offaly), fols 160r: Deposition of Edward St Larence, 163r: Deposition of Grace Smith, 219r: Deposition of John Hodgson, 235r: Deposition of Thomas Morley, 270r: Deposition of Charles Jewell.

96 Raymond Gillespie, *Conspiracy: Ulster Plots and Plotters in 1615* (Belfast: Ulster Society for Irish Historical Studies, 1987), p.15.

97 George Hill, 'The Stewarts of Ballintoy: With Notices of Other Families of the District in the Seventeenth Century', *Ulster Journal of Archaeology*, 2nd series, 6:1 (1900), pp.17–23.

soldiers, along with their wives and children.[98] However, the terrifying speed with which the mutineers crossed the Bann and raised the Route afterwards suggests that Portnaw was a not a panicky reaction but a carefully planned strike. Soon, Coleraine was virtually the only settler stronghold in the entire arc of Irish territory between Derry and Larne.

Coleraine was ever more tightly blockaded after 'Black Friday' on 11 February when Archbald Stewart led out 600 foot soldiers, one-third English and two-thirds Scots, and a troop of horse to 'get prey'. He met about the same number of Irishmen under Mac Colla at Bendooragh:[99]

> ... the Scots aiming the glory of the day strove for the Van, & having made their body full for battaile charged the Enemy: when after about a few shot betwixt the Enemy & the Scots (only one Scot being slain) the whole body of the Scots suddenly wheeled about: Crying We are all Slain we are all slain: & so running confusedly amongst the English ...[100]

Simon Harcourt landed on in Dublin on New Year's Day, two days before Portnaw, with the first increment of massive reinforcements to come. Charles Coote, military governor of the capital, now felt confident enough to pounce on the Fingallians who lay uncomfortably close to the northern suburbs. Coote first fell on Santry, two miles north of Dublin, where Luke Netterville, in a scarlet coat, did not 'stand to fight'. Though outnumbered two to one, Netterville put up stiffer resistance when Coote fell on Swords with 3,000 men at dawn on 11 January 1642.[101] Netterville's musketeers shot at Coote from the ditches on either side of a boreen until some of Coote's men broke down the embankments, rolled up Netterville's shot and killed, according to English reports, about 100 of them in the 'hot skirmish'.[102] The English admitted to losing four men, including Sir Lorenzo Carey, brother of one-time Lord Deputy Falkland, shot in the head 'by mischance'.[103] But sacking Swords did not open the road to Drogheda. The priest Laurence Rowan still lurked at Artane, four miles to the north of Dublin, his object being to 'keep corn and other provisions from the market'.[104] In response to the reverse at Swords, Hugh Mac Phelim O'Byrne erected a fortified camp beside nearby Kilsallaghan Castle and manned it with 1,350 foot soldiers, two-thirds

---

98   TCDL: 1641 Depositions, MS 838 (County Antrim), fols 78r: Examination of Donnell crone McCart, 160v: Examination of Any ny Cary.
99   TCDL: 1641 Depositions, MS 839 (County Derry), fols 96v–97r: Deposition of Charles Anthony.
100 Hogan (ed.), *History of the Warr of Ireland*, p.22.
101 Ó Donnchadha, 'Cín lae', p.36.
102 Richard Chappell, *A true and good Relation of the Valliant Exploits, and Victorious Enterprises of Sir Simon Harcourt, and Sir Charles Coote ...* (London: F. Coules and W. Ley, 1642), pp.1, 3.
103 TNA: *HMC Report on the Manuscripts of the Earl of Egmont*, vol. I, pp.159–60, 'Paul Davys to Sir Philip Percival, 11 January Dublin'; Margaret M. Verney, *Memoirs of the Verney Family during the Seventeenth Century* (London: Longmans, Green and Co., 1892), vol. II, p.133.
104 TCDL: 1641 Depositions, MS 810 (County Dublin), fol. 114r: Deposition of Daniell Barwick and MS 816 (County Meath), fols 16r, 16v: Examination of James Grace.

of them transferred from County Kildare.[105] Coote promptly turned his attention south-west to the latter county, seized Castle Lyons and 'thoroughly burnt' 15 nearby villages.[106]

Meanwhile, in Munster, forays across the Shannon from north Tipperary into County Clare set off a spate of cattle rustling in the week before Christmas. Thomond, governor of the county, made 'divers of his own kindred' captains, and they pretended to put down the cattle rustlers while Thomond pretended to believe that they were doing so. The pretence worked, for a while. The moment of decision, when settlers finally fled their homes to seek safety behind castle walls, came six weeks later than in the adjacent parts of Munster across the Shannon.[107]

At the beginning of February 1642, Mountgarret led a host of up to 6,000 men – whose 'many pikes made as great a show as a spacious wood' – west from County Tipperary into County Limerick by way of Kilmallock and then south through a gap in the Bayllyhoura Hills into County Cork.[108] President of Munster Sir William St Leger, a grizzled veteran of the Nine Years' War, chose to abandon open countryside and pull back to the port towns and a few inland strongholds, like the 'great thoroughfare' of Mallow and its bridge over the River Blackwater. A 'well fortified and flanked' castle held by a strong garrison of 200 soldiers loomed within 100 yards of the bridge. At the northern end of the town was Castlegar, a smaller castle. On Friday and Saturday, 11–12 February, the throng of drovers, sutlers and servants poured into town to be followed by the soldiery, who were short of gunpowder, 'ignorantly disciplined' and 'carelessly commanded'.[109] Having failed to intimidate the defenders of the main castle, Mountgarret's followers occupied a nearby line of houses, knocked loopholes for muskets and 'suffered not the defendants to put their heads over the wall'. Meanwhile, the County Cork contingent prised out Castlegar's kitchen window, smashed the surrounding stonework and sent a storming party through the hole in the wall. As the attackers tentatively probed the dark recesses, swordsmen on either side of the breach cut off the pike heads (a pike shaft was only about as thick as a broom handle towards its tip) while a sniper in a dark nook

---

105 TCDL: 1641 Depositions, MS 813 (County Kildare), fols 46r, 46v, 47r: Information of Walter Hussey.
106 TCDL: 1641 Depositions, MS 840 (County Dublin), fol. 8v: Letter from Philip Bysse to his brother.
107 Trinity College Dublin Library (TCDL) 1641 Depositions, MS 815 (Queens County), fol. 376r: Deposition of John Brereton; TCDL: 1641 Depositions, MS 821 (County Tipperary), fol. 202r: Examination of Jane Cooper, MS 829 (County Clare), fols 29r: Deposition of Urias Reade, 70v: Deposition of Edmund Manwaring, 95v: Deposition of Andrew Chaplin, and MS 829 (County Limerick), fol. 150v: Deposition of Thomas Browne.
108 Urban Vigors, 'Urban Vigors' Relation', *Journal of the Waterford and South-East of Ireland Archaeological Society*, 15 (1912), p.85; Trinity College Dublin Library (TCDL) 1641 Depositions, MS 822 (County Cork), fol. 14v: Deposition of George Chimery; The National Archives (TNA) *HMC 7th Report, Manuscripts of Sir Harry Verney* (London: HMC, 1879), p.437, 'John Leeke to Edmund Verney, 4 March 1642'.
109 Robert Cole, *More good and true news from Ireland sent from Dublin by Master Robert Cole merchant, to his brother Iohn Cole here resident in London …* (London: F. Coules, 1642), p.2; Herbert W. Gillman, 'The Rise and Progress in Munster of the Rebellion, 1642', *Journal of the Cork Historical & Archaeological Society*, 2nd series, 2:13 (1896), pp.11–63.

'shot so fast as three people appointed for the purpose could charge some three or four muskets' and 200 were, gloated a Protestant source, 'sent apace to hell'. Being promised that their lives would be spared, they capitulated at first light. There was a tense moment when some of the Corkmen growled that 'there was no quarter to be kept with such English dogs', and the English appealed to Sergeant Majors Purcell and Michael Wall of Coolnamuck, County Waterford, both 'bred abroad in the wars', to honour their promises. With swords drawn, Purcell and Wall escorted the frightened English to the bigger castle and safety.[110]

And that was it. The Irish pulled back on the afternoon of 16 February, burning what they could not pillage and leaving behind two 'sows', musket-proof shelters that could be manhandled on wheels or rollers. Mountgarret had been in two minds about pushing on even as far as Mallow, but local notables Dermot MacCarthy of Duhallow (who was confusingly called 'Mac Donagh') and Maurice Roche, Viscount Fermoy, had promised him abundant supplies. The Tipperarymen came but without Mountgarret. Fermoy had inherited a dispute over precedence between his late father and Mountgarret and, consequently, would not serve under 'so mean a man' as Sergeant Major Purcell. This dreary quarrel would undermine the Catholic war effort in Munster for years to come, with William Bourke, Baron Castleconnell, and Theobald Bourke, Baron Brittas, supporting their kinsman Fermoy and Donough MacCarthy, 2nd Viscount Muskerry, backing his Butler in-laws.[111] Ikerrin reluctantly took charge only to pull back which was a colossal mistake as he should have laid close siege to the Great Castle, which controlled the only bridge over the Blackwater before Cappoquin, County Waterford, 40 miles downriver.

Patrick Fitzmaurice, 19th Baron of Kerry, had been appointed military governor of the county, but here – as in Westmeath, Kildare, Mayo and Clare – those mustered to defend the county defected, including Fitzmaurice's half-brother. Tralee Castle was beleaguered as early as 14 February 1642, even as the attack on Mallow petered out.

The pivotal siege of Drogheda also stalled. Phelim O'Neill had blockaded the town and threw a boom across the Boyne Estuary. A relief fleet broke the boom on 20 February, and, the very same day, almost 2,000 fresh English soldiers disembarked at Dublin.[112] At four o'clock in the morning, on 21

---

110 Gillman, 'Rise and Progress', pp.20, 22, 23, 25.
111 Gilbert (ed.), *Irish Confederation*, vol. I, p.67; TCDL: 1641 Depositions, MS 821 (County Cork), fol. 327r: Depositions of Francis Bettrige and Richard Williams; Patrick McCarthy, 'The 1641 Rebellion in Cork to the Battle of Liscarroll, 3 September 1642', *The Irish Sword*, 22:90 (2001), p.377; House of Commons, *A relation touching the present state and condition of Ireland. Collected by a committee of the house of Commons, out of severall letters, lately come from the Lords Justices of Ireland and others, and printed by order of the said house. And also the examination of Hubert Petit, taken the 19. of February, 1641. by the direction of the Lords Justices, and counsell of Ireland* (London: E. G., 1642), p.6; Micheál Ó Siochrú, 'Roche, David', *Dictionary of Irish Biography* (2009), <https://www.dib.ie/biography/roche-david-a7742>, accessed 18 Nov. 2020.
112 TCDL: 1641 Depositions, MS 810 (County Dublin), fol. 12: Deposition of George Stockdale; Gilbert (ed.), *Irish Confederation*, vol. I, pp.45–50; Carte, *History of the Life of James Duke of Ormonde*, vol. I, pp.282–83; Pádraig Lenihan, *Confederate Catholics at War, 1641-49* (Cork: Cork University Press, 2001), pp.46–47.

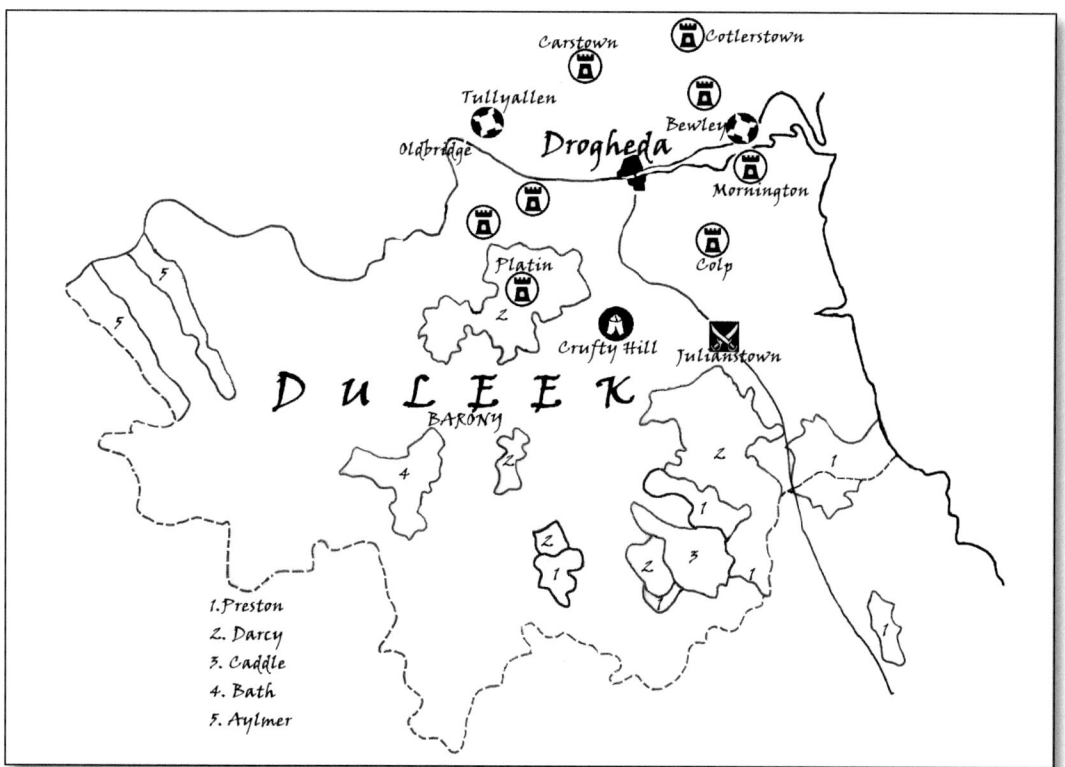

Duleek and Drogheda. (Author's illustration)

February, Phelim's men placed scaling ladders 'at a low private Corner where sometimes a Sentinel had been omitted'. Such was not the case this night. A sentinel raised the alarm, and the attack was aborted.[113]

Three days after the reinforcements landed, Ormond, lieutenant general of the Crown army, marched on Kilsallaghan Castle. Outnumbered and outgunned, the insurgents were winkled out of the entrenchments that they had dug in a churchyard opposite the castle gate with the loss of over 100 men.[114] The road to Drogheda now lay open.

A week later, on the last day of February, Tichborne surprised the siege camp at Tullyallen and routed Colla Mac Brian's men.[115] The next day, he secured control of the south bank in a sharp skirmish around Stameen and Colp, after which Phelim 'hid in a furze bush' before fleeing to Dundalk.[116] With the siege raised, the Pale lords begged in vain for 'furtherance & assistance'

---

113 Bernard, *The whole proceedings of the siege of Drogheda*, p.69; TCDL: 1641 Depositions, MS 838 (County Antrim), fol. 297r: Examination of John Morris.
114 R. C. Simington and John MacLellan, 'Oireachtas Library List of Outlaws, 1641-1647', *Analecta Hibernica*, 23 (1966), p.351; TCDL: 1641 Depositions, MS 813 (County Kildare), fols 10v: Examination of Thomas Ash, 39r, 39v: Examination of Charles Connor, 46r, 46v: Examination of Walter Hussey and MS 816 (County Dublin), fols 83r, 85r, 87r: Examination of Patrick Dillon, 196r: Examination of Teige Kelly.
115 Pilib Ó Mórdha, 'The MacMahons of Monaghan (1600 — 1640)', *Clogher Record*, 2:2 (1958), pp.311-27.
116 John Temple, *The History of the General Rebellion in Ireland. Raised Upon the Three and Twentieth Day of October, 1641. Together with the Barbarous Cruelties and Bloody Massacres which Ensued Thereupon* (Cork: Phineas and George Bagnell, 1766), pp.202, 299, 303, 307.

from their fellow countrymen.[117] Nugent of Carlanstown responded by urging that Gormanston invite Phelim O'Neill and Mountgarret to a sit-down 'to make up all jealousies and differences between them, or at least to send some lawyers and clergy as their Commissioners to do it'.[118] That is why Archbishop O'Reilly of Armagh convened that synod at Kells in March 1642 that would be the institutional progenitor of the Confederate Catholic regime.

That winter saw many Droghedas writ small. Insurgent murders of Protestant civilians in the first months of the 1641 rising were soon elaborated into a black legend of 'Hell-taught Furies, [who] in one black dismal night One hundred thousand Murther, e're 'twas light'.[119] Froude's preface to Mary Hickson's *Irish Massacres* (1884) also asserts that the murders 'held a place of infamy by the side of the Sicilian Vespers and the Massacre of St Bartholomew'.[120] Nonetheless, the murders were not a single explosive outburst. Settlers living in regions overrun by natives had days and weeks to recognise the increasing danger of robbery, injury, prison or death and to flee or to be escorted to a castle, walled town or tract of country held by friendly Catholics or more usually by countrymen and co-religionists. Some of the worst massacres, like that on Portadown bridge, were inflicted on refugees doing just that.[121]

Their destination was usually a castle, the focus of many plantation schemes. The typical planter castle had a rectangular bawn or walled enclosure with a gatehouse and rounded turrets or flankers bellying out at all or some of the corners.[122] Within stood a tower house or the more horizontal fortified mansion, the latter giving preference to comfort over defence as evidenced by amenities like mullioned windows. The tower house could be free standing or form one side of the enclosure. Typical of the type was Augher in County Tyrone, a substantial three-storey building enclosed by a bawn with four flankers, behind which about 1,000 women and children huddled.[123] It was less common for the castle to nestle within a square fort with regular corner bastions and a moat in the modern mode. Castlecomer provides a good example, not that it did the 300 people sheltering within much good since they capitulated as early as 2 March 1642.[124]

---

117 TCDL: 1641 Depositions, MS 816 (County Meath), fol. 71r: Examination of Nicholas Dowdall; Perceval-Maxwell, *Outbreak of the Irish Rebellion*, p.225.

118 Charles W. Russell and John P. Prendergast (eds), *The Carte manuscripts in the Bodleian Library, Oxford. A report presented to the Right Honourable Lord Romilly, master of the rolls* (London: G.E. Eyre and W. Spottiswoode, 1871), p.195.

119 William Mercer, *The moderate cavalier, or, The soldiers description of Ireland and of the country disease, with receipts for the same* (Cork: Publisher unknown, 1675), p.4.

120 Mary Hickson, *Ireland in the Seventeenth Century, or, The Irish Massacres of 1641–2: Their Causes and Results* (London: Longmans, Green and Co., 1884), vol. I, p.v, 'Preface' by J. A. Froude.

121 Mícheál Ó Siochrú and Mark S. Sweetnam, 'The 1641 Depositions and Portadown Bridge', *Seanchas Ard Mhacha: Journal of the Armagh Diocesan Historical Society*, 24:1 (2012), p.77.

122 Paul M. Kerrigan, 'Castles and Fortifications of County Offaly c. 1500-1815', in W. Nolan and T. P. O'Neill (eds), *Offaly: History & Society* (Dublin: Geography Publications, 1998), p.400.

123 TCDL: 1641 Depositions, MS 836 (County Tyrone), fol. 128v: Examination of Michaell Harrison and MS 839 (County Tyrone), fol. 21 v: Deposition of Roger Markham.

124 Cóilín Ó Drisceoil, 'Excavation of a Seventeenth Century Bastioned Fort at High Street, Castlecomer, Co. Kilkenny', *Old Kilkenny Review*, 70 (2018), pp.54, 76.

By the end of February 1642, when the tide of insurgency reached its highest, very few Protestant 'zones of control' survived, apart from the Laggan of north-west Ulster and Clandeboye in east Ulster. 'Zones of disruption' were, however, almost countrywide.[125] Loeber counted 19 sieges across Laois alone in 1642–1643.[126] Ulster probably contained 42 percent of the total settler population, Leinster had 31 percent, Munster 21 percent, and Connacht a mere 7 percent. Yet Ulster has relatively few strongholds and fewer yet that endured long sieges (Coleraine, County Derry, and Keelagh and Croaghan, County Cavan, are the only ones discussed) because the distribution of Protestant strongholds maps only on to those regions where newcomers were thickest on the ground and where they had time enough to pack up and flee to a friendly castle or walled town. Many of the 16 incorporated plantation towns in Ulster – including Dungannon, Charlemont, Mountjoy, Cookstown, Moneymore and Dungiven – had not enough warning and were amongst the first places to fall.[127]

The seventeenth-century siege was 'an affair of artillery', but the Irish had no proper artillery. The Lords Justices would complain that the culverin had to fire too many shots and took too long to knock a breach in walls, but those who knew better considered the culverin 'a good battering gun'. Good, that is, except that it was too heavy to be transported overland except in high summer on an arterial route.[128] The demi-culverin, shooting a nine-pound ball, represented a better trade-off between punch and portability. Anything smaller would not do. When the Mastersons loosed seven shots from 'one small ordinance' against Carnew Castle, County Wicklow, or when Phelim Rua knocked a hole in the roof of Augher with a field gun, the attackers probably knew that their guns were too light to batter and that they were using them as terror weapons.[129] Homemade contrivances like Viscount Clanmalier's tin cannon 'did not prosper', and the leather gun fired at Ballyalla 'broke & so gave fire backward'.[130] Daniel O'Dunne was more fortunate when

---

125 Robert Armstrong, *Protestant War: The 'British' of Ireland and the Wars of the Three Kingdoms* (Manchester: Manchester University Press, 2005), p.35.
126 Rolf Loeber, 'Warfare and Architecture in County Laois through Seventeenth Century Eyes', in P. G. Lane and W. Nolan (eds), *Laois: History & Society: Interdisciplinary Essays on the History of an Irish County* (Dublin: Geography Publications, 1999), p.385.
127 William J. Smyth, 'Towards a Cultural Geography of the 1641 Rising/Rebellion', in M. Ó Siochrú and J. Ohlmeyer (eds), *Ireland: 1641: Contexts and Reactions* (Manchester: Manchester University Press, 2013), p.75; Annaleigh Margey, '1641 and the Ulster Plantation Towns', in E. Darcy, A. Margey, and E. Murphy (eds), *The 1641 Depositions and the Irish Rebellion* (London: Pickering & Chatto, 2014), pp.79–96.
128 James Hogan (ed.), *Letters and Papers Relating to the Irish Rebellion between 1642–46* (Dublin: Stationary Office, 1936), p.73, 'Lords Justices to Parliamentary Commissioners, Dublin Castle, 8 July 1642'; Antoine de Pas, *Memoirs of the late Marquis de Feuquieres: Lieutenant-General of the French army. Written for the instruction of his son. Being an account of all the wars in Europe, from the year 1672, to the year 1710 ...* (London: T. Woodward and C. Davis, 1737), vol. 2, 'Military Dictionary'.
129 TCDL: 1641 Depositions, MS 811 (County Wicklow), fol. 80r: Deposition of John Millington, MS 836 (County Armagh), fol. 128r: Examination of Michaell Harrison, and MS 839 (County Tyrone), fol. 21 v: Deposition of Roger Markham.
130 TCDL: 1641 Depositions, MS 829 (County Clare), fol. 96r: Deposition of Andrew Chaplin.

he took Castlecuffe, County Laois, with a mock-up gun carved from a block of half-burned timber and drawn by eight oxen.[131]

Sometimes, the attackers struck lucky. Phelim *a chogaidh* (of the wars) O'Neill found a door left ajar at Mountjoy, County Tyrone.[132] Redmond O'Fallon took Grange in County Roscommon when the warders opened the door for him.[133] In County Tipperary, a servant's betrayal and a sneak shooting opened Rochestown Castle's doors.[134] The followers of Morgan Kavanagh of Clonmullen and Walter Bagnall of Dunleckny (like Mac Thomas, he had been a captain appointed and armed by Dublin Castle) met feeble resistance while knocking a hole 'with pickaxes iron Crows & other instruments' in Rathellin Castle's keep.[135]

Boasts that the 50 defenders of Elphin slew no fewer than 52 attackers 'one time when they attempted to scale the walls with ladders' are probably an exaggeration.[136] If it proved necessary to attack, climbing over the walls on ladders was 'most hazardous' since ladders were so easily spotted (in daylight or bright moonlight, at any rate) and were almost as easily pushed away. Scaling was too hazardous for some faint hearts who deserted the storming party told off to climb the walls of Lismore Castle, County Waterford.[137] Redmond Barry made up ladders to scale Annagh and Liscarroll in County Cork, but nothing came of his preparations.[138] Richard Mac Thomas O'Dempsey had his men place scaling ladders against the walls of Monasterevan Castle, County Kildare, 'in the dark of the night' and was shot dead, probably before anyone put their foot on a rung. His soldiers 'ran away', not even stopping to carry off his body.[139] The only successful escalade that comes to mind was when Dermot MacCarthy's followers scaled the walls of Newmarket at three o'clock in the morning on 7 January 1643 and surprised the warders.[140] Dungarvan Castle, County Waterford, provides an

---

131 John W. Wright, 'Sieges and Customs of War at the Opening of the Eighteenth Century', *American Historical Review*, 39:4 (1934), p.633; TCDL: 1641 Depositions, MS 829 (County Clare), fol. 29r: Deposition of Urias Reade; Frederick Fitzgerald, 'Lettice, Baroness of Offaly, and the Siege of Her Castle of Geashill, 1642', *Journal of the County Kildare Archaeological Society and Surrounding Districts*, 3 (1899–1902), p.422; John O'Hanlon and Edward O'Leary (eds), *History of the Queen's County* (Dublin: Sealy, Bryers & Walker, 1914), vol. II, p.515.
132 TCDL: 1641 Depositions, MS 839 (County Tyrone), fol. 91: Examination of Turlough Grome O Quin.
133 TCDL: 1641 Depositions, MS 830 (County Roscommon), fols 30r–31v: Deposition of John Dodwill.
134 TCDL: 1641 Depositions, MS 821 (County Tipperary), fol. 231r: Examination of David Powell and MS 829 (County Tipperary), fol. 209r: Deposition of ffaieth Grady.
135 TCDL: 1641 Depositions, MS 812 (County Carlow), fols 69r: Deposition of Ann Butler, 144r: Examination of John Thomson.
136 TCDL: 1641 Depositions, MS 831 (County Roscommon), fol. 217r: Ismah Darby.
137 Christopher Gravett, *Medieval Siege Warfare* (Oxford: Osprey, 1990), p.30; Jim Bradbury, *The Medieval Siege* (Woodbridge: Boydell & Brewer, 1994), p.275; Gilbert (ed.), *Irish Confederation*, vol. I, pp.71–72.
138 Trinity College Dublin Library (TCDL) 1641 Depositions, MS 827 (County Cork), fol. 14r: Examination of Phillip Holmes.
139 TCDL: 1641 Depositions, MS 813 (County Kildare), fol. 312v: Deposition of Edward Williamsonn.
140 Trinity College Dublin Library (TCDL) 1641 Depositions, MS 824 (County Cork), fol. 68v: Deposition of George Tanner.

example of someone capturing a castle with a ladder in an unexpected way. John Hore was returning a borrowed ladder, and, as the warders raised an iron grate, the six men carrying the ladder thrust it into the gap, whereupon Hore's followers 'entered the castle and took it'.[141]

A month later, more O'Dempseys came back with three sows. The sow was a solidly built hut that was wheeled up to walls and fancifully named from the image of a sow suckling her bonhams – the men crouched underneath – or rooting around in the ground with her snout.[142] One account describes this medieval contraption:

> … having its three sides made musket proof with boards; it was drawn on four wheels, each a foot high, with folding doors to open inwards, and several loopholes to shoot through, without a floor, that 10 or 12 men who went therein might drive it forwards. These machines were set against castle walls whilst the men within them attempted to make a breach with crows and pick-axes.[143]

O'Dempsey's sow would have been proofed against muskets, being double planked, the cavity stuffed with wool, and swathed in cowhides. Alas, a few shots from a two-pounder gun drove O'Dempsey's pioneers to flee. Lady Elizabeth Dowdall defended Kilfinny, County Limerick, with 'more than amazon courage', and her men 'pierced the sow with iron bullets and killed her pigs'. Sows were also trundled out at nearby Geashill, against Carnew, at Longford Castle, at Golden and Rochestown in County Tipperary, at Elphin in County Roscommon, at Ballyalla in County Clare, at Ballybeggan near Tralee in County Kerry, at Mallow in County Cork and no doubt at other places across three of the four provinces.[144] The outcomes were equally unhappy for the attackers, largely because it was all too easy to drop heavy rocks or masonry down on the roof of the sow, cracking it open.

Fire was sometimes used alongside other methods. Connock O'Farrell's men tried to scale the walls of Longford Castle with ladders before rolling a barrel of pitch against the gate to set it ablaze.[145] The attackers of Elphin also used pitch, together with dry wood and a 'fuel' of some sort, to set a fire at the gate.[146] Henry Jones, Dean of Clogher, told about the followers of Maolmhuire O'Reilly, a 'heady young man', who thrust 'sheaves of oats, and straw burning on the tops of their pikes' into the musket loops of Keelagh Castle for upwards of three-quarters of an hour, blinding the enemy, but then milled about aimlessly, having brought no scaling ladders.[147]

---

141 Trinity College Dublin Library (TCDL) 1641 Depositions, MS 820 (County Waterford), fol. 282r: Deposition of Walter Bartram.
142 Jeanette M. A. Beer, *A Medieval Caesar* (Geneva: Libraire Droz, 1976), p.113; Bradbury, *Medieval Siege*, p.272.
143 John Caball, 'The Siege of Tralee, 1642', *The Irish Sword*, 2:9 (1956), p.315.
144 TCDL: 1641 Depositions, MS 811 (County Wicklow), fol. 175r: Deposition of Calcott Chambre, MS 815 (Queens County), fol. 324r: Deposition of Samuell Franck, and MS 821 (County Tipperary), fols 56r–57v: Deposition of Thomas Grove.
145 TCDL: 1641 Depositions, MS 817 (County Longford), fol. 292v: Examination of Raph Griffin.
146 TCDL: 1641 Depositions, MS 831 (County Sligo), fols 216r, 216v: Deposition of Ismah Darby.
147 Scott (ed.), *Dr Henry Jones' Account*, pp.53–54.

Ladders, sows, barrels of pitch or sheaves of straw – all were ineffectual. Jones continued the story of Maolmhuire O'Reilly's assault on Keelagh: '… hereupon they altogether retreated; now applying themselves to what they are more skilful in, the gathering together and taking away all the cattle that were without the castle, which they did, doing the like through all the way they went back, for six miles together, lest any should fall into the hands of our men for their supply'.[148]

Here, and elsewhere, the besiegers sooner or later pulled back to impose a loose blockade.[149] For example, at least 400 refugees sheltered in the town and castle of Newcastle West, County Limerick. The closest friendly outpost was John Southwell's Castle Matrix, another one-time Desmond castle, standing about eight miles to the north-west. The besiegers set 100 men at each of five or six posts and pinned the defenders to an inverted triangle of three square miles formed by the Deel and its tributary stream the Daar. Five captured foragers were hanged, and their bodies were tied to stakes to be 'left standing [as] their bodies rotted' to discourage others.[150] On 11 April 1642, the besiegers burnt the town of Newcastle West. The next day, John Southwell led a 140-strong party to break the blockade but was blocked at an outpost on the Deel and shot dead by a sharpshooter.

Whether and how quickly a Protestant stronghold succumbed depended on how deeply it was embedded in enemy territory and how tightly the attackers could draw their cordon. Coolnashinny or Croaghan Castle and Keelagh lay less than a mile north-west and east, respectively, of Killashandra, County Cavan. Sir Francis Hamilton had 286 armed men in Keelagh. He burnt Killeshandra to deny the besiegers roofs over their heads, but he was eventually boxed in tight, and his followers were reduced to eating 'grass, roots and weeds'.[151] Croaghan had only half as many armed men as Keelagh, and the O'Reillys built trenches by night to within half a musket shot of the castle gate, thereby 'shutting them up' from their water supply, presumably a spring just outside the gate. This would not have been immediately fatal in an Irish winter, but the defenders must have been forced to drink tainted water, which probably accounts for the 'mortal and infectious sickness' that struck them down.[152]

Coleraine was packed tight with newcomers, and the O'Cahan and Mac Donnell besiegers camped close to the charred suburbs. A soldier recalled seeing 140 corpses buried at one time 'in one deep hole or pitt, & laid so thick

---

148 Scott (ed.), *Dr Henry Jones' Account*, pp.53–54.
149 Thomas Bartlett, '*The Academy of Warre*': *Military Affairs in Ireland, 1600 to 1800* (Dublin: National University of Ireland, 2002), pp.18–19.
150 TCDL: 1641 Depositions, MS 829 (County Limerick), fols 136r: Deposition of Richard Lacky, 137r: Deposition of Ralph Billing, 142v: Deposition of Samuell Wishlade, 145r: Deposition of Richard Turnor, 148r: Deposition of John Billal, 183v: Deposition of Jane Meriett, 190r–91v: Deposition of Bushopp Planke and Ann Reynes, 200v: Deposition of John Massey, 202r: Deposition of John Cottrell, 257v: Deposition of Anne Sowthwell, 327r: Depositions of Walter James & Thomas Atkins, 347r: Deposition of John Cox.
151 TCDL: 1641 Depositions, MS 833 (County Cavan), fols 165r: Deposition of John McKewne, 264v: Deposition of John Simpson.
152 Gilbert (ed.), *Contemporary History*, vol. II, pp.485–86, 492, 'Henry Jones, "Proceedings in Cavan"'.

& close together as he may well compare it to the making or packing up of herrings'. The hungry and sickly survivors were 'scarce able to bury the dead', and 'those that could get the flesh of dogs Cats horses, raw hides, rats or such like coarse food, would account themselves happy'. He recalled that when his comrades 'would desperately sally & adventure out to fetch relief prey or forage few of them & sometimes none of them could return alive but were from time to time cut off & slain by the wicked & cruel Irish'.[153]

Cumulatively, the winter war tied down thousands of Catholic troops at any one time. Take the 10-week siege of Carlow Castle, the 22-week siege of Carnew, County Wicklow, and the (at least) seven-month siege of Duncannon, County Wexford. Arthur Fox, a character almost as ubiquitous as Rory O'More, directed a close siege of Carlow Castle. He had been sergeant major of the Mac Mahon camp at Tullyallen during the siege of Drogheda, a post that surely suggests that he was a veteran of continental warfare.[154] Four hundred persons were sheltered within the castle, or in bothies without, 'most of them like to starve for want of food'. It was even dangerous to fetch water from the Barrow for fear of being shot.[155] Carnew sheltered 180 persons and was even more closely pressed by 'great shot *of a field piece,* undermining & with an engine called a sow' so that the besieged were driven to risk 'their lives in the gaining in & getting of docks nettles & other weeds to eat'.[156] Finally, the promontory fort of Duncannon on the Hook Peninsula threatened the vital artery of Waterford Harbour while its landward face presented formidably thick ramparts kinked into salients and re-entrants. The 300-strong English garrison also maintained a satellite outpost at Tintern. The Irish enveloped both Duncannon and Tintern in a loose blockade. Their main camp sat at the base of the Hook Peninsula, with outposts at Burkestown, Ballyhack, Redmond's (Loftus) Hall, Fethard and Dungulf – all between two and four miles from Duncannon.[157] A sea-borne attack on Redmond's Hall in July cost 80 men from a garrison already thinned out by sickness. Tintern was lost soon afterwards, and the main fort was 'blocked up'.[158]

Despite setbacks, these operations amounted to a strategic victory for the English: these three sieges – Carlow, Carnew and Duncannon – absorbed the attention of all the troops raised in County Wexford, the southern part of County Wicklow and all of County Carlow, together with the adjacent

---

153 TCDL: 1641 Depositions, MS 830 (County Roscommon), fol. 41v: Deposition of Anthony Stephens.
154 Donald M. Schlegel, 'An Index to the Rebels of 1641 in the County Monaghan Depositions', *Clogher Record*, 15:2 (1995), pp.69–89.
155 TCDL: 1641 Depositions, MS 812 (County Carlow), fols 2v: Deposition of Hugh ffisher, 74r: Deposition of Edward Harman, 83v: Deposition of Edward Briscoe.
156 TCDL: 1641 Depositions, MS 811 (County Wicklow), fols 121r: Deposition of Peter Poore, 174r: Deposition of Calcott Chambre.
157 TCDL: 1641 Depositions, MS 819 (County Wexford), fols 229r–29v: Examination of Edward Synnot; Elaine Murphy, 'Siege of Duncannon Fort in 1641 and 1642', in E. Darcy, A. Margey, and E. Murphy (eds), *The 1641 Depositions and the Irish Rebellion* (London: Pickering & Chatto, 2014), pp.153–54.
158 Hogan (ed.), *Letters and Papers*, pp.92–94, 'Lawrence Esmond to Earl of Cork, Duncannon, 25 July'.

barony of Slewmargy in Laois. Yet the exigencies of so many winter sieges across the country do not excuse why the Palesmen were thrown to the wolves. County Westmeath contained no English garrisons; nonetheless, the county waged a 'defensive war only'.[159] Moreover, Counties Kilkenny and Tipperary were relatively uncommitted, and Mountgarret should surely have been able to help when, in the opening days of March, the lords of the Pale begged for help.[160]

Spring 1642

The Tipperarymen's retreat from Mallow gifted St Leger a full month's grace until Donough MacCarthy, Viscount Muskerry, driven by fear of religious persecution, led west Munster into revolt. His throng of 3,000 'ill-armed foot' and 50 horse leaguered beside Rochfordstown Castle, three miles to the south-west of Cork City, in order to discourage St Leger's forces from spoiling Muskerry's estates, which lay on the city's doorstep.[161] A second camp at Belgooly helped isolate settler forces in Bandon, Kinsale and Cork from each other.[162]

Muskerry practiced aristocratic mobilisation with a Gaelic twist. All four branches of the old MacCarthy clan were represented at Rochfordstown Camp: Mac Donagh, MacCarthy Reagh of Carbery to the south-west, MacCarthy Mór of County Kerry and the Muskerry MacCarthys, the most recently dominant branch. The most obvious difference between Muskerry present and past was that the lord of Gaelic Muskerry had maintained a standing force of 300 infantrymen and 20 horse, in addition to the temporary 'rising out' of another 1,000 freemen. Donough MacCarthy, Viscount Muskerry, had no such body of armed retainers and had to make do with 1,000 tenants 'armed but with skeans, darts, javelins and pikes'.[163] Garrett Barry, a veteran of Spanish service and one of the recruiting 'colonels', had 1,000 recruits ready to embark at Kinsale, and no doubt they joined Muskerry as a body.[164]

The pyramid of landed wealth in Muskerry was attenuated at the top, compared to Bargy or even Duleek, with Donough MacCarthy now owning most of the barony while his chief followers, like O'Herlihy and O'Leary, owned relatively small estates or none at all.[165] Mac Sweeney was described as 'captain of Muskerry's gallowglasses', a nod to the family's mercenary

---

159 Gilbert (ed.), *Contemporary History*, vol. I, p.17.
160 TCDL: 1641 Depositions, MS 816 (County Meath), fol. 71r: Examination of Nicholas Dowdall; Perceval-Maxwell, *Outbreak of the Irish Rebellion*, p.225.
161 Gilbert (ed.), *Irish Confederation*, vol. I, pp.70–73.
162 George Bennett, *The History of Bandon* (Cork: Henry and Coghlan, 1862), p.71.
163 Gilbert (ed.), *Irish Confederation*, vol. I, pp.68, 75.
164 R. A. Stradling, *The Spanish Monarchy and Irish Mercenaries: The Wild Geese in Spain, 1618-68* (Blackrock: Irish Academic Press, 1994), p.38.
165 William F. T. Butler, *Gleanings from Irish History* (London: Longmans, Green and Co., 1925), pp.103, 122.

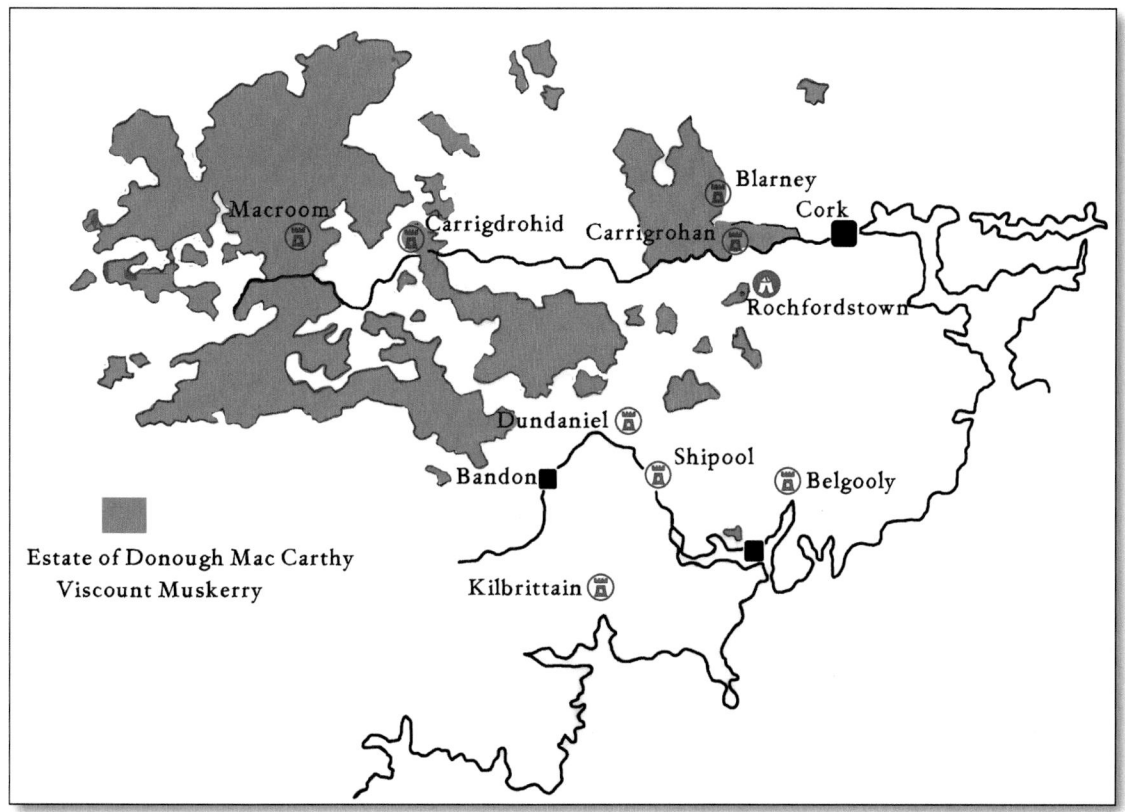

Muskerry and Cork. (Author's illustration)

origins.[166] O'Cronin, Muskerry's colonel, was a 'freeholder', that is, a tenant who rented extensive lands, enjoyed security of tenure and had some status, but a tenant for all that.[167]

Present were three brothers from the Mac Finghins of Glanerought, County Kerry, an offshoot of the MacCarthy Mór, the middle brother known as 'Captain Suggane'.[168] The name probably derived from the twisted hay or straw rope (*súgán*) that the Irish often wore as a mark to distinguish friend from foe.[169] Captain Suggane had obeyed 'the Lord of Muskerry's order', left the siege of Tralee and marched a company of soldiers to Rochfordstown.[170] After the rest of Muskerry's army were routed, he stood his ground and went

---

166 Trinity College Dublin Library (TCDL) 1641 Depositions, MS 823 (County Cork), fol. 166v: Deposition of Walter Baldwin.
167 Butler, *Gleanings from Irish History*, pp.101, 121–22, 268–69, 272–74; TCDL: 1641 Depositions, MS 822 (County Cork), fol. 22r: Deposition of Ralph Steeres and MS 823 (County Cork), fols 166v: Deposition of Walter Baldwin, 171r–72v: Deposition of Symon Bridges.
168 S. T. McCarthy, 'The Clann Carthaigh (Continued)', *Kerry Archaeological Magazine*, 3:13 (1914), p.61.
169 Trinity College Dublin Library (TCDL) 1641 Depositions, MS 825 (County Cork), fol. 20v: Deposition of Thomas Reymond and MS 828 (County Kerry), fol. 199r: Deposition of Arthur Blenerhasset.
170 Trinity College Dublin Library (TCDL) 1641 Depositions, MS 826 (County Cork), fol. 66r: Examination of James Roch.

down in hand-to-hand fighting, alongside an uncle and a foster brother.[171] Rather than loyalty to the shadow of a clan, Captain Suggane's heroism may be best explained by religious zealotry: he was a 'real Machabee, not just warlike but pious also' and was related to another zealot named Oliver Stephenson of County Limerick, whose 'only commotion was for religion'.[172] In Ireland, as in England, it was those who 'felt more strongly about religion who began the war'.[173]

On the whole, nobles like Muskerry were reluctant insurgents, and the rising was driven by the gentry and especially by members of that class who were burdened by particular experiences and expectations: zealots, priests, lawyers, members of Parliament, recruiting army officers and anyone who had suffered from, or had been threatened by, state-sanctioned theft. While recognising the importance of residual clan affiliations, I see recruitment and motivation through the prism of class and, specifically, the nexus of dependency and deference between nobles and gentry on the one hand and common folk on the other while also remembering that class lines were smudged and that some rankers self-identified as 'gentlemen' and they would be driven by much the same motivations as their wealthier brothers, nephews or uncles.

The common man in the ranks every man from copyholder down to cottager, seems to have been less invested in the Catholic cause than the gentry. He might believe that he would go straight up to heaven if an English musket ball should kill him and that the devil would claim his enemy's soul.[174] He might 'swell a progress' and steal a cow or two, but would he grip a length of stick tightly while a wall of horseflesh and thundering hooves bore down on him? Or would he clamber onto a breach, whose shadows were ominously lit by glowing match? Or suffer the long watches of a winter's night? All too often, the gentry bemoaned their 'runagate' followers with neither 'courage nor heart'.[175] The poet Turlough O'Connor assumed the persona of a cowardly and landless ("*'s gan fód don dúthchais agam*") common

---

171 TCDL: 1641 Depositions, MS 823 (County Cork), fols 166v: Walter Baldwin, 183r: Deposition of Abrame Ashtone and MS 828 (County Kerry), fols 124v: Deposition of Stephen Love, 194v: Deposition of Thomas Dight, 198v: Deposition of William Seames, 237r: Deposition of William Dethick, 263r: Deposition of William Goode, 265v: Deposition of Margaret Percy, 273r: Deposition of William Hayles, 284v: Deposition of Edward Vauclier.

172 IMC: Kavanagh (ed.), *Commentarius Rinuccinianus*, vol. I, p.313; Gilbert (ed.), *Contemporary History*, vol. I, pp.50, 66.

173 John Morrill, *Revolt in the Provinces: The People of England and the Tragedies of War, 1630-1648* (Harlow: Longman, 1999), p.73.

174 TCDL: 1641 Depositions, MS 817 (County Westmeath), fols 37v: Deposition of Thomas Fleetwood, 38r: Deposition of Thomas Fleetwood, MS 820 (County Waterford), fol. 309r: Deposition of John Clement, MS 823 (County Cork), fol. 4v: Deposition of Arthur Bettsworth, and MS 838 (County Armagh), fol. 104v: Deposition of Elizabeth Price; Mac Cuarta, 'Religious Violence', pp.169–70.

175 TCDL: 1641 Depositions, MS 836 (County Armagh), fol. 108v: Relation of Francis Sacheverell; The National Archives (TNA) *HMC Report on Franciscan Manuscripts in Dublin* (London: HMC, 1906), p.209, 'Edmund Dwyer to Luke Wadding, La Rochelle, 29 October 1642'.

soldier, who complained that the officers hogged the booty, 'even though I can run away just like them' ("'s go dteíchim féin mar iadséin").[176]

And run they did from Rochfordstown. The man in charge there, Garrett Barry, had been picked as a compromise candidate between the squabbling Munster 'men of quality'.[177] He had served the Spanish since 1600, rising from the ranks to make major of a paper regiment by 1636, but he had never commanded anything bigger than a company.[178] Officer veterans of the Spanish and French service were fairly numerous. Two of the 19 officers of captain rank or above in Philip Mac Hugh O'Reilly's regiment had 'lately come over out of the Low Countries', and one of these served as the major. Philip Mac Hugh himself had fought in the Army of Flanders as a young man, probably as a volunteer in search of experience, education and even renown, like Richard Butler of Ikerrin.[179] Veterans like Hugh O'Reilly or Michael Wall, Mountgarret's sergeant major on the march to Mallow, always filled the sergeant major slot and were responsible for drilling raw troops and forming them up in battle array.[180]

Barry was regarded as a 'good soldier', but now he showed 'as much motion as in a stone' as he sat tight while the English in Cork were inexorably reinforced.[181] On 12 April, a remonstrance from Barry's camp complained that the 'puritans' in the House of Commons wished to 'abolish the Catholic religion and to root out the nation of the Irish'.[182] The remonstrance was a prelude to action or at least a rheumatically slow twitch. Next day, a small Irish force approached Cork City and goaded St Leger's men into coming out. The Irish '… made a bold but disorderly charge upon the English foot who, having the advantage of a ditch where they had planted themselves, wounded so many of the Irish officers, as there were hardly any left to lead on the men, which occasioned their sudden retreat'.[183]

The 'bold' charge faltered outside of Cork City, when it had worked so well at Julianstown, because the charge depended on inspirational leadership. Homeric heroes like Mac Colla are incalculable assets, but success should not depend on them. Moreover, St Leger's musketeers were well drilled, numerous, firing from behind cover and had powder to burn. The English pursued and fell on Barry's camp, scattering all of his forces except for Captain Sugán, who put up a 'strong defense' as long as his gunpowder held out. Indeed, Cork admitted that the English owed much of their success to

---

176 Mhág Craith Cuthbert, 'Toirdhealbhach Ó Conchubhair (floruit circa 1645)', in Franciscan Fathers (eds), *Father Luke Wadding: Commemorative Volume* (Dublin: Clonmore and Reynolds, 1957), pp.423, 428.
177 Gilbert (ed.), *Irish Confederation*, vol. I, p.74.
178 Brendan Jennings (ed.), *Wild Geese in Spanish Flanders 1582-1700* (Dublin: Irish Manuscripts Commission, 1964), pp.12, 265.
179 TCDL: 1641 Depositions, MS 833 (County Cavan), fols 105r–06v: Deposition of Ambrose Bedell, 162r: Deposition of William Jameson, 280r: Deposition of Richard Parsons.
180 TCDL: 1641 Depositions, MS 825 (County Cork), fol. 20v: Deposition of Thomas Reymond.
181 Gillman, 'Rise and Progress', pp.11–63.
182 Willson H. Coates, Anne S. Young, and Vernon F. Snow (eds), *The Private Journals of the Long Parliament: 7 March to 1 June 1642* (New Haven, CT: Yale University Press, 1987), p.222.
183 Gilbert (ed.), *Irish Confederation*, vol. I, p.76; TCDL: 1641 Depositions, MS 823 (County Cork), fols 171r–72v: Deposition of Symon Bridges.

the fact that the Irish were so 'sparingly furnished'.[184] Cork gloated about what happened next:

> … in the end they entred and gave them Condon's quarter at Coole, for they killed the captain and all the rest that were in it, being about 400, except three pipers, whom they carried to play before their captain's head, which they brought on a pole to Cork, and then they were put out of tune and their music ended, for they were all hanged up.[185]

The significance of the reference to 'Condon's quarter' was that, a few days before Rochfordstown, a party led by Richard Condon had surprised 22 soldiers of David Barry, Earl of Barrymore and Cork's son-in-law, who had been threshing corn at Coolecarron in the no man's land between the Condon strongholds of Careysville and Ballyderown on the Blackwater and Barrymore's Castlelyons.[186] The soldiers had fled to a nearby farmhouse, recalled a survivor Trooper Andrew Lacy:

> … they instantly fired the house where our men were who still kept on fighting until the fire flamed all about them then the musketeers in the lower room cried out for quarter, upon that Richard Condon aforesaid promised them, (upon the yielding up of their arms) quarter for their lives, our men instantly came forth, and resigned their arms, that done the Rebels fell a stripping of our men, and as soon as they were stripped they were all slain cruelly murdered one by one, the said Richard Condon always struck upon them the first blow with his sword, and then the rebels would fall upon them with their skeins & pikes, till they were murdered …[187]

Four Irish civilians in the farmhouse were taken to Cloghleagh, and three of them were later hanged. A month after Rochfordstown, the catchcry 'Condon's quarter' was raised to excuse the slaughter of up to 300 persons at Ballymacpatrick Castle during operations in which Barrymore pushed the Condons north and clear across the Blackwater. A poet commented sourly on this double dealing: '*A leithsgéal ann gach feall dá ndéinid / gur ceathrú phonncúil Chonndúin chaomhnaid*' (Their excuse for every one of their decits / they are observing Condon's quarter to the letter).[188]

By the summer of 1643, the English would dominate the Blackwater Valley all the way from Mallow to Cork's vast estates in the crook of the Blackwater, around Cappoquin and Lismore and thence downriver to the port of Youghal. In spring 1642, as many as 1,200 men from County

---

184 Richard Boyle, *A letter of the Earle of Corke to the state at Dublin …* (London: Edward Blackmore, 1642), p.2.
185 Richard Caulfield (ed.), *The Council Book of the Corporation of Kinsale, from 1652 to 1800* (Guildford: J. Billing and Sons, 1879), p.xxxix.
186 Canny, *Making Ireland British*, p.309.
187 TCDL: 1641 Depositions, MS 824 (County Cork), fol. 56r: Deposition of Andrew Lacy and MS 826 (County Cork), fols 21v: Examination of William Higgins, 22r: Deposition of William Merricke.
188 O'Rahilly (ed.), *Five Seventeenth-Century Political Poems*, p.87.

Waterford forded the Blackwater and occupied the town of Lismore. They summoned the castle defended by one of Cork's sons, Roger, Baron Broghill, and gathered scaling ladders to scale the walls at night 'in several places'.[189] The attackers were led by two continental veterans, Edmund Fennell and Thomas Butler, but one amateur officer led his men away, protesting that he had no intention of 'fighting against walls'. This desertion dampened the morale of the rest, who promptly went home.[190] It was Mallow Castle all over again. On the last day of April 1642, Fennell returned to burn the town and slaughter 10 civilians, all but one being women.[191]

Mountgarret had fixed his attention on Munster in February and March, but his attention was drawn back to Leinster when Ormond set out on 2 April 1642 towards Naas with an army of 3,000 foot and 500 horse. On the march, the English 'put all to the sword', 'banished, hanged, and killed all the Irish, and Papists in the Town of Naas' and stormed Tipper Castle, slaughtering the garrison.[192] The half-dozen English wounded in the storm of Tipper were sent back under cavalry guard, but Irish partisans drove off the escort near Rathcoole and slaughtered the wounded men. Ormond owned only the ground over which his soldiers trod as he continued his march by way of Athy, and Carlow, pitched camp at Stradbally, and sent off detachments to relieve Portlaoise, Borris, Ballynakill and Birr.

In 1597, the Earl of Tyrone insisted that he would not 'fight upon the plain' against Crown forces but would 'lay all passes and straits' against them.[193] By 'strait', Tyrone meant any defile where a route narrowed and troops in a column bunched up. As their grandfathers had done against the Earl of Essex at the 'Pass of the Plumes' in 1599, the men of Laois entrenched passes through the many midland bogs. At Ballaghmore (*Bealach Mór*), on the road from Portlaoise to Borris-in-Ossory, for instance, they dug a trench six feet wide across the road and cast up a breastwork on either side of the obstacle.[194] One of Ormond's detachments bullied through Ballaghmore but, on the way back, was forced to detour around yet another entrenched pass to be benighted and lost in trackless bog. Forty-eight hours of continuous riding destroyed over 100 horses.[195]

---

189 Patrick Little, *Lord Broghill and the Cromwellian Union with Ireland and Scotland* (Woodbridge: Boydell & Brewer, 2004), p.26; Gilbert (ed.), *Irish Confederation*, vol. I, p.71.
190 Thomas Fitzpatrick, *Waterford during the Civil War (1641-1653)* (Waterford: Downey and Co. Publishers, 1912), p.125.
191 TCDL: 1641 Depositions, MS 820 (County Waterford), fols 92v: Deposition of Edward Crockford, 152v: Deposition of Samuell Hill, 290r: Deposition of Elizabeth Facy.
192 B. D., *Tvvo letters from tvvo chief officers under the command of the Earle of Ormond Particularly relating their good and happy successe in their late expedition* (London: H. Blunden, 1642), p.3; A. L., *A true relation of the late expedition of the right honorable, the Earl of Ormond, and Sir Charles Coote Knight, and Baronet, into the severall counties of Kildare, Queens county, Kings county, and the county of Catherlagh ...* (London: Joseph Hunscott, 1642), p.3.
193 G. A. Hayes-McCoy, 'Strategy and Tactics in Irish Warfare, 1593-1601', *Irish Historical Studies*, 2:7 (1941), p.272 and 'The Tide of Victory and Defeat: II. The Battle of Kinsale, 1601', *Studies: An Irish Quarterly Review*, 38:151 (1949), pp.307–17.
194 Loeber, 'Warfare and Architecture', p.407.
195 BHO: Rushworth, 'Historical Collections', pp.504–59.

RAW GENERALS AND GREEN SOLDIERS

A skirmish on 14 April 1642, near Athy, illustrates the potential benefits of harrying Ormond's homeward trek and picking off stragglers. A troop of Irish horse swam over the Graney, each horse bearing a cavalier and a musketeer riding pillion, to attack scattered foragers. The captains of two English troops, who were keeping watch on the foragers, gathered their riders and counterattacked: two English troopers were shot dead, but the English 'killed one of their Horsemen, hurt divers of the rest, [and] killed all the Foot'. As well as illustrating possibilities, the skirmish illustrates the danger for commanded musketeers in combined operations with cavalry, in that they were liable to be abandoned when things went awry.

The next day, Mountgarret chose to disregard the precepts of his father-in-law and confront Ormond. This would be near a point where Ormond's column would slosh across a muddy stream near Kilrush in County Kildare.

English sources routinely credit the Irish with absurdly large numbers because the bigger the enemy, the greater the triumph and the more compelling the proof of God's favour. Two English 'chief officers' counted 50 to 60 Irish colours at Kilrush. The count was probably accurate, though not the extrapolation that the Irish fielded up to 8,000 men. A colour was carried by a company of foot or a troop of horse with nominal strengths of 100 infantrymen or 40 to 60 troopers, respectively, or 5,000 to 6,000 men altogether.[196] However, paper strength was one thing; boots on the ground were quite another. Eleven County Kildare companies mustered on the Curragh before marching south to rendezvous with militiamen from adjacent counties, and at least one of these companies had a mere 28 men.[197] Mountgarret's army was not, in fact, 'exceedingly dishevelled and

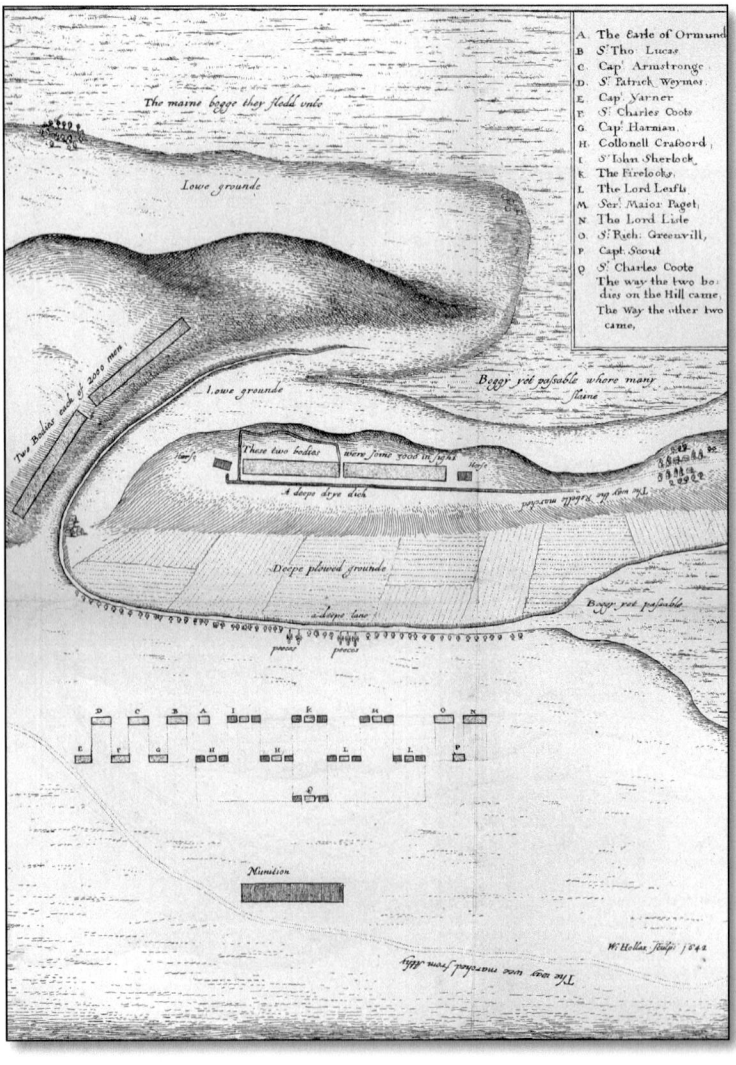

Battle of Kilrush, Wenceslaus Hollar, 'Battle of Kilrush'. (John T. Gilbert (ed.), *History of the Irish Confederation and the War in Ireland 1641-1649* (Dublin: M. H. Gill and Son, 1879–1880), vol. I, p.89)

---

196 Gilbert (ed.), *Irish Confederation*, vol. I, p.79.
197 TCDL: 1641 Depositions, MS 810 (County Dublin), fol. 23v: Examination of Daniel Enos and MS 813 (County Kildare), fols 57v: Examination of John Magawly, 63r: Information of Edward Walsh.

miscellaneous', but it was understrength.[198] The Irish probably had nearer to 4,000 foot soldiers, which matches a pictorial map showing the Irish regiments drawn up in four large squares or squadrons (Spanish '*cuadro*' or 'square'). The term 'square' will normally be used to denote battle formations even where, as here, the 'squares' were much wider than they were deep. Two squares stood on the slope of Bull Hill, or 'Cnocaterife' (*Cnoc an Tarbh*), and two more, flanked by horsemen, stood an inexplicable three-quarters of a mile away to the south on a lower slope, in the eponymous townland of Kilrush. The Boherbaun stream trickled between the two hills. Wenceslaus Hollar's illustration of the Battle of Kilrush exaggerates the height and bulk of the two hills on which the Irish stood. A photograph looking northeast towards Bull Hill from Ormond's left wing reveals Bull Hill as a slight undulation on a flat plain.

View from Ormond's left wing towards Bull Hill. (Author's photo)

Battle squares normally combined about equal numbers of pikemen and 'shot', or musketeers, though the preferred proportions for Irish armies would shift to one-third pike before the end of the decade. Pike formations functioned by having multiple ranks of tightly packed men forming a rectangular block that operated as a single unit. Steadiness, the capacity to stand and take a pounding, was all important, and, if one man fell or broke ranks, his neighbours had to hold their nerve and trust their comrades or the whole unit would disintegrate.[199] Affective bonds like this grew only from long service: '… a formation of waving, clinking pikes would have advertised its wielders' collective unease, exhaustion or inexperience'.[200] Squares clashed

---

198 Kelsey, 'Butler, Richard'.
199 Adrian K. Goldsworthy, 'The Othismos, Myths and Heresies: The Nature of Hoplite Battle', *War in History*, 4:1 (1997), pp.6–14.
200 Thomas F. Arnold, *The Renaissance at War* (London: Cassell, 2006), p.86.

RAW GENERALS AND GREEN SOLDIERS

in 'push of pike' only once, at Benburb in 1646, and pikemen might have fought other pikemen in only three fights out of 20.[201] Usually, the pikemen held each other at bay whilst the sleeves of shot loosed volleys until one side broke.[202] Increasingly, the pike would be dismissed as having 'no other merit than its length', and the pikeman just one more sharp thorn in the bramble to frighten horses.[203]

Battle square, detail from 'Bataille de Nortlingue' (1634). (*Bibliothèque nationale de France*)

The Irish pikemen probably stood in the middle of the square, with the musketeers wrapped around them, in the manner illustrated by a detail from a contemporary print of Habsburg forces at Nördlingen. A military primer written in 1647 criticises this wraparound formation as old fashioned and explains that the musketeers should be placed in wings on either side.[204] That proposed alternative is the so-called 'Dutch' formation practiced by the English at Kilrush, according to Hollar's illustration, with blocks of musketeers on each side of the pikemen.

The idea of putting battle squares on Bull Hill might have been to attack the vanguard of the English as they struggled out of the defile where the highway dipped into the stream. Mac Thomas was in charge here with his Kildare men, along with, probably, O'More's contingent from Laois and Mountgarret's from Kilkenny. His advice, and that of his fellow professional, Hugh O'Byrne, had been not to throw these 'fresh water soldiers' into battle,

---

201 Frank Tallett and D. J. B. Trim (ed.), *European Warfare, 1350–1750* (Cambridge: Cambridge University Press, 2010), p.231.
202 Bert S. Hall, *Weapons and Warfare in Renaissance Europe: Gunpowder, Technology, and Tactics* (London: Johns Hopkins University Press, 1997), p.187; Peter H. Wilson, *Europe's Tragedy: A New History of the Thirty Years War* (London: Allen Lane, 2009), p.461.
203 Jacques François de Chastenet, *Art de la guerre, par principes et par règles* (Paris: C. A. Jombert, 1748), p.70.
204 Jacques II de Castlenau, *Le Marechal de Bataille* (Paris: Etienne Migon, 1647), pp.245, 259.

Column of march, Claes Jansz. Visscher, 'Siège de Maastricht en 1632'. (Rijksmuseum, Amsterdam)

but Mountgarret and Ikerrin disregarded this counsel and further insisted that they would see to the 'fitting of the field'.[205] The second two battle squares may have been placed to swoop on Ormond's rearguard as it trudged across the stream, now churned up by thousands of feet, hooves and cart wheels into glutinous mud.[206]

To frustrate this, Ormond sought a fight. He had some trouble forming his men up in battle formations and might have been 'in some hazard' if the Irish had attacked at this opportune moment. Instead, a commanded body of Irish musketeers marched forwards of the main array: '… being not in posture of an army body, in battle array, or any either horse or foot assigned to second or relieve them, that one would think them rather exposed to slaughter, or give grounde, then for service to advance or gain any foot'.[207]

P. S. was being unfair – the commanded musketeers were not on a suicide mission. They enjoyed the shelter of 'ditches and high banks' less than a musket shot forwards of the main body. It was common to send musketeers a short distance ahead of the main position with orders to fire on the advancing enemy, disorganise him and get back out of there.

One of the few detailed descriptions of an Irish musketeer describes 'his Bandoliers about him, his Musket in his hands and match lighted at both ends'.[208] Irish shot probably carried not only muskets but also whatever firearms they could beg, borrow or steal – including the lighter caliver, which weighed eight pounds compared to the larger calibre musket's 16-pound weight. He carried ammunition on a bandolier, a leather band that he draped over his torso and one shoulder and from which dangled eight to 12 wooden or tin flasks, each holding a measure of propellant gunpowder. He stored the finer priming powder loose in a separate flask or horn. The match was a cord steeped in saltpetre that burned slowly as he held it between the fingers of his

---

205 Gilbert (ed.), *Contemporary History*, vol. I, p.30.
206 D., *Tvvo letters from tvvo chief officers*, p.3.
207 Gilbert (ed.), *Contemporary History*, vol. I, pp.30–31.
208 TCDL: 1641 Depositions, MS 813 (County Kildare), fol. 30r: Examination of Richard Harris.

left hand. Forked rests were passing out of use as muskets grew lighter, and a list of weapons imported for the Confederate Catholics in 1645 included 2,000 muskets, complete with bandoliers but with no rests.[209] Even without a musket rest, the matchlock musketeer was 'the most heavily encumbered infantryman the armies of Europe have ever employed', who had to move slowly and carefully, not least because his match could touch off the powder in his flasks.[210]

At length, Ormond untangled his ranks, and opened files and spacings before dispatching his own commanded musketeers across 'deep ploughed ground' to the 'very breast' of the Irish forlorn hope and fired 'thick and sure' at them. Behind was the main body, with only the pike heads and fluttering flags peeping above high embankments. Ormond's field guns fired 10 ineffectual shots at the main body, and two bodies of shot fired 'fiercely' on the forlorn hope. This '... struck the Rogues [the usual term for the Irish] into such a fear, that some of the Pikes began to retreat: At sight whereof a great shout was in our Army in derision, crying, O hone, O hone, O hone, and the Rebels still discharging, though faintly against our men'.[211] . 'Ochón' is an exclamation meaning 'Woe is me!'

If Baroque battle was a moral clash, the English had won already as they picked up on the signs of hesitancy and apprehension in the Irish ranks and mocked their enemy.

The Irish fired less than 100 shots in this one-sided firefight, before their shots faltered, they 'having but a barrel of powder' in the whole army.[212] After some time (the published accounts telescope events), six troops of English cuirassiers, or armoured horsemen, under Sir Thomas Lucas, commissary general of the Horse, found a gap in the hedgerows. With 'divers of Horse and Men that were with him being hurt', Lucas charged the forlorn hope at 'a good and round Trot'.[213]

Ormond had two other types of horsemen besides cuirassiers. Most common was the carbineer, whose main weapon was a short-barrelled firearm with a mechanical mechanism (e.g., a wheellock or a snaphance) that did not depend on lighting a match on horseback. Less common was the dragoon, a foot soldier who rode into combat but dismounted to fight. Cuirassiers and carbineers could trot through the killing zone of musketry very quickly, and, given the limitations of the matchlock, the musketeer

---

209 Gary D. Peterson, *Warrior Kings of Sweden: The Rise of an Empire in the Sixteenth and Seventeenth Centuries* (Jefferson, NC: McFarland & Company, 2007), p.136; IMC: Kavanagh (ed.), *Commentarius Rinuccinianus*, vol. II, pp.39–40.
210 Ewart Oakeshott, *European Weapons and Armour: From the Renaissance to the Industrial Revolution* (Rochester, NY: Boydell & Brewer, 2012), p.41.
211 Anon., *A Full relation, not only of our good successe in generall, but how, and in what manner God hath fought his own cause miraculously* (London: G. Miller, 1642), p.10; Anon., *A true and perfect diurnall: of the most remarkable passages in Ireland …* (London: Edward Blackmore, 1652), p.5.
212 Gilbert (ed.), *Irish Confederation*, vol. I, p.80; TCDL: 1641 Depositions, MS 813 (County Kildare), fol. 63v: Examination of Edward Walsh.
213 Maurice Eustace, *A letter from Sir Maurice Eustace Knight, His Maiesties serjeant at law in the kingome of Ireland, and speaker of the House of Commons, in Parliament there being a perfect relation of the last true newes from Ireland* (London: E. G, 1642), p.3.

simply could not stand in the open. The order sequence beginning 'Advance your Pikes' involved each pikeman in the front rank anchoring the butt of the pike against his right foot and holding the staff with his left hand so that it stood at a 45-degree angle. The man in the rank behind held the pike staff (an ash staff some 16 feet long) horizontally at shoulder level.[214] When pressed, musketeers cowered under this hedge of protruding steel. The pike heads might have a narrow point, the better to punch through armour, or a broader lozenge shape.[215]

In 'the end', Lucas broke the forlorn hope and then the two squares, and they all ran from Kilrush 'towards a bog'. Meanwhile, more troops of English cavalry overwhelmed the troop that stood on the southern flank of the Irish squares. Ormond's army, after a shaky start, had managed to coordinate the manoeuvre of foot and horse.[216]

All the while, the Irish on Bull Hill looked on until a troop of horse and a detachment of 300 foot soldiers approached them. Sixty English musketeers darted forwards and fired. The Irish returned fire for a time, but, at length, they shuffled off, keeping up an 'orderly retreat' for a little while before running 'with all speed possible' to a bog.[217]

Old Charles Coote had lost his hat but chased the Irish from Kilrush Hill literally with a vengeance and 'scoured about the field, crying, Kill, kill'. For all his exhortations, English cavalry cut down only 100 and lost about 40 – we can disregard boasts that the Irish dead 'lay like a sheet upon the ground, all stripped'. Two troops of County Carlow horsemen, Walter Bagnall's and Sir Roger Harpole's, covered the withdrawal from Kilrush Hill to a 'great bog', inaccessible to horsemen, a mile away.[218] Here, the fleeing foot soldiers paused so that the bog 'looked

'Charge to horse', O'Neill regiment's camp at Benburb, 27 November 2021. (Author's photo)

---

214 Anon., *The Military discipline wherein is martially showne the order for drilling*, p.3; Jeremy Black, *European Warfare, 1494-1660* (London: Routledge, 2002), p.39.
215 Ignacio and Iván Notario López, *The Spanish Tercios 1536-1704* (Oxford: Osprey, 2012), p.38; Blackmore, 'Destructive and Formidable', p.38; Elton, *Compleat Body of the Art Military*, p.57.
216 Fissel, *English Warfare*, p.253.
217 BHO: Rushworth, 'Historical Collections', p.513.
218 TCDL: 1641 Depositions, MS 815 (Laois), fol. 402v: Examination of Robert Doughtie; Abraham Yarner, *Relation of the battaile fought at Kilrush ...* (London: F. Coules, and G. Badger, 1642), p.3;

even black (for their apparel was generally black) being all covered over with them', and they cried, we are told, 'Ohone, Ohone, Ohone; some bewailing the loss of Fathers, some of Brothers, some of their Cousins, and others of their Masters and friends'.[219]

A vanguard of English foot soldiers was about to enter the bog when they were ordered back, 'having got honour enough for that day'. Edmund Borlase left the impression that Ormond deliberately let his grand-uncle's men escape, though Mountgarret did lose his cart loaded with provisions and fine clothes.[220] In fact, Ormond's army was probably too exhausted for any further heroics, and the Irish may have looked steadier than the bombastic pamphleteers would have us believe.

In pulling back to the bog, the Irish lost three colours: 'In one of the Colours there is three Pictures, one of the Trinity in visible shapes, and of Joseph, and Mary and Christ, like a child in one place: The second is of Mary Magdalen: The third of S. Patricke'. The first flag probably resembled Francisco Camilo's 'The Holy Family or Trinity on Earth' in the Prado, showing the Christ Child looking out at the viewer sandwiched by Mary on his right and Joseph on his left, both looking at Him. The dove of the Holy Ghost hovers above them. Thomas Messingham's, 'Florilegum Insulae Sanctorum' (Paris, 1624), had popularised the icon of the bearded national saint accoutred as a Tridentine bishop with mitre and staff and trampling a nest of vipers underfoot.[221] The choice of Mary Magdalen is bewildering.

The English cut down four captains of Sir Morgan Kavanagh's Wexford regiment, '… whose heads we brought along with us', slavered a newsletter, 'and placed them on the gates of *Dublin*'.[222] One of the captains was Dermot Kavanagh, who rose from his sickbed 'because there must a way have been found to bring him to be engaged in the battle of Mullaghmast' so that he might fulfil 'an old prophesy'.[223] This is, without doubt, a reference to the Prophecies of Colmcille, a 'history of the past and the future' deriving from the twelfth-century *Cogadh Gaedhel re Gallaibh* (*War of the Gael against the Foreigner*), which were very popular in the seventeenth century.[224] The prophecies identify two places where the Irish, at last united, would rout the foreigner. One such site of destiny was Mullaghmast, just three miles away

---

Anon., *The last joyfull newes from Ireland being the copies of two severall letters sent from Dublin the 28 of Aprill, 1642 to a noble person in this city* … (London: T. Fawcet, 1642).
219 Anon., *Full relation*, p.11.
220 Edmund Borlase, *The History of the Execrable Irish Rebellion Trac'd from Many Preceding Acts, to the Grand Eruption the 23. of October, 1641. And Thence Pursued to the Act of Settlement, MDCLXII* (London: Robert Clavel, 1680), p.75.
221 Francisco Camilo, 'The Holy Family or Trinity on Earth', *Museo del Prado*, <https://www.museodelprado.es/en/the-collection/art-work/the-holy-family-or-trinity-on-earth/caf18f44-eb03-4f68-bd7f-139f6b304372>, accessed 13 May 2023; Bernadette Cunningham and Raymond Gillespie, '"The Most Adaptable of Saints": The Cult of St Patrick in the Seventeenth Century', *Archivium Hibernicum*, 49 (1995), p.90.
222 Most English accounts put the number of killed at upwards of 600. Carte, *History of the Life of James Duke of Ormonde*, vol. I, p.316; D., *Tvvo letters from tvvo chief officers*, p.4; TCDL: 1641 Depositions, MS 818 (County Wexford), fols 25r: Examination of Donnogh Murphy, 164r: Examination of William Oulton, 323: Examination of Ralph Waddington re Bryan Cauanagh.
223 Gilbert (ed.), *Irish Confederation*, vol. I, p.80.
224 O'Riordan, *Poetics and Polemics*, p.277.

across the fields from Kilrush. The horsemen who were killed included a brother of Hugh O'Byrne and Garret Fitzgerald of Castleroe, County Kildare, 'an excellent scholar, an exceeding good antiquarist in both Latin, English and Irish, a traveller, a courtier, and a brave horseman'.[225]

For all that the body count was low, there can be no denying the strategic importance of Kilrush, which sustained the Protestant outposts of south Leinster for many more months and let Ormond bring his army back to Dublin.[226]

---

225 Gilbert (ed.), *Contemporary History*, vol. I, p.30.
226 TCDL: 1641 Depositions, MS 813 (County Kildare), fol. 350r: Deposition of Francis Hilgrove.

2

Summer and Autumn 1642

Having secured beachheads in Dublin, Cork, Kinsale, Youghal and Carrickfergus, the Lords Justices and their Scottish Covenanter allies in Ulster were, by the early summer of 1642, able to deploy massive armies of 44,800 men in aggregate and push deep into insurgent territory.[1] By then, the insurgents may have had, on paper, about 70,000 soldiers.[2]

Irish Military Strength

Province	Soldiers
Leinster	25,000
Ulster	20,000
Munster	20,000
Connacht	5,000
Total	**70,000**

But to compare the Irish's 70,000 with the English and Scottish's 45,000 is to compare apples and oranges. The Irish total represents part-timers answering the *gairm-slua* (this word is almost the same as the Scots Gaelic *slua-gairm* or 'slogan'), who were raised occasionally and locally and who were not redeployed to counterbalance the increasing local superiority in numbers enjoyed by government forces. This failure dictated the general course of the war from March to September 1642, with the insurgents being driven out of Ulster altogether and the Palesmen beaten back out of striking range of Dublin. A breathless Catholic account captures this near collapse:

> … the heretics regained their courage and spirits, gathered in safer refuges, mustered in troops and regiments and began to scorn our men. Presently, once

---

1 Hugh Hazlett, *A History of the Military Forces Operating in Ireland 1641-49*. 1938. Queen's University of Belfast, PhD, p.45; Hogan (ed.), *Letters and Papers*, p.127; Scott Wheeler, 'Four Armies in Ireland', in J. Ohlmeyer (ed.), *Independence to Occupation: Ireland 1641–1660* (Cambridge: Cambridge University Press, 1995), pp.50–51.
2 Lenihan, *Confederate Catholics at War*, p.48.

they had been reinforced they drew up battalions, put them in battle formations and in pitched battle they not only defended themselves against the Catholics but attacked them so threateningly that they drove them in sometimes shameful flight.[3]

The English could track fire and sword across north Leinster again and again. To give a taste of these *chevauchées*, and the Palesmen's hapless response, it will suffice to describe one such operation. The Irish especially abhorred Charles Coote, who, as the eponymous Cola of the drama *Cola's Furie*, vows 'to hang, to racke, to kill, to burne, to spoile, / untill I make this land a barren soile'.[4] In late May 1642, Coote took Daingean, whose 70 musketeers 'withstood us valiantly, but in vain'. Thirty were killed outright, and 'the rest taken by us and hanged'. He next relieved Geashill and then made for Castlejordan, detouring slightly to within musket shot of Ticroghan, hoping to lure Luke Fitzgerald out from behind his ramparts. Finally, Coote lunged at Trim, the biggest inland town of the Pale, and the defenders of the town 'betook themselves to their heels'.[5] But the castle held out and cost the attackers 20 men and three officers killed before it capitulated. The English massacred the 80 men in the garrison, but, like 'valiant Knights errant', as one of them put it, they let the womenfolk go free.[6] An Irish counterattack cut off 20 soldiers and carters who had scattered in search of plunder, and Coote himself stopped a bullet in the back, which surely means that 'friendly fire' killed him as he was not in the habit of turning his back on an enemy.[7] So passed an 'accursed scourge' (*sciúrsa mallachta*) of the Irish.[8] After losing Trim, many Palesmen fled north to County Cavan: 'Day & night there came through Virginia great Droves of Cattle of all sorts, great Carts laden with trunks and all kinds of good housholdstuff, great store of wheat and Malt'.[9]

Why were Gormanston's forces so ineffectual? Courage was not wanting. The Palesmen doggedly defended castles and tower houses that lay closest to Dublin's expanding enclave: these included Carrickmines, Daingean, Tipper, Bert, Dunmahon, Baldongan, Trim, Blackwood, Lynch's Knock, Blackhall, Rathcoffey, Clongoweswood and Syddan.[10] In March 1642, Simon Harcourt's regiment assailed Carrickmines Castle in south County Dublin. A sniper picked off Harcourt and discouraged the siege gunners from their battery, but the assailants nonetheless succeeded in smashing open the door

---

3   John Hagan, 'Miscellanea Vaticano-Hibernica', *Archivium Hibernicum*, 6 (1917), pp.94–155.
4   Henry Burkhead, *A tragedy of Cola's furie, or, Lirenda's miserie* (Kilkenny: Publisher unknown, 1646), p.16.
5   Anon., *Admirable, good, true and joyfull newes from Ireland …* (London: John Wright, 1642), pp.2–3.
6   Verney, *Memoirs*, vol. II, p.135.
7   Kevin Forkan, 'Inventing an Irish Protestant Icon: The Strange Death of Sir Charles Coote, 1642', in D. Edwards, C. Tait, and P. Lenihan (eds), *Age of Atrocity: Violence and Political Conflict in Early Modern Ireland* (Dublin: Four Courts Press, 2007), pp.204–18.
8   Ó Donnchadha, 'Cín lae', p.36.
9   TCDL: 1641 Depositions, MS 832 (County Cavan), fol. 152v: Deposition of George Creighton.
10 Pádraig Lenihan, 'Siege Massacres in Ireland: Drogheda in Context', in M. Bennett, R. Gillespie, and R. S. Spurlock (eds), *Cromwell and Ireland; New Perspectives* (Liverpool: Liverpool University Press, 2021), pp.45–48.

with axes and bursting through. Harcourt's men were 'highly provoked' and 'put all they found therein to the sword'. Baldongan, just 12 miles north of Dublin, held out as long as it did because the defenders trusted Gormanston's promises of relief. However, in early June, two battering guns quickly opened a breach, and the English burst in on the 120 rebels, 'whom immediately they put to the sword'. The term 'rebels' often included civilians: two burial pits excavated at Carrickmines contained the remains of 15 victims of frenzied attacks – men, women and children from three to 45 years of age who were shot and struck multiple times from behind or when on the ground by swords and musket butts.[11]

A few days after Baldongan, Colonel George Monck summoned the defenders of Summerhill, County Meath. The keep was a four-storey tower, and there is no trace of earthworks having been dug to strengthen either bawn or keep. With unwarranted confidence, the defenders bade the attackers, 'Be gone yee Parliament Rebells'.[12] They withstood battery and assault for five days until '… some were of opinion they should accept of a quarter, others that it were more honourable to fight out to the last man to avenge themselves of these perfidious round heads, who would never observe quarter unto them'.

The mistress of the house had beseeched the soldiers to capitulate. Upon marching out, 'the lieutenant and all the rest his soldiers were there executed; the gentlewoman only was saved'.[13] The English accounts are similar in their essentials except that they deny any promise of quarter was given to

Lynch's Knock. (<https://lynchscastlesummerhill.weebly.com>)

---

11 Damian Shiels, 'Siege, Storm and Slaughter: 17th Century Mass Graves', *Archaeology Ireland*, 33:4 (2019), p.36.
12 Anon., *A Briefe relation of the proceedings of our army in Ireland, since the tenth of June to this present July 1642 together with the petition of the Parliament there assembled, to the lords, iustices, and counsell* (London: R. Oulton and G. Dexter, 1642), p.3.
13 Gilbert (ed.), *Contemporary History*, vol. I, p.392.

the men within the castle. According to these accounts, grenades cast in through a breach set the castle ablaze, at which many of the defenders 'cried for quarter, but none being granted but to the women and children, they resolutely defended themselves, and kept our men almost two hours at the breach at push of pike' until they were dragged out, 'begging for quarter', stripped and 'immediately slain'.[14] In what seems to be a reference to this episode, 'Tibernus', a trusted follower of 'Cola', tells his soldiers that he will pretend to '… promise what ever they will demand, until / we gaine this place of strength, our losse is much / already; when that is done, gentlemen, / and brother souldiers, their lives shall be at / each of your disposalls, as our poore countrymen / hath been at theirs'. An Irishman emerging from the castle protests, 'Hold we had quarter promist us!' An English soldier replies, 'Believe him not he lyes, kill, kill, let not a bastards / brat of that unhappy brood, escape your hand'.[15]

By August, the Flemings were desperately defending the last of their castles at Syddan on the northernmost fringe of the Pale: 'we storm'd it thrice and when the castle was batter'd about them they fought us out of the ruin'.[16]

The Lords Justices hoped that the 'sharpness' at Baldongan would 'discourage' the Palesmen 'from presuming to keep castles from us hereafter'.[17] It certainly helped encourage some of them to build ramparts thick enough to absorb repeated shots from the culverin, which was the lightest siege gun that could be hauled from Dublin in dry weather and could penetrate up to a 12-foot thickness of tightly rammed earth.[18] The earliest example of artillery earthworks was the 'great work of earth & sodds' thrown up at Kilmeague, County Kildare, on the bog island of Allen, which provided sanctuary after Irish troops had been swept out of the plains country.[19]

Adversity taught the Palesmen a second painful lesson. The Catholics had no central body capable of mobilising resources and directing them where they were most needed, and so the Palesmen had been left to bear the brunt of the fighting on their own. So, as we saw, the first step to creating a national government and running this 'lawful and pious' war was taken at Kells, on the marches of the Pale, by a clerical synod convened in March.[20] Later,

---

14 Mark Empey, 'The Diary of Sir James Ware, 1623–66', *Analecta Hibernica*, 45 (2014), p.110; Anon., *True intelligence from Ireland. Relating many passages of great consequence …* (London: John Sweeting, 1642), p.1.
15 Burkhead, *Cola's furie*, p.24.
16 British Library (BrL) Sloane MS 190 (12): 'A collection of letters and papers formerly belonging to Edmund Borlase', p.70; Empey, 'Diary of Sir James Ware', p.111; Anon., *A True relation of the latest occurrences in Ireland. Sent from the postmaster there, to a friend of his in London. Dated in Ireland, August 17. 1642* (London: Benjamin Allen, 1642), p.8.
17 F. E. Ball (ed.), *Calendar of the Manuscripts of the Marquess of Ormonde, K. P., Preserved at Kilkenny Castle* (London: HMSO, 1902–1920), vol. II, pp.100, 142, 144, 'Lords Justices to Earl of Leicester, 31 March 1642 and 7 June 1642'.
18 Cathal J. Nolan, *Wars of the Age of Louis XIV, 1650-1715: An Encyclopedia of Global Warfare and Civilization* (Westport, CT: Greenwood Press, 2008), p.17.
19 TCDL: 1641 Depositions, MS 810 (County Dublin), fols 235r, 236r: Deposition of William Hollis.
20 Thomas L. Coonan, *The Irish Catholic Confederacy and the Puritan Revolution* (Dublin: Clonmore and Reynolds, 1954), p.138; Charles P. Meehan, *The Confederation of Kilkenny* (Dublin: James Duffy, 1846), pp.20, 23.

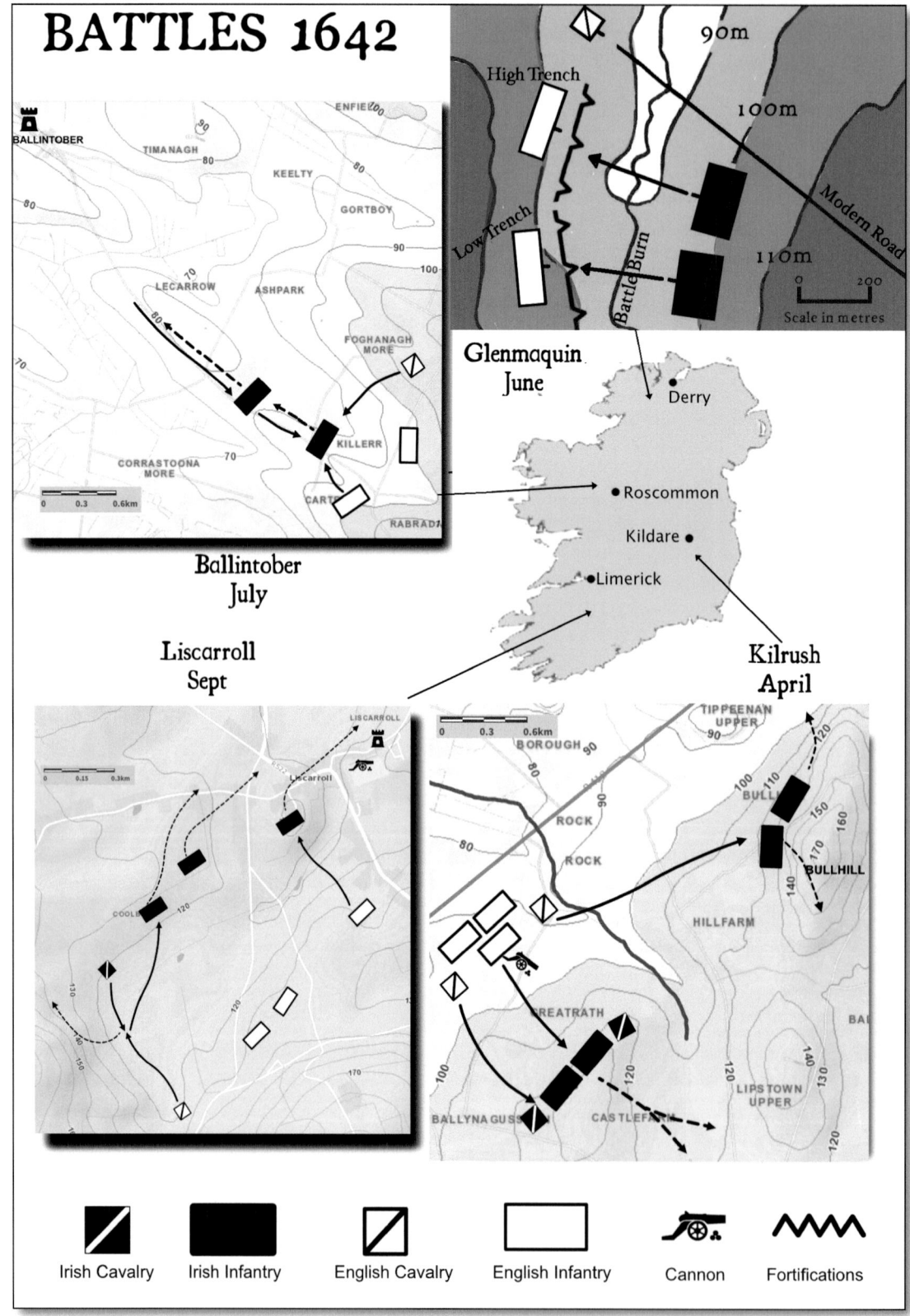

Kilrush, Glenmaquin, Ballintober and Liscarroll. (Kevin Glynn)

Charles agreed with Parliament to finance the cost of reconquest by loans secured on two-and-a-half million acres of Irish lands, that is, almost all the Catholic-owned land. This brought home to the insurgents countrywide that they could not conclude a negotiated settlement in the short term. The clergy took the initiative in creating a government of Confederate Catholics and convened a general assembly, or unicameral parliament, at Kilkenny on 24 October. Old Mountgarret would preside over a standing executive, or Supreme Council. It was a long way from coordinating a national war effort, but it was a start.

Like the Palesmen, the Catholic forces in Ulster endured severe pressure. Robert Monro's 'invincible Scots' represented the biggest single military intervention of all, and the insurgents closest to hand, Manus Rua O'Cahan and the Mac Colla brothers, crossed the Bann in April and May to flee their wrath.[21] Having lost Newry and Armagh, Phelim set Armagh ablaze and so earned the soubriquet 'Totane', or 'firebrand'. He was not alone. It became routine for both sides to burn habitable buildings to deny shelter to enemy soldiers. Often, for good measure, they massacred or banished the inhabitants. Phelim Totane incorporated O'Cahan and the Mac Collas in his own army to make up a host of 4,000 men and led them north-west, penetrating to the heart of the Laggan, the settler-planted lowlands of north-east County Donegal environed by river, mountain and sea.[22] The outnumbered Laggan men had burrowed into an escarpment on the westerly slopes of Tully Hill, overlooking a stream later called the 'Battleburn'. Across the stream, the Irish camped on the night before what came to be known as the Battle of Glenmaquin (16 June 1642). The next day, Sir Robert Stewart, 'an old soldier', sent a detachment downhill to goad Phelim's men, and two formations of Irish foot duly charged uphill, endured 'continual shot' at close range for 15 minutes and then 'turned faces'.[23]

Why did the Irish attack? They were in the heart of the enemy's breadbasket, but no doubt Stewart's cavalry deterred them from scavenging and ravaging at will, and so they were probably pinched by hunger and could not wait much longer. Having chosen to be the ones to charge, rightly or wrongly, why pick an axis of advance to their front, where they must climb a steep scarp? But an advance to their left would have demanded an even stiffer climb. The ground to their right sloped more gently, but Stewart's horsemen were probably waiting there and would have made short work of any Irish foot soldiers coming that way. Today, the escarpment is (and was) shrouded in brush and offered attackers some cover from view and fire. The axis of advance was as good as Phelim Totane and Mac Colla were going to get, but it was not good enough.

The Irish marched uphill 'close together' in two 'brigades', by which term Stewart probably meant bigger battle squares than usual. One formation

---

21 Siobhan Talbott, '"Causing Misery and Suffering Miserably": Representations of the Thirty Years' War in Literature and History', *Literature & History*, 30:1 (2021), p.6.
22 Hogan (ed.), *History of the Warr of Ireland*, p.23.
23 Hogan (ed.), *Letters and Papers*, p.50, 'Sir Robert Stewart to Sir John Borlase, Culmore, 21 June 1642'.

comprised O'Cahans and Mac Colla's County Antrim followers, together with 'many [Scots] Highlanders', who 'cried up their valour as invincible champions' and, recalled Stewart, 'assailed my brigade fiercely insofar as they were not far from coming to push of pike'. The Laggan men stood their ground and 'galled' Mac Colla's brigade with 'continual shot' for 15 minutes at close range.[24] Why did Mac Colla's charge fail at Glenmaquin when the charge had worked so well before and would so again?

An 'immediate and dramatic change' in fire discipline followed the opening clashes of the English Civil War. Rather than fire once the enemy came within musket range, musketeers held their fire until the enemy approached to within the length of a pike or two, which is five to 10 yards. Three ranks then fired a single salvo rather than follow the cumbersome fire-by-ranks procedure attempted at Julianstown. At Glenmaquin, Stewart had anticipated this development.[25]

Put like that, it must seem no contest since charging men could hardly beat troops unleashing volleys at close range. In theory, the musket was reasonably accurate. A seventeenth-century matchlock tested in modern times against a man-sized target hit the target half the time at 100 metres. Fear, physical exhaustion, haste and other variables would have impaired the theoretical optimum performance. The shooter had to hold his aim on a moving target for an appreciably long time as the arm, onto which he had screwed the glowing end of a match, swung down several inches into the open priming pan and ignited the powder and the trail burned into the main charge. A Dutch illustration purporting to show Irish musketeers defending Athlone in 1691 shows the muzzles of the three front ranks belching clouds of black smoke, which must have seriously degraded accuracy. An eyewitness of a black-powder battle remarked that, at 60 paces, he 'saw through the smoke cloud nothing but flashes, the glint of bayonets and the tops of grenadier's caps'. Ardant du Picq, a nineteenth-century proponent of shock over firepower, argued that firepower, the material, counted for less than what he called the 'moral' or psychological effect and insisted that, when troops are forced to wait anxiously and passively, the order to fire finally releases their tension such that the 'shots are fired into the air. If anybody is killed it is an accident'.[26] Moreover, a trained musketeer could fire only two shots a minute and that only for a short time, if it was not raining or windy. The clue to the defining limitation is in the name: a matchlock's wick was a slow burner and would often fail to ignite the priming powder in the pan, which lay exposed to wind and rain.[27]

The outcome hung in the balance on the scarp for 15 minutes, not least because it was so steep that the attackers were hard put to close the final few

---

24 Patrick McCarthy, 'Preserving Donegal - The Battle of Glenmaquin, 16 June 1642', *The Irish Sword*, 23:94 (2003), pp.361–82.
25 Blackmore, *'Destructive and Formidable'*, p.42.
26 Charles Ardant du Picq, *Études sur le combat* (Paris: Librairie Hachette, 1880), pp.110, 160–61.
27 B. P. Hughes, *Firepower: Weapons Effectiveness on the Battlefield, 1630-1850* (London: Arms and Armour Press, 1974), pp.81–83; Philip T. Hoffman, *Why Did Europe Conquer the World?* (Princeton: Princeton University Press, 2015), pp.56–58; Peter Gaunt, *The English Civil War: A Military History* (London: Bloomsbury, 2019), p.108.

SUMMER AND AUTUMN 1642

Fire by ranks, Romeyn de Hooghe, 'Verovering van Athlone, 1691', (Leiden: Johannes Tangena, 1691). (Rijksmuseum, Amsterdam)

yards and strike with sword or pike and that most of Stewart's shots must have flown over the heads of Mac Colla's men. However, one ball hit Mac Colla, and that made all the difference. The Mac Colla–O'Cahan formation began to unravel when pikemen at the rear 'broke': the rearmost soldiers were usually the first to slip away because they were usually filled by raw or less reliable troops and they could melt away more easily than the men standing in the front ranks. The disorder probably began when Mac Colla was shot and an O'Cahan cousin brought him off in a horse-litter. Seeing Mac Colla's square breaking up, the second square under Red Phelim soon disintegrated. To judge from the captains who were killed, an O'Donnelly, an O'Hagan and an O'Neill, it was Phelim's brigade that took up the rear and so bore the brunt of the subsequent pursuit.

O'Mellan noted that the Irish lost 180 men and three captains, which he considered a 'lot' (*iomad*). Stewart said that his men killed 500, which may be nearer the truth, considering he 'had the chase and execution of them for 6 or 7 miles'.[28] One source claims a 'company of lame beggars' were 'all lost because they could not run', but O'Neill was hardly that strapped for manpower, and the story may have 'grown legs' from another anecdote about a cripple who struck a pursuing cavalryman with a blow of his crutch and made off on his horse.[29] Whatever the body count, Glenmaquin was a decisive defeat for O'Neill.

In the aftermath of Glenmaquin, Stewart caught up with O'Cahan at Gelvin near Dungiven, County Derry. O'Cahans men attacked 'with the greatest fury that I think ever any men were seen to charge', but a volley from

---

28   Ó Donnchadha, 'Cín lae', p.12; Hogan (ed.), *Letters and Papers*, p.50.
29   Hogan (ed.), *History of the Warr of Ireland*, p.24; Ó Donnchadha, 'Cín lae', p.12.

80 musketeers broke the charge, leaving Stewart free to push on to relieve Coleraine.[30] Pressing into mid-Ulster from the opposite direction, Monro launched forays deep into the interior, even over the Blackwater. In despair, the Ulster chiefs declared that 'every man should look out for himself'.[31] Conn O'Neill had been sent home by his uncle Eoghan Rua to prepare the ground, and he argued strenuously that they should wait for his uncle to disembark. Just then, a footman dashed in, bearing news that Eoghan Rua had landed at Doe Castle, County Donegal, with men, arms and munitions.[32]

Spain had sponsored Tyrone in the Nine Years' War (1594–1603), and France would support the Irish in the Williamite War (1689–1691). This time, neither of the rival great powers had skin in the game.[33] Moloch's appetite was not sated, and that 'whole complex of conflicts' known as the Thirty Years' War had seven years to run, and the Franco–Spanish conflict had another 18 years.[34] The Spanish offered scant help until English encouragement of Portuguese rebels stung them into releasing Irish soldiers and officers from their service.[35] Richelieu followed suit. The two up-to-strength Irish tercios, Tyrone's and Tyrconnell's, had been transferred to Spain, leaving behind one-time *Maestre de Campo* Thomas Preston's company and Eoghan Rua O'Neill's understrength regiments behind. The Spanish could afford to lose a rump that was top-heavy with officers and pay their arrears in arms and munitions if it created goodwill towards Spanish recruiters in the future.[36] In a further beneficent gesture, Spanish authorities paid 20,000 escudos to the Augustinian James Talbot to buy weapons and ammunition.[37] Encouraged by the papal nuncio Grimaldi, the French also quietly facilitated shipments of men and munitions. In June 1642, Condé gave licenses to 36 officers from the Fitzwilliam and Belling regiments to go home.[38] By allowing some officers and men to return, the French and Spanish were baiting their hooks with sprats to catch mackerel.

---

30 Hogan (ed.), *Letters and Papers*, p.58.
31 IMC: Kavanagh (ed.), *Commentarius Rinuccinianus*, vol. I, p.331–32; Ó Donnchadha, 'Cín lae', pp.12–13; Jerrold I. Casway, *Owen Roe O'Neill and the Struggle for Catholic Ireland* (Philadelphia: University of Pennsylvania Press, 1984), p.60.
32 TCDL: 1641 Depositions, MS 836 (County Armagh), fol. 107r: Deposition of Frauncis Sacheverell; Casway, *Struggle for Catholic Ireland*, p.54; Gilbert (ed.), *Contemporary History*, vol. III, p.198.
33 TNA: *HMC Report on Franciscan Manuscripts in Dublin*, pp.122, 127.
34 Jeremy Black, 'The Thirty Years' War', *Teaching History*, 63 (1991), p.44; Jerrold I. Casway, 'Owen Roe O'Neill's Return to Ireland in 1642: The Diplomatic Background', *Studia Hibernica*, 9 (1969), pp.54–55, 61.
35 Tadhg Ó hAnnracháin, 'Vatican Diplomacy and the Mission of Rinuccini to Ireland', *Archivium Hibernicum*, 47 (1993), <http://hdl.handle.net/10197/7900>, pp.77–88; Eduardo de Mesa, 'The Career of Owen Roe O'Neill in the Spanish Army of Flanders (1606-42): Documentation Held in Spanish Archives', *Archivium Hibernicum*, 67 (2014), pp.11, 21.
36 Eduardo de Mesa, *The Irish in the Spanish Armies in the Seventeenth Century* (Woodbridge: Boydell & Brewer, 2014), pp.29–30.
37 De Mesa, *The Irish in the Spanish Armies*, pp.29, 92, 129, 163, 171; Rafael Valladares Ramírez, 'Un reino más para la monarquía? Felipe IV, Irlanda y la guerra civil inglesa, 1641-1649', *Studia historica. Historia moderna*, 15 (1996), p.268.
38 Pierre Gouhier, 'Mercenaires irlandais au service de la France (1635-1664)', *Revue d'histoire moderne et contemporaine*, 15:4 (1968), p.678.

O'Neill ran the blockade and disembarked 300 officers and men at Doe Castle. Phelim led a strong escort and met Eoghan Rua at Killybegs, whence they marched hard by Ballyshannon back to the interior of Ulster. While Phelim's army was stealing back and forth across enemy-dominated south County Donegal, Monro and his local allies burst into the heart of his country, destroying his home at Caledon, where 'nothing was left quick [alive] but angry dogs and embers', and capturing Dungannon and Mountjoy for a time.[39]

Charlemont held out, and, taking the long view, the survival of this forward base, taken together with O'Neill's arrival there on 13 August, changed what might have been Monro's 'complete success' into a 'very limited victory'.[40] But it must not have seemed like that at the time. With Mountjoy and Dungannon in their hands, the 'British' (i.e., the inclusive term used to denote English and Scottish settlers as distinct from Monro's Covenanters) of east Ulster had inserted what threatened to be a permanent and irksome presence right in the heart of Irish Ulster. Cattle raiders from Mountjoy were especially troublesome: once, when closely pursued, the raiders halted, fired a 'full volley', raised a 'great shout' in imitation of the Irish and charged, chasing them for four miles and killing 'many of their best men who could not get their soldiers to stand'.[41] In August, Alexander Leslie, Earl of Leven, marched in a wide and unstoppable circuit over the Bann and counterclockwise around Lough Neagh, halting to let off a celebratory volley at Dungannon before continuing through Armagh to Newry. Leven's second expedition was designed to capture Charlemont, but he made it less than halfway from the rendezvous at Lisburn to his objective when he had to turn back, thwarted by dwindling provisions and too few draft animals to haul the guns and baggage over 'extremely bad' ways. Leven returned to Scotland, his forays having achieved 'almost nothing'.[42] However, the cumulative pressure was unrelenting as the enemy killed 'without mercy or remorse all man, woman, and child, that came in his way', drove off cattle as booty, ruined grain stores and burnt growing crops so that the peasants could no longer grow their oats, graze their cattle or feed the armies.[43] Fleeing from Leven, the creaghts of County Derry had drifted south and east as far as Slieve Veagh in the south-easternmost corner of County Tyrone. This flight was temporary, but later flights would be permanent.

In September 1642, Lord Conway complained that his British troops 'at the end of a wet summer are entering into winter without hay for our horses, without houses for our men, it rains continually, everyone is sick,

---

39 Quoted in Richard Bagwell, *Ireland Under the Stuarts and during the Interregnum* (London: Longmans, Green and Co., 1909), vol. II: 1642–1660, p.24.
40 David Stevenson, *Scottish Covenanters and Irish Confederates: Scottish-Irish Relations in the Mid-Seventeenth Century* (Newtownards: Ulster Historical Foundation, 1981), p.120.
41 Anon., *A True Relation of the Taking of Mountjoy in the County of Tyrone by Collonell Clotworthy* ... (London: R. Oulton and G. Dexter, 1642), p.5; Gilbert (ed.), *Contemporary History*, vol. I, part 2, p.514.
42 Stevenson, *Scottish Covenanters and Irish Confederates*, pp.124–25.
43 Gilbert (ed.), *Contemporary History*, vol. I, p.41.

few clothes, little money, ill meat, worse drink'.[44] It was this wet summer that granted Eoghan Rua breathing space. He had no more than 1,000 full-time soldiers, even including the warders of Charlemont and Cloughoughter. Others were called out 'the best they could from the incursions of the enemy, to wit, each county to defend themselves'.[45] In summer 1642, the two Red O'Neills between them could muster 4,000 occasional soldiers in the whole block of mid-Ulster encompassed by the south-eastern extremity of County Derry, east Tyrone and north Armagh – from which one can extrapolate a paper strength of about 18,000 Irish soldiers in all of Ulster.

The Irish position in Connacht was also weak. In June 1642, a relief expedition from Dublin had smashed through to Athlone and installed a strong garrison of some 2,000 men in the town and castle. Urged on by his subordinates, on 14 July, President of Connaught Viscount Ranelagh attacked Ballagh Castle, where the highway between Athlone and Roscommon grazed Lough Funshinagh.[46] Ranelagh's troops knocked a breach but were forced back, and a 'great many' were killed by shot, 'besides what perish'd by Stones, and other Materials thrown from the top of the Castle'. That night, the warders stole away, and Ranelagh linked up with well-manned strongholds sprinkled across the maghery: Elphin had 50 men, Roscommon Abbey had 40, and most of the others (e.g., Lissadorn, Roscommon Castle, Knockvicar, Canbo and Tulsk) were probably about that size, too.[47] Charles Coote the younger (the elder had been shot in the back at Trim) proved to be a natural warrior thrown up by the challenges of the time. The Irish had built a standing camp at Creggs to 'molest and pen up' the garrison of Castlecoote, County Roscommon, until Coote scattered them in March 1642.[48] Castlecoote would metastasise into an engorged garrison, mainly filled with native desperadoes and renegades.[49] Robert King of Boyle had captained a troop of horse in the standing army, and, in April 1642, he had loosened the Mac Dermott stranglehold of Elphin.[50] Reinforced by troops from the maghery garrisons to about 2,000 men, Ranelagh's column pressed farther north to Ballintober, where Charles O'Conor Don had 'began to awake out of his Ale and Aqua-vitae' and was gathering 2,000 infantry and 160 horsemen. At first, the Irish stayed within a secure position almost encircled by bogs and abutting Ballintober Castle, a massive keepless structure that enclosed a bawn of one-and-a-half acres. But, for some reason, a battle square of 1,200 Irish pikemen lumbered forth from the fastness towards Ranelagh. King's troop of cavalry in the vanguard

---

44 Stevenson, *Scottish Covenanters and Irish Confederates*, p.125.
45 Gilbert (ed.), *Contemporary History*, vol. III, p.199.
46 Borlase, *Irish Rebellion*, p.80; Burke, *Memoirs and Letters of Ulick*, p.190; Gilbert (ed.), *Irish Confederation*, vol. II, pp.134–37; Hogan (ed.), *Letters and Papers*, pp.45–51; Carte, *History of the Life of James Duke of Ormonde*, vol. I, p.345.
47 TCDL: 1641 Depositions, MS 830 (County Galway), fol. 15v: Deposition of John Ridge.
48 Borlase, *Irish Rebellion*, p.76.
49 Robert Armstrong, 'Coote, Sir Charles', *Dictionary of Irish Biography* (2009), <https://www.dib.ie/biography/coote-sir-charles-a2027>, accessed 2 April 2020; Clarke, *Old English*, p.53; Victor Treadwell, *Buckingham and Ireland 1616-1628: A Study in Anglo-Irish Politics* (Dublin: Four Courts Press, 1998), pp.59, 144, 200–02, 266.
50 TCDL: 1641 Depositions, MS 831 (County Sligo), fols 216r, 216v: Deposition of Ismah Darby.

Pike at 'charge for horse'. (Jacques II de Castlenau, Le Marechal de Bataille (Paris: Etienne Migon, 1647), p.99) (Author's collection)

fired their carbines from a close range of about 12 yards while a nearby forlorn hope of English musketeers also blazed away.

Some pikemen fell, their pikes entangling those of their comrades, and King seized on the disorder to fall on a corner (always a weak point) of the rectangle while Coote and others charged the sides and broke the square apart. Just at this inopportune time, a body of Irish musketeers shambled up, saw their comrades run and also took to their heels. It was not English practice to keep pike and shot in separate bodies, but we see French infantry attacking in just this manner in a print depicting the curtain-closing act of the tragedy, or farce, that was Buckingham's descent on the Isle of Ré in 1627.

The battle, as a contest, was over, but not the cavalry cutting down runaways. Given the long distance they had to flee, the Irish foot soldiers must have taken heavy losses (Michael Earnley, one of Ranelagh's officers, estimated them at 600) and lost nearly all their weapons. One soldier

Pike at 'charge'. (Jacques II de Castlenau, Le Marechal de Bataille (Paris: Etienne Migon, 1647), p.79) (Author's collection)

stood his ground in the corner of a field and held off five horsemen with his pike until an English foot soldier slipped past the pike head and slew the soldier. When it came to stripping the body, the scavengers first took off the mountero (a soft cap with a rounded crown, sometimes endowed with a peak and flaps), and 'there fell down long Tresses of flaxen hair, who being further search'd, was found a woman'.[51] This 'mountero' may denote the soft cap described by a Frenchman who traversed Leinster and Munster in 1644: 'a little blue bonnet, raised two fingers breadth in front, and behind covering their head and ears'.[52]

Earnley claimed that they had now broken the enemy in Connacht and grumbled that Ranelagh was not following up the victory, but this was to ignore the difficulties that Ranelagh would have faced. Follow-up operations would surely have meant a siege of Ballintober. Meanwhile, in Ranelagh's absence, Sir James Dillon attacked Athlone's weakened defences, broke into the Leinster side of town and set it ablaze in an attack that may have been coordinated with his brother Lucas. Yet Earnley may have had a point. It would take four years and external help for the Catholic position in County Roscommon to recover from the Ballintober setback.

From Munster came the first glimmering of sustained Irish offensives. On 15 May 1642, Barry's new army began its attack on King John's Castle, whose squat round towers dominated the bridge over the Shannon to County

---

51 Borlase, *Irish Rebellion*, pp.81–82.
52 Corpus of Electronic Texts (CELT) T100076: 'The tour of the French traveller M. de La Boullaye Le Gouz in Ireland, A.D. 1644', p.43.

SUMMER AND AUTUMN 1642

Pike and shot advancing, Laurent de La Hyre, 'Défaicte des Anglois en l'isle de Ré par l'armée françoise'. (Gallica, Bibliothèque nationale de France)

Clare.[53] Barry's force was mainly drawn from north Munster. Barry's second-in-command was now Patrick Purcell from Kildimo, County Limerick, 'bred in the wars of Germany'.[54] Other County Limerick leaders included Castleconnell, Baron Brittas and Oliver Stephenson. From Tipperary came the veteran of Smolensk Richard Butler of Ikerrin and Purcell of Loghmoe. County Clare's most notable officer present was Christopher O'Brien, younger brother of Murrough, Baron Inchiquin, soon-to-be leader of the Munster Protestants.

Wanting siege artillery to knock breaches in the ramparts, Barry nonetheless surprised an isolated castle on the western bank of the Shannon at 'Mockbegger'. The besiegers next fashioned a boom of long ash trunks fastened with iron links to two mill stones at Mockbegger and at the other end to the tower of the Quay. This blocked access to the quay and, with that, all hope of 'relief by sea'.[55] The steeple of St Mary's Cathedral overlooked much of the space within the walls, and snipers shot at least six men over the course of those weeks and no doubt forced the besieged to huddle more closely in lean-tos against the southern curtain wall.[56]

Barry was short of gunpowder, which probably explains why a man who so delighted in exploding devices nonetheless had to settle for old-fashioned burnt prop mining. A trench was dug between the castle and the houses on High Street so that miners could safely tunnel from the backyards. For three weeks, Barry's men drove a tunnel wide and high enough for a man to walk almost fully erect towards the bastion.[57] The idea was to dig under the walls

---

53 TCDL: 1641 Depositions, MS 829 (County Limerick), fol. 101v: Deposition of John Comyne.
54 Gilbert (ed.), *Irish Confederation*, vol. V, p.21.
55 TCDL: 1641 Depositions, MS 829 (County Limerick), fol. 380r: Deposition of James Craven.
56 TCDL: 1641 Depositions, MS 829 (County Limerick), fol. 132v: Deposition of John Lilles.
57 TCDL: 1641 Depositions, MS 840 (County Limerick), fols 91–97: 'A relation of the rebellion in and about Limerick with the taking of the castle of Limerick' and 'John Rastalls relation';

RAW GENERALS AND GREEN SOLDIERS

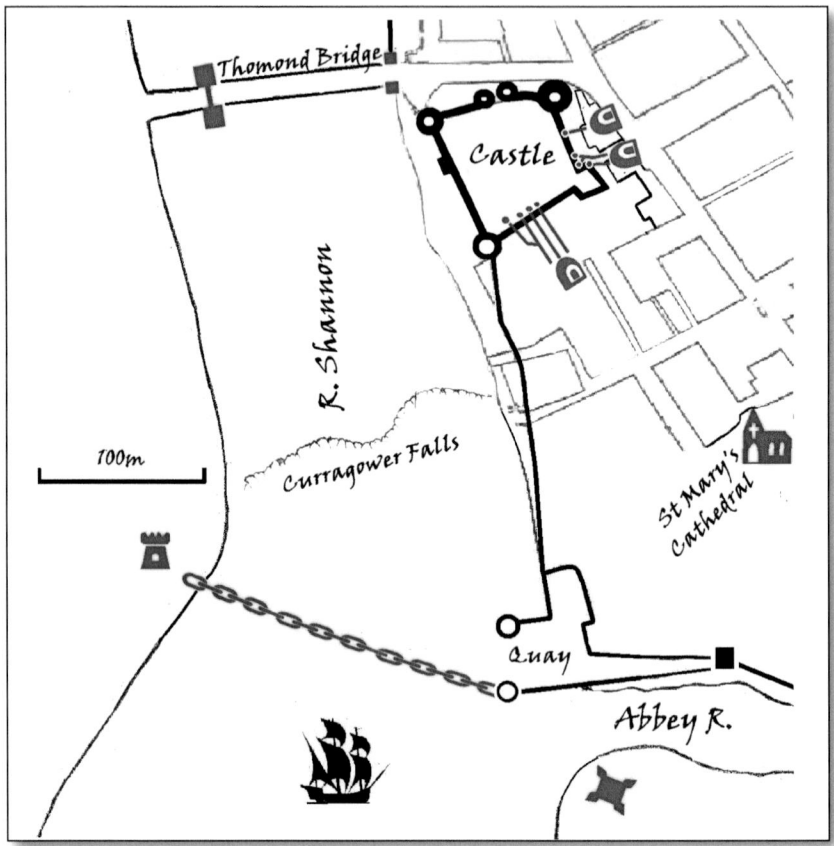

Mines and countermines. (Kenneth Wiggins, *Anatomy of a Siege: King John's Castle, Limerick, 1642* (Woodbridge: Boydell & Brewer, 2001))

and then collapse the mine by burning the props, thereby causing a length of wall to subside. Hearing the scrape of shovel and pick, the defenders began their own countermines to intercept and destroy the tunnel. On 7 June, the first of the attacker's tunnels emerged prematurely into the dry ditch around the castle, whereupon the defenders flooded the tunnel, and Barry was forced to abandon that approach. However, he regrouped and drove several more tunnels forwards from different directions. On 20 June, an underground gun battle in acrid blackness drove the Irish back again. Nonetheless, the next day, stretches of the ramparts were collapsed, and the governor, Captain Courtenay, capitulated, 'wanting men, ammunition and victuals'.[58] By now, over a third of the men, women and children in the castle had perished from disease and privation.

Inchiquin would soon take command of English forces in Munster from his father-in-law, St Leger, and, a week after the capitulation of King John's Castle, Inchiquin scattered Irish forces gathering at Newtown, near the Ballyhoura Gap, but he did not push forwards through the gap. It was too late for that.

Kenneth Wiggins, *Anatomy of a Siege: King John's Castle, Limerick, 1642* (Woodbridge: Boydell & Brewer, 2001), pp.48, 57, 73, 87, 170–74, 253–54; Lenihan, *Confederate Catholics at War*, pp.57, 112; Carte, *History of the Life of James Duke of Ormonde*, vol. I, p.341.

58 TCDL: 1641 Depositions, MS 829 (County Limerick), fol. 380r: Deposition of James Craven.

Musketeer. (*Jacques II de Castlenau, Le Marechal de Bataille* (Paris: Etienne Migon, 1647), p.29)

Barry had used 'industry rather than gallantry'.[59] Several of the defenders were miners who had fled from Silvermines, and Barry was no doubt also able to draw on mining expertise.[60] But technical expertise was not the sole reason why Barry succeeded where Phelim had failed at Drogheda. He had some 1,500 men under his command to contain just 300 able-bodied defenders, which gave him a comfortable 5:1 margin of superiority.

While Inchiquin was trying to organise the relief of King John's Castle, his factional enemies, the Boyles, were busily expanding their control from the Lower Blackwater Valley. Two of Boyle's sons – Richard, Viscount Dungarvan, and Broghill – planted a culverin against Ardmore Castle, County Waterford, and the adjacent round tower. When the gun was 'ready to play', the defenders 'asked quarter for goods and life, but that being denied, they were content to submit themselves to the mercy of the Lords, who gave the women and children their clothes, lives, and liberty to depart, the men we kept prisoners'. Between the castle and the tower, the Boyles took 154 prisoners: 'The next day we hanged 117. The English prisoners [held by the Irish] we freed'.[61]

---

59 Borlase, *Irish Rebellion*, p.119.
60 The naturalist Gerald Boate insists that the miners at Silvermines were all Englishmen. Dermot F. Gleeson, 'The Silver Mines of Ormond', *Journal of the Royal Society of Antiquaries of Ireland*, 7th series, 7:1 (1937), p.109.
61 James Buckley, 'The Siege of Ardmore Castle, 1642', *Journal of the Waterford and South-East of Ireland Archaeological Society*, 4:1 (1898), pp.58–59.

Barry dismounted two cannons from the castle ramparts. One gun was ferried by water up Bunratty Creek towards Ballyalla while 'Bess', a monster weighing over three tons, was shipped down the Shannon Estuary. Barry now deployed the biggest siege gun in the country, offloaded and mounted on a hollowed-out tree trunk to prevent it from sinking in soft ground and dragged by a team of 50 oxen. County Limerick's enemy strongholds fell like nine pins.

Barry's Sieges in County Limerick, July–August 1642[62]

Capitulation	Place	Total Numbers[63]	Soldiers[64]
29 July	Kilfinny	*400*	80
1 August	Croom	100	*20*
6 August	Newcastle	1,000	*200*
14 August	Askeaton	*600*	200

Reading English accounts, one might believe that they fell to a body of men that numbered 6,000 to 7,000 men and was stable enough to be considered an army. Just because witnesses saw 'colonel' so-and-so at a particular siege, it does not follow that an equivalent regimental-sized formation was also present. Usually, the 'colonel' brought only a company or two, or he was preoccupied with other operations. From 25 March until the beginning of August, Castleconnell, for one, was fully engaged in beleaguering Loughgur, and Stephenson commanded the two forts built to constrict Castle Matrix from April to August 1642.[65]

The mopping-up campaign in County Limerick, then, was carried out by bodies of men from that county, reinforced by smaller contingents coming and going from neighbouring counties. Muskerry and Purcell of Loghmoe were still with the army that took Askeaton, for example, together with a small contingent from across the Shannon Estuary led by Thomond's nephew Dermot O'Brien of Dromore, 'colonel in the field' of the County Clare regiment and a future diplomat and supreme councillor. The army, on this occasion, comprised 18 companies, or less than 2,000 men, from west and mid-County Limerick.[66] By the time the travelling roadshow

---

62   Gilbert (ed.), *Irish Confederation*, vol. II, p.72; TCDL: 1641 Depositions, MS 829 (County Limerick), fols 132r: Deposition of John Lilles, 136r: Deposition of Richard Lacky, 138r, 138v: Deposition of Elizabeth Dowdall, 145r: Deposition of Richard Turnor, 183v: Deposition of Jane Meriett, 377r: Examination of Anthony Sherwyn; Westropp, 'Ancient Castles', p.159.

63   Estimated figures in italics.

64   Estimated figures in italics.

65   TCDL: 1641 Depositions, MS 829 (County Limerick), fols 190v: Deposition of Bishop Planke and Ann Reynes, 209v: Deposition of ffaieth Grady, 345v: Deposition of George Man and Robert Willies.

66   Gilbert (ed.), *Irish Confederation*, vol. II, pp.51–53; TCDL: 1641 Depositions, MS 823 (County Cork), fols 157r–58v: Deposition of William Eams, MS 829 (County Clare), fol. 67r: Deposition of John Hawkins, and MS 829 (County Limerick), fols 132r: Deposition of John Lilles, 136r: Deposition of Richard Lacky, 147r: Deposition of John Billal, 153r: Deposition of John Howell, 254r: Deposition of Thomas Ragg, Robert Ragg and Henry Briggs; Jane Ohlmeyer,

crossed into County Cork, it had doubled in size. After the tiny garrison of Liscarroll capitulated on 2 September, one of the besiegers sneered at the enemy that 'we will beat you from here to Mallow and then to Cork and from thence into the sea'.[67] Howbeit, Liscarroll would mark the end of Barry's triumphal progress.

The Boyles, at last, cooperated with Inchiquin, so he could now scrape together about 2,800 men, and he chose to stake all on one battle rather than see his garrisons snuffed out one by one. An English account marvelled that 'we were but a handful in respect of them', and Barry had more foot soldiers than Inchiquin, for what that was worth.[68] Barry had 3,000 to 4,000 infantrymen, corresponding to the 'three great bodies', coming in more or less equal numbers from Counties Cork, Limerick and Tipperary, with a handful from County Kerry. Four hundred cavaliers converged from right across Munster.[69] All but three of the identifiable fatalities in the table below were horsemen.

'Ireland Independent: Confederate Foreign Policy and International Relations during the Mid-Seventeenth Century', in J. Ohlmeyer (ed.), *Independence to Occupation: Ireland 1641–1660* (Cambridge: Cambridge University Press, 1995), p.92.

67 TCDL: 1641 Depositions, MS 825 (County Cork), fol. 21r: Deposition of Thomas Reymond.

68 Richard Gething, *Digitus dei, or, A miraculous victory gained by the English upon the rebels in Munster expresst in two letters written to Lievtenant Colonell St.Leger, sonne and heire to the Right Honourable Sir William St. Leger, knight, late Lord president of Munster* (London: Thomas Bates, 1642), p.4; McCarthy, '1641 Rebellion in Cork', p.384; TCDL: 1641 Depositions, MS 812 (County Kilkenny), fol., 173r: Deposition of Richard Costalla and MS 829 (County Limerick), fols 173r: Deposition of Dauid Counagh, 350r, 351r: Deposition of John Welsh.

69 Hogan (ed.), *Letters and Papers*, p.149, 'Lords Justices to the Parliamentary Commissioners, Dublin, 29 September 1642'; Anon., *A iournall of the most memorable passages in Ireland. Especially that victorious battell at Munster, beginning the 25. of August 1642. and continued. Wherein is related the siege of Ardmore Castle; together with a true and perfect description of the famous battell of Liscarroll* (London: T. S., 1642), p.10; TCDL: 1641 Depositions, MS 820 (County Waterford), fol. 171r: Deposition of Henry Howell; Brian Ó Dálaigh, 'Mícheál Coimín: Jacobite, Protestant and Gaelic Poet 1676-1760', *Studia Hibernica*, 34 (2006–2007), p.137.

Known Irish Fatalities at Liscarroll

Name	County
Garrett Mac Patrick Pierse	Kerry
Florence or Finghin MacCarthy[70]	Kerry
Phelim Mac Finghin MacCarthy[71]	Kerry
Oliver Stephenson	Limerick
Thomas Burgett[72]	Limerick
Walter Mac Ricard Bourke[73]	Limerick
Thomas Butler[74]	Waterford
Domhnall Mac Domhnall O'Brien[75]	Clare

Two of Barry's squares (comprising mainly shot) stood astride a 'main body consisting most of pikes', which was pulled back slightly.[76] A limestone outcrop poking south from Liscarroll Castle must have covered the flank of the easternmost of the three squares, which was further protected by a stream flowing sluggishly north past the castle and seeping into a boggy sump. 'Bess' sat ineffectually behind a 'great high ditch' in a fort between the easternmost square and the castle.[77] The western square stood on a knoll in rolling meadow, so Barry deployed all his horsemen close by to protect the square's vulnerable flank. The layout calls to mind formations depicted in Barry's *Military Discipline*, while the discrete pike-and-shot formations echo those of the 1636 Spanish ordinance that were applied at Ballintober.[78]

Inchiquin's formation mirrored Barry's, as he put 800 pike in his main body, with 600 musketeers under Colonel Vavasour to the east and 300

---

70   Son of Mac Carthy Mór of Pallis, Aghadoe Parish, appointed governor of County Kerry. Gething, *Digitus dei*, p.5; TCDL: 1641 Depositions, MS 828 (County Kerry), fols 211r–13v: Deposition of John Abraham.
71   Of Tullaha, Kilkaha parish. TCDL: 1641 Depositions, MS 828 (County Kerry), fols 124v: Deposition of Stephen Love, 284r: Deposition of Edward Vauclier.
72   Probably a son of John of Kilmallock, one of the three commissioners for setting enemy estates. TCDL: 1641 Depositions, MS 829 (County Limerick), fol. 138v Deposition of Elizabeth Dowdall.
73   Of Killonan or Ballyvarra (Killeenagarriff parish), County Limerick. TCDL: 1641 Depositions, MS 829 (County Limerick), fol. 210v: Deposition of Faith Grady; Alan O'Driscoll and Brian Hodkinson, 'Who Was Who in Early Modern Limerick', <https://www.limerick.ie/sites/default/files/atoms/files/who_was_who_in_early_modern_limerick_1.pdf>, accessed 22 May 2021.
74   Thomas Butler of Ringagonagh parish near Dungarvan, hanged at Cork after the battle. TCDL: 1641 Depositions, MS 820 (County Waterford), fol. 89r: Deposition of Gilbert Gamage and MS 823 (County Cork), fol. 170r: Deposition of Symon Bridges.
75   Son of Daniel O'Brien of Dough. Thomas J. Westropp, 'Notes on the Sheriffs of County Clare, 1570-1700', *Journal of the Royal Society of Antiquaries of Ireland*, 5th series, 1, part 1 (1890), pp.68–80.
76   Barry O'Brien, 'The Battle of Liscarroll – 3 September 1642', *The Irish Sword*, 22:90 (2001), p.399.
77   William Brocket, *Good newes from Ireland. Or, A true relation of a great victory obtained by the Protestants in the province of Munster in Ireland …* (London: I. Thomas, 1642), p.4.
78   Barriffe, *Military Discipline*, pp.24–25; Pierre Picouet, *The Armies of Philip IV of Spain 1621-1665: The Fight for European Supremacy* (Warwick: Helion & Company, 2019), p.141.

musketeers under a 'Captain Cooper' to the west.[79] At nine o'clock in the morning, the encounter began and, one might very well say, ended with cavalry combat. Inchiquin's own troop, led by Captain William Jephson, and assorted gentlemen joined the 30 outriders and rode up to within half a mile of Barry's position. Boyle's contingent of foot and gentlemen riders included his son-in-law Barrymore and four of his sons – Broghill, fresh from the Ardmore slaughter, Dungarvan, Lewis, Viscount Kinalmeaky, and plain Francis Boyle. 'But because the ground where the enemy [the Irish] stood was extremely disadvantageous, they determined a full troop should march a good distance before our men, with orders, as the enemy advanced, to retreat; this we did to draw them from their Quarters, which we heard they had fortified.'[80]

If they were coat-trailing, they got more than they bargained for because Barry's cavalry steadily advanced, carefully coordinating their movements with the scurrying shot. They had performed a similar manoeuvre near Cappoquin, where the horse sheltered behind a 'quick set hedge' and musketeers in a 'ditch adjoining made some few shot'.[81] The side that was weaker in cavalry was the one that sent out 'commanded' shot in 'sleeves', or 'platoons', for extra firepower, like the *'enfants perdus'* (lost boys). Commanded shot did not win battles, but they might force a draw or prolong the experience of losing.

Cavalry combat, Jan Martszen de Jonge, 'Drie ruiters in gevecht Cavaleriegevechten'. (Rijksmuseum, Amsterdam)

---

79 Anon., *A iournall of the most memorable passages*, p.6.
80 Anon., *A iournall of the most memorable passages*, p.4.
81 Fitzpatrick, *Waterford*, p.120.

Inchiquin's party pulled back, facing about from time to time in a show of bravado, but the Irish came on relentlessly, 'resolved to put the whole stake on the game', with 'their musketeers running before them to bushes and ditches from whence with security they played on us, their body of Horse following to second their muskets'.[82] Notwithstanding Kinalmeaky's full armour, a fowling piece fired from behind a hedge shot him in the neck. Armour would not have been proofed against that 'old fowler' of Edmund Fennell's, who 'did usually run by his horse side'.[83] The dying man grasped the reins of his brother's horse, but the latter was too harried to recover his body, which was quickly stripped naked. By now, Inchiquin had pulled back, almost back to his own position: 500 of his musketeers fired on the Irish horse and 'blinded them so with the smoke of our guns' that they 'confusedly' pulled back to their starting positions.[84]

Inchiquin's whole army now advanced. The artillery on both sides fired at each other for half an hour: one English shot 'slew five', which suggests a shot hit a file, which was typically six men deep.[85] Next, Inchiquin's left wing (Jephson's and Dungarvan's cavalry troops) broke alignment and trotted ahead towards some huts clustered in a little meadow. The commanded musketeers hurried back to the Irish main body, pursued by Inchiquin's outriders, who now presented their vulnerable flank. Fancying that he had caught all the English horse at a disadvantage, Stephenson gave the order to charge. Then, Inchiquin assailed Stephenson.

Before they come to blows, let us pause to consider the Irish cavalry's appearance, weapons, and manner of fighting. The cavalryman was a mixture of cuirassier and harquebusier. The cuirassier was so called from his cuirass, a back and breastplate fastened together and blackened against rust. He brandished a carbine, a brace of pistols and a sword. The harquebusier was defined by his firearm, which had been the eponymous harquebus, later the petronel and still later the carbine. The Irish horseman might wear a helmet and bits and pieces of armour, depending on how far from home his horseboy could carry these burdensome items. A pen picture of the 'proud cavalier' picks out the 'scarf', 'hat', and 'buff coat' of thick leather (worn over a doublet, or short jacket) as his distinguishing articles of dress.[86] Buff coats could withstand the force of bladed weapons and even a pistol ball. P. S. told of how one cavalry officer was shot twice in the chest by pistol balls, which singed his buff coat 'as if two coales of fire were laid upon it', though he attributed the officer's survival to divine protection rather than the thickness of his coat:

---

82 James Buckley, 'The Battle of Liscarroll, 1642', *Journal of the Cork Archaeological and Historical Society*, 2nd series, 4:38 (1898), p.94.
83 Fitzpatrick, *Waterford*, p.120.
84 Brocket, *Good newes from Ireland*, p.4.
85 McCarthy, '1641 Rebellion in Cork', p.385.
86 Cuthbert, 'Toirdhealbhach Ó Conchubhair', p.432; Lynch (ed.), *Castlehaven's Memoirs*, p.74. Keith Dowen, 'The Seventeenth Century Buff-Coat', *Journal of the Arms and Armour Society*, 21:5 (2015), pp.157–88.

SUMMER AND AUTUMN 1642

Killing ground: view of *Féith na Fola* (Bloody Stream) to north-east of Liscarroll Castle. (Author's photo)

He never armed himself with breast plate or other proof only his coat of buff and carried still about him three agnus dei's [discs impressed with the image of the Lamb of God] encased in silver boxes—one hung at his breast, another at his shoulder, and the third at his right arm. He had such confidence in the divine virtue of those holy things that he would not trouble himself to wear any armour, those, he said, surer then any how steely soever, which was true for true believers.[87]

The Irish horseman had a holstered pistol or two draped over his horse's shoulders, and, if he carried a two-handed firearm, it was as likely to be a petronel as a carbine given the job lots of old and obsolescent firearms that were being dumped on the Irish market.[88] Irish cavaliers did not really rely on firepower, other than pistols for close work, and trusted to the sword and to the headlong charge, like a Mac Colla on horseback, and for similar reasons. At Liscarroll:

[they] did suppose that the English were better experienced and armed with guns (most of them being a furnished with a carbine and a case of pistols) than themselves. They put on a resolution Pell Mell … to fall in amongst them, that they should have little time to discharge, none to recharge, and by that means to make their swords and numbers to be decisive. The first, second, and third ranks

---

87 Gilbert (ed.), *Contemporary History*, vol. I, p.54–55.
88 TCDL: 1641 Depositions, MS 810 (County Dublin), fols 25r: Deposition of George Cashell, 107r: Deposition of Francis Sacheverell and MS 812 (County Carlow), fol. 144v: Examination of Mary Thomson.

of the English squadron gave fire as they were directed, and wheeled off to the rear. This the hindmost rank interpreted as retreat, and they began to rout.[89]

Clearly, English troopers were much given to what was still called the 'caracole', which usually denoted a charge in which the lead ranks would fire and pull aside to let the following ranks charge home with the sword and, necessarily, turn their backs on an attacking enemy. Inchiquin's cavalry mistook the manoeuvre for a rout and fell into confusion. To add to the muddle, Inchiquin had split the two troops, leaving Dungarvan's troop to hold Stephenson's attention, and he himself rode off with Jephson's troop to one side with the apparent intention of hitting Stephenson's flank.[90]

There are two Irish accounts of what happened next. P. S. represents the battle's point of articulation as a single combat in which the English champion was a cheat and the Irish champion a dupe. Stephenson, the Irish champion who commanded the Irish horse, had beseeched his mother's blessing as he set off:

> … she would not impart the same unto him, other than upon condition, he would spare the life of Inchiquin in case he had the upper hand on him (this Inchiquin was her nephew, her brother's son). The obedient child answered that it was a hard condition for him to observe, going unto a field, against an enemy, to use so much humanity towards his foe, in case they came to handy blows, if he were so tied to spare him, and not to draw his blood, that twenty to one in such a case, but would perish by it himself and desired vehemently his mother not to endanger his proper life to save another …

The lady insisted, and her son promised, 'telling her by that hereby she would never see him again'. Stephenson seized cousin Murrough and held him prisoner at sword point, whereupon Inchiquin's followers plunged into the mêlée and one of them fired his pistol into the 'eyelight' of Stephenson's helm. In his last moments, Stephenson swung his sword high and contrived to 'cleave' the rescuer 'down to his very shoulders' in the manner of a Greek epic hero.[91] Most of this is literally untrue, though Stephenson's helm sounds like a colourful detail of the kind often captured by folklore: a closed burgonet with a mask-like visor containing small slits for eyes and nostrils was common among armoured cuirassiers at the time.

Bellings described the combat more prosaically. Stephenson 'shot off his pistol and missed'. Inchiquin then killed Stephenson just as the latter's sword 'was raised to strike', but, meanwhile, the English cavalry proved 'unable to resist the enemy's shock' and promptly 'turned off and ran away', leaving Inchiquin fighting three vengeful men. One of the three gripped Murrough

---

89   TCDL: 1641 Depositions, MS 840, no. 20: A Discourse of the Battle of Liscarroll.
90   Thomas Johnson, *A true relation of Gods providence in the province of Munster in delivering them from the hands of ther enemies and giving them a great victory : related in a letter / sent from a gentleman, a vounltier in the Lord Dungarvans troope to a worthy friend of his in London* (London: L. N., 1642), p.3.
91   Gilbert (ed.), *Contemporary History*, vol. I, p.39.

by the arm while the other two 'struck and thrust' at him. Captains Bridges and Jephson piled in. Jephson was cut on the hand, and Murrough on the head and hand.[92] Elsewhere, Dungarvan shot and wounded a charging cavalier with one pistol, but, before he had a chance to draw his second pistol, the cavalier was on him and 'gave him such a stroke' with his falchion (a single-edged sword with a slight curve on the blade towards the point) that he 'cut quite through' his armour before Dungarvan managed to draw his second pistol and fire.[93] Barrymore, the patron to whom Barry had dedicated *Military Discipline*, sustained wounds from which he died on Michaelmas Day, almost a month later.[94] One can imagine in that meadow the thump of carbines, the tinny clang of swords, the growls and grunts of yellow- and black-clad men in harsh exertion and the groans of the wounded as horsemen slashed, shot and stabbed at one another.[95]

Colonel Charles Vavasour led his musketeers forwards to give close fire support, letting Inchiquin hack his way to safety, where he slowly and painfully set to pulling his cavalry back into rank and file. He sent the first handful of horsemen forwards under Bridges while he and Jephson rounded up more. Meanwhile, the Irish horsemen 'scattered all the field' in pursuit of fugitives and stragglers 'so as hardly could twenty be seen in a body'. Bridges routed them and also scattered the sleeve of shot, which had again crept forwards, 'thinking there was no more to be done than follow the execution'. The men in the other two bodies, the one in the middle and the one on the east closest to Liscarroll Castle, looked on passively until, seeing another body of horse that Inchiquin and Jephson were rallying, they melted away 'without fighting a stroke more'.[96]

A problem with the English and most Irish accounts is that they focus on the cavalry-against-cavalry combat and telescope subsequent events into a sentence or two, which makes it seem as if the three bodies of Irish infantry collapsed almost instantly. But a *caoineadh* (elegy) for a captain of foot named Garret Pierse suggests that some of the foot soldiers put up a fight.[97] Poetic heroism puffs up the lament, as one would expect. We are told that hundreds of enemy corpses piled up and that Pierse felled a dozen men with his own sword even as he stood on just one foot (*ar aonchus*) after he had been shot in the leg. Once he was finally killed, it was all over: 'When the tree fell, the branches withered' (*Do thit an crann do chaill a ghéaga*).[98] Shortly before noon, Pierse's company was cut off from the rest, and 18 named 'Followers of Garret' (*Gearóidí*) were slaughtered and are said to lie together in a rath named 'Lisgarret', which lay on the extreme right, or west, of the Irish position.

---

92 Gilbert (ed.), *Irish Confederation*, vol. I, p.93; Anon., *A iournall of the most memorable passages*, p.7.
93 Johnson, *Gods providence in the province of Munster*, p.4.
94 Little, *Lord Broghill*, p.198; Verney, *Memoirs*, vol. II, p.56.
95 Anon., *A iournall of the most memorable passages*, p.7.
96 Gilbert (ed.), *Irish Confederation*, vol. I, pp.93–94.
97 My thanks to Marc Caball of University College Dublin for this reference.
98 Pádraig de Brún and John H. Pierse, 'Lament for Garret Pierse of Aghamore, Slain at Liscarroll, 1642', *Journal of the Kerry Archaeological and Historical Society*, 20 (1987), pp.16, 23–24.

Another version propagated by the Boyles gives credit to Sir Charles Vavasour, rather than Inchiquin, for the decisive stroke and insists that he, at the head of 600 musketeers, fell on the Irish square closest to Liscarroll Castle and the artillery. It would have been an uneven contest. Vavasour had more musketeers who could stand off and pour salvoes into a body of pike and shot at their leisure, as had happened to the unfortunate Whitecoats in the last hours of Marston Moor.[99]

As discussed before, casualties in actual engagements were always surprisingly light. The engagement was a test of fortitude, and the side that blinked first was the one that suffered heavy and disproportionate loss of life in the final, or 'execution', phase of combat, even if it had inflicted the most casualties up to that point. Pride and dutifulness were finely balanced against the urgent wish not to die. A square could disintegrate into a panicky mob if that balance tilted ever so slightly. A wall of equine flesh thundering down on a square of foot soldiers may look unstoppable, but horses -sensible creatures- will pull away at the last moment rather than run onto an unwavering line of spear points. So long as the pikemen did not panic (and what a big 'if' that was), they were safe. Fear is inescapable, but men were loath to be seen acting in fearful ways that their comrades might stigmatise as cowardice. However, when other men begin to slink away, typically from the rear ranks, that social pressure could lift when each man knew his personal failure to be inconspicuous in the general dissolution.

Foot soldiers could drop their muskets and pikes and outrun pursuing infantrymen. But they could not outrun horsemen, and we are assured that the 'execution was bloody and cruel' – 600 Irish were killed, another 60 taken prisoner, and all were hanged but for Richard Butler of Ikerrin, 'the last man that stood of that whole army'.[100] Some Irish sources agree. A contemporary Gaelic notation names three prominent men killed at Liscarroll and speaks of 'many' (*morán*) of the Irish having fallen while a poet of the Condons said hundreds fell.[101] Yet most Irish sources claim their losses were 'inconsiderable'. The usual tokens of victory yield contradictory results: 14 colours were apparently captured, but 'few' weapons, while other sources claim that 200 to 300 muskets were picked up together with 'so many pikes they served us as firewood'.[102]

To judge how many Irish were cut down in any post-battle execution, the key question must be asked: how near, and how big, was the nearest bog? Horse could not tread soft ground, and pursuing foot soldiers invariably lagged behind their mounted comrades. Some 140 yards north of Liscarroll Castle, low-lying ground beckoned. A photograph shows the north-eastern corner tower and the fields, peacefully grazed by cows, sloping downwards towards that fatal wetland. Encompassing little more than 100 acres, the wetland named '*Féith na Fola*' (Bloody Stream) was rather circumscribed

---

99   McCarthy, '1641 Rebellion in Cork', p.387.
100 Anon., *A iournall of the most memorable passages*, p.8; Gething, *Digitus dei*, p.8.
101 Gilbert (ed.), *Irish Confederation*, vol. I, p.93; IMC: Kavanagh (ed.), *Commentarius Rinuccinianus*, vol. II, p.338.
102 Gething, *Digitus dei*, p.5.

SUMMER AND AUTUMN 1642

The cattle drive, detail from Stefano della Bella, 'Siège d'Arras en 1640'. (Rijksmuseum, Amsterdam)

and likely to have proven to be a death trap. One of the English accounts describes how Inchiquin's cavalry surrounded this wetland and waited for kill squads to be sent in on foot. But Inchiquin called them back, according to a version of events touted by his Boyle rivals. This supposedly happened when he returned to the battlefield from gathering his cavalry and, seeing troops in a position formerly occupied by the Irish, assumed that they were, in fact, Irish. The delay gave the Irish a chance to skip two miles farther north to the streams and ponds that formed the headwaters of the Deel.[103]

Or, the muddle may have been a Boyle-inspired smear. Though it was still only late afternoon, Inchiquin's cavalry had been fighting for nigh on seven hours and were no doubt bone weary and impaired by that psychological reaction of inertia and passivity that overtakes men after a hard-fought day, even one that they had been winning. For instance, by the time Prince Rupert returned to the battlefield of Edgehill with most of his triumphant cavaliers, a concerted attack was out of the question.[104] In other words, Inchiquin's cavalrymen may have been in no fit condition to hunt down runaways.

Pierse's company from County Kerry was in the westernmost of the three Irish squares: two officer fatalities and who knows how many other ranks from the company of Daniel MacCarthy Mór, colonel of the County Kerry forces, suggest that there was a second company from County Kerry in that luckless square.[105]

For all that, the body count was lighter than it might have been, and so, especially because it had been such a close-run thing, Liscarroll was

---

103 Barry O'Brien, *Munster at War* (Cork: Mercier Press, 1971), pp.331–35; O'Brien, 'Battle of Liscarroll', pp.391–402; McCarthy, '1641 Rebellion in Cork', pp.381–89.
104 Burne and Young, *Great Civil War*, p.30.
105 TCDL: 1641 Depositions, MS 828 (County Kerry), fol. 236v: Deposition of William Dethick.

nonetheless a 'major setback': 'Defeated, routed, broke and beaten blind, / Their baggage, arms and cannon left behind'.[106] Liscarroll was important for what did not happen. Inchiquin recovered Liscarroll Castle but little else. Had Inchiquin lost, the Protestants would quickly have been left clinging to a few Munster ports.

The Irish could have held Liscarroll Castle if Barry had thought to put more men inside. Like Ballintober, Liscarroll had no central keep but comprised a spacious rectangular bawn (at three-quarters of an acre, the bailey was the third biggest in Ireland after Ballintober and Trim) with circular towers at the corners, a rectangular tower or keep built into the north wall and a gate tower in the south wall. Richard Butler had evidently taken refuge there, and his life was spared when he surrendered the place after the rout. All 60 men who were taken prisoner that day were probably in the castle with him, and they would have been enough to hold out: the English garrison had been even smaller.[107] All were hanged except for Butler, who later escaped from the provost marshal's custody in Cork and fled, along with two of his goalers. Had Barry left his guns inside for safe keeping, and half a dozen companies, Liscarroll would have been impregnable. He could then have pulled out the remaining infantrymen safely, leaving the horse as a rearguard, and denied Inchiquin a victory. Instead, with wholly unjustified confidence in his abilities, he chose to accept battle when it was avoidable.

Barry allowed the component parts of his array to be defeated in detail, and, without a guiding hand, his followers made a throng, not an army.[108] The contrast with Inchiquin is instructive. When occasion demanded, he conspicuously displayed the sort of heroic leadership from the front that men demanded in that stern age. But he did not let blood lust distract him from his responsibilities as a commander. After escaping from the mêlée and gathering some troopers, he did not plunge back in but instead left Bridges to do so while he, quite properly, continued to rally his shaken men. What made his cavalry so formidable, like the Roundhead cavalry at Naseby, was not ferocity in hand-to-hand combat, still less skill with pistol and carbine, but rather persistence, namely, 'the thickness' of his reserves and 'their orderly and timely coming on'.[109] Inchiquin fed in his slightly bigger number of horse (he had 360 to 300 Irish) gradually, incrementally and carefully, whereas Stephenson gave all in a do-or-die effort.[110] Whoever, if anyone, stepped into Stephenson's boots would have had a great deal of trouble regrouping once his cavaliers were scattered and their horses blown. But someone should have tried.

MacCarthy Reagh was not at Liscarroll because he faced a threat closer to home. The 'Adventurers', as subscribers to Irish war loans were called, funded an expedition of 18 ships and 1,000 soldiers under Alexander Baron

---

106 David Plant, *British Civil Wars, Commonwealth & Protectorate 1638-1660*, <http://bcw-project.org/>, accessed 20 May 2021; Ó Dálaigh, 'Mícheál Coimín', p.137.
107 Empey, 'Diary of Sir James Ware', p.112.
108 IMC: Kavanagh (ed.), *Commentarius Rinuccinianus*, vol. I, p.338.
109 Burne and Young, *Great Civil War*, p.206.
110 Empey, 'Diary of Sir James Ware', p.112.

SUMMER AND AUTUMN 1642

Forbes, a Scottish veteran of the Swedish service. The plan had been for the 'Sea Adventurers' to operate in support of an Adventurer-funded land army, which was no sooner raised than it was diverted to fighting for the English Parliament in England. Forbes sailed for Munster on 1 July, landed at Kinsale and chose to disregard Inchiquin's pleas for help. He allied with the Boyles, and, in concert with the Bandon town companies, he marched to relieve Rathbarry Castle, beset since the middle of February. The column swept through the countryside, burning and killing, and scooped up an enormous prey of 2,000 sheep, cattle and horses.

Camp, detail from Jacques Callot, 'Les Petites Misères de la Guerre'. (*Bibliothèque nationale de France*)

Forbes left three of his own companies, together with a Bandon company, behind at Clonakilty to guard the livestock. Up to 400 men would seem adequate, but, evidently, Cormac MacCarthy Reagh's soldiers had been lurking nearby and quickly 'beset the said town'. Most of the English fled for safety to a nearby 'fort' (probably an old earthen rath) except for one of Forbes's companies and some Bandonmen, who stood and opened fire, but 'after the first discharge the enemy fell in upon them & routed them'.[111] The margin between firepower's success at Glenmaquin and failure at Clonakilty was probably quite narrow. The survivors were 'beleaguered' by MacCarthy's 'varlets', drawn up 'in a square Battle', but held out until Forbes turned back and rescued them.[112]

---

111 TCDL: 1641 Depositions, MS 840, fols 47v, 48r: Account of the Rising in Munster by James Cleland.
112 Hugh Peters, *A true relation of the passages of Gods providence in a voyage for Ireland ...* (London: Luke Norton, 1642), p.7; TCDL: 1641 Depositions, MS 823 (County Cork), fol. 143v:

Battle squares, detail from pictorial map of Galway City. (<https://library.nuigalway.ie/digitalscholarship/projects/17th-century-map-of-galway-city/>)

On 25 July, Forbes sailed away to the islands and promontories of the south-west, harrying, burning and blowing up the O'Donovan castle of Castlehaven and the O'Driscoll castle of Baltimore. He next planned on disembarking in north Kerry to assist David Crosbie, who maintained a promontory castle and fort at Ballingarry. Crosbie brought Forbes victuals, and Forbes delivered firearms in return, but, having reached a live-and-let-live accommodation with his neighbours, Crosbie persuaded Forbes to be on his way.[113]

Forbes next sailed to Galway at the behest of Captain Willoughby, where his long boats resupplied Forthill with food, arms and ammunition. He then called on Mayor Walter Lynch to surrender the town. Stung by Lynch's refusal, Forbes asked Clanricarde and Ranelagh for help against the townspeople. But both were Royalist in sympathy, wanted to continue the ceasefire and warned Forbes that indiscriminate severity would confirm fears that the government was bent on 'utter extirpation' of the Irish. Forbes next ranged up and down the coast of Connemara killing O'Flahertys before returning to Galway and debarking men on the western, or Claddagh, bank of the Corrib, which looked across the rushing waters at the quays. Forbes set two pieces of ordnance at the Dominican church and no doubt knocked down walls and slates within the town, but he could not have hoped to actually take the town that way. The pointless violence was of a piece with the 'piracy and rapine' that had marred the whole enterprise.[114] Ranelagh quietly hoped that Forbes would sail for Sligo, a prospect that gave Lucas Taaffe 'no

---

Deposition of Edmond Mc Carty.
113 TCDL: 1641 Depositions, MS 828 (County Kerry), fol. 220r: Deposition of William Haynes.
114 Karl S. Bottigheimer, 'English Money and Irish Land: The "Adventurers" in the Cromwellian Settlement of Ireland', *Journal of British Studies*, 7:1 (1967), p.17.

SUMMER AND AUTUMN 1642

Sickness, detail from Jan Luyken, 'Pest Straatbeeld met stervende pestlijders straatbeeld'. (Rijksmuseum, Amsterdam)

little occasion of fear' because Forbes could have stepped ashore and linked up with Frederick Hamilton of Manorhamilton, who had burned the town only the month before.[115] But Forbes sailed away south and might have been in time to relieve Tralee had he not tarried to lay waste the Aran Islands. Writing from the Shannon Estuary, he complained that many of his men were falling sick of 'the Country diseases', but he stayed delusionally upbeat to the end, reckoning that 5,000 to 6,000 men could quickly take Galway and Limerick and so 'end the war before Christmas'.[116] That is the last we hear of his coastal descents, which never amounted to more than strategic pinpricks.

Despite Liscarroll, Inchiquin's grip was slack: Dromana Castle, an outlier of Cappoquin, fell just a fortnight after the battle.[117] In October 1642, the governor of Youghal sent a dozen men and women over the ferry to the County Waterford bank of the Blackwater 'to reap & bind some of the rebells corn', but they 'no sooner fell to work' than a company of Irish soldiers

---

115 BHO: Rushworth, 'Historical Collections', pp.504–59.
116 Peters, *Gods providence in a voyage for Ireland*, p.5.
117 David Edwards, 'Holding On: The Earl of Cork's Blackwater Army and the Defence of Protestant Munster, 1641–43', in P. Little (ed.), *Ireland in Crisis: War, Politics and Religion, 1641–50* (Manchester: Manchester University Press, 2020), pp.20–42.

snatched them.[118] That same month, the Irish surprised a party of soldiers 'fetching home' corn to Cork, Inchiquin's general headquarters. Rather than retreat, the captain in charge of the foragers reckoned that he and his 50 men could shelter in a nearby rath and drive off the attackers with musketry. But the attackers came on 'in too great numbers', and Inchiquin's troops were slaughtered to a man.[119]

Away in the western recesses of the county, John Óg Barry and 300 besiegers dug trenches to 'half a musket shot' of the main gate of Rathbarry Castle and blocked up the castle tight. A messenger slipped out by night, and, detecting Barry's sentries in the gloom 'by their matches', he tiptoed around them to beg for help. His efforts were in vain. Vavasour, Kinalmeaky's replacement as governor of Bandon, ordered that Rathbarry be evacuated.[120]

Dublin's hinterland was hardly more secure. As early as mid-September, three companies of Sir James Dillon's regiment took Moymet Castle in a night assault. Moymet was an outpost of an outpost, about halfway between Trim and Athboy, was held by only 14 soldiers but was a straw in the wind.[121] In that same month, a party of 20 or so Irish riders cheekily set about extorting ransom from travellers on the highway near Gormanstown. These raiders belonged to the 'Slowbegg', the little band that was 'very frequent and dangerous' in Fingal and 'up and down the county of Kildare' that winter.[122] The guerrilla band comprised over 100 men under three captains driven from Fingal to Kilmeague in the Bog of Allen, a Carmelite friar named Oliver Walsh, Father Lawrence Rowan of Finglas and John Finglas (later sergeant major general of the Leinster Horse) of Westpalstown. In October 1642, raiders repeatedly swooped from Powerscourt and Bray onto the plain country between there and the Dodder, two miles south of Dublin, cattle-rustling, burning isolated farmsteads and killing those who tried to stop them. James Goodman's company burnt Laughlinstown Castle and killed five warders while others burned a 'great barn' even closer to the capital at Palmerstown, 'it being full of wheat'.[123] It would get worse as winter drew on. An English observer remarked how the 'summer war maketh us superior' but the fact that the English had more and better horses counted for little during 'the long and dark nights'.[124]

Sickness was another seasonal problem. English and Scottish soldiers were struck down by 'fluxes', the debilitating diarrhoeas of late summer. Newly raised and disembarked British armies typically suffered a sickness

---

118 TCDL: 1641 Depositions, MS 820 (County Waterford), fol. 230r: Deposition of Roger Greene and Garrett Barry.
119 Hogan (ed.), *Letters and Papers*, p.161, 'Inchiquin to Parliamentary Commissioners, Cork, 28 October 1642'.
120 Herbert W. Gillman, 'Siege of Rathbarry Castle, 1642', *Journal of the Cork Historical and Archaeological Society*, 2nd series, 1:1 (1895), p.18.
121 Ball (ed.), *Calendar of the Manuscripts of the Marquess of Ormonde*, vol. I, p.52, 'Examination of John Sturden'.
122 TCDL: 1641 Depositions, MS 810 (County Dublin), fols 25r: Deposition of George Cashell, 235r: Deposition of William Hollis.
123 TCDL: 1641 Depositions, MS 810 (County Dublin), fols 183r: Deposition of Simon Swayen, 213v: Examination of John Lalis.
124 TCDL: 1641 Depositions, MS 840, fol. 35r: Henry Jones, 'Observations'.

rate of up to 25 percent, and Ireland in 1642 was probably no better.[125] By September, one-half of the soldiers were out of action, lying sick, having deserted or having been killed in action – doubtless in that order.[126] Only 1,000 out of 3,000 surviving soldiers were fit to fight in Munster probably because so high a proportion of them were English-born and not inured to flux, the 'country disease'.[127] According to Sir James Turner at Newry:

> This great fatigue and toil, a very spare diet, lying on the ground, little sleep, constant watching, Sir Phelemy being for most part always within a days march of us, all these, I say, added to the change of the air, made most or rather indeed all our officers and soldiers fall sick of Irish agues, fluxes and other diseases of which very many died.[128]

The statistical evidence would suggest that Scots forces escaped more lightly than their English allies. By September, Glencairn's regiment of Monro's army had lost 9 percent of its strength in under five months, and over 7 percent of the rest were sick, which was not a high mortality or morbidity rate by the standards of the time.[129]

Flux laid nearly every soldier low for a time but seldom killed outright. In January 1643, an 'ague' (acute fever) brought Turner himself 'to death's door'.[130] 'Fever' was deadlier than flux, especially what would be later called 'typhus', a name that derives from the Greek word '*typhos*', which described another symptom besides very high fever, namely, stupor or delirium. When the commander of Duncannon reported that his men were succumbing to 'smallpox, fevers and calenture [delirium]', it is the latter that was the most ominous sign.[131] A third symptom was the presence of dark or purplish spots, or petechiae: the English soldiers in Munster 'die in heaps' of a 'contagious disease resembling a spotted fever'.[132] The mechanism of typhus is the human body louse sucking the infected host's blood and thereby ingesting rickettsia bacteria.

---

125 Andrew Bamford, *Sickness, Suffering, and the Sword: The British Regiment on Campaign, 1808–1815* (Norman: University of Oklahoma Press, 2021), p.223.
126 Hazlett, *Military Forces Operating in Ireland*, p.44.
127 Gilbert (ed.), *Irish Confederation*, vol. I, p.77 and vol. II, pp.53–54, 61; Anon., *Severall passages of the late proceedings in Ireland* (London: Henry Overton, 1642); Carte, *History of the Life of James Duke of Ormonde*, vol. I, p.342; Alexander Grosart (ed.), *The Lismore Papers (Second Series)* (London: Chiswick Press, 1888), vol. V, p.105.
128 Hogan (ed.), *Letters and Papers*, pp.135, 157, 159.
129 Edward M. Furgol, *A Regimental History of the Covenanting Armies, 1639–1651* (Edinburgh: John Donald, 1990), pp.85–86; Pádraig Lenihan, *Fluxes, Fevers and Fighting Men: War and Disease in Ancien Régime Europe 1648-1789* (Warwick: Helion & Company, 2019), pp.54, 86, 109; Frank Tallett, *War and Society in Early Modern Europe 1495-1715* (London: Routledge, 1992), p.105.
130 James Turner, *Memoirs of His Own Life and Times* (Edinburgh: Bannatyne Club, 1829), pp.23, 25.
131 Hogan (ed.), *Letters and Papers*, pp.92–94, 'Lawrence Esmond to Earl of Cork, Duncannon, 25 July'.
132 TNA: *HMC Report on Franciscan Manuscripts in Dublin*, p.174, 'Don Jayme Nochera to Luke Wadding, London, 8 August 1642'.

O'Neill. (Anon., 'Owen "Roe" O'Neill', *Ulster Journal of Archaeology*, 1st series, 4 (1856), pp.25–39)

When the original human host burns with fever, or cools with death, the louse will crawl to another lousy host. And there were plenty of those. An English soldier in *Cola's Furie* complains of 'vermin' that 'creepe, bite, and keepes a damnable quarter / on my shoulders'.[133] Louse bites precipitates an allergic reaction in the new host's skin, which causes the host to scratch and thereby rickettsiae expelled in the louse's faeces is rubbed into the skin. Dried faeces in clothes or bedding can also be inhaled. As body lice live in the seams of clothing and require the warm habitat of a human's body temperature, they were common in cold weather and carceral contexts like army camps, ships, prisons and hospitals, where the hungry, cold and unwashed huddled together for warmth.[134] In late summer and autumn, typhus ripped through the ranks. In August, we are told by a gleeful Catholic source that Inchiquin's soldiers 'die in heaps' of a 'contagious disease resembling a spotted fever'.[135] By 21 September, typhus had broken out in Dublin and its outposts: 'All our soldiery is wasted through sickness and death having a most pestilential spotted fever raging here that is little better than a plague', many of the soldiers were 'starved', and 'the rest weak and half-eaten up with lice'.[136]

Smallpox was another disease of person-to-person contact. As refugees crowded into Dublin in February 1642, it was reported that 'Here are very many dead Lately, especially of the poorer sort, and the Children die very thick of measles and pox'.[137] While smallpox mainly afflicted children, soldiers, too, fell victim.[138] The thinning of the ranks by epidemic disease and combat would have been made good by reinforcements except that, in the months before the opening Battle of Edgehill on 23 October 1642, both

---

133 Burkhead, *Cola's furie*, p.37.
134 John Pringle, *Observations on the Diseases of the Army, in Camp and Garrison. In Three Parts. With an Appendix, Containing Some Papers of Experiments, Read at Several Meetings of the Royal Society* (London: A. Millar, D. Wilson, T. Durham, and T. Payne, 1753), p.243.
135 TNA: *HMC Report on Franciscan Manuscripts in Dublin*, p.174, 'Don Jayme Nochera to Luke Wadding, London, 8 August 1642'.
136 Bodleian Library (BoL) Carte MS 3, fols 487, 516: Sir Nicholas Loftus to unk, Dublin, 21 September 1642.
137 John Cunningham, 'Sickness, Disease and Medical Practitioners in 1640s Ireland', in J. Cunningham (ed.), *Early Modern Ireland and the World of Medicine, Practitioners, Collectors, and Contexts* (Manchester: Manchester University Press, 2019), p.64; TCDL: 1641 Depositions, MS 836 (County Armagh), fols 57v: Deposition of John and Isabell Gowrly, 121r: Examination of Magdalen Duckworth and MS 840 (County Dublin), fol. 10v: Letter from Philip Bysse.
138 Hogan (ed.), *Letters and Papers*, pp.92–94, 'Lawrence Esmond to Earl of Cork, Duncannon, 25 July'.

SUMMER AND AUTUMN 1642

Charles and the English Parliament diverted 'men, money, arms, powder and match' to their own use, and so English operations in Ireland floundered.[139]

Returning veterans were slotted into positions of command. Richard Cullen, a Dubliner, David Synott from Wexford, Gormanston's uncle Thomas Preston and John Bourke of County Mayo all disembarked at Wexford in mid-September.[140] Preston and Eoghan Rua would be the most important of the returned officers. The portrait of the latter as a square-jawed, full-bearded man in his prime, wearing a shaggy Gaelic mantle and bejewelled bonnet, is a romanticised image of a 51-year-old with a high forehead and hair 'longer than ordinary', which had no doubt turned from russet to grey over the preceding decades as he fought for one 'scabbed town' or another in Flanders.[141] *Maestre de campo* of an Irish regiment for an appreciable time and governor of Arras during the celebrated siege of 1640, O'Neill had exercised more senior command than any of the other returned military exiles. Thomas Preston had been one of O'Neill's captains and had his own regiment for only a brief interlude before it was fed into the meat grinder of the Thirty Years' War. Flowing hair parted in the middle and a Van Dyke beard accentuated Preston's long face, which was set off by a proud aquiline nose. He was '… a delicate person in his diet, fine in his deportment, wavering in his resolutions [and] imperious in his precepts'. A friendlier witness described him 'as brave a soldier to keep a town or to take a town as was any in the three kingdoms'.[142]

The flow of munitions was even more important than the returned veterans.[143] Apothecaries made up batches of gunpowder at Kilkenny, Leighlin, Kileen Castle, County Meath, Limerick City and no doubt other places that we do not know about but only in small quantities because one vital ingredient had

Preston. (John T. Gilbert (ed.), *History of the Irish Confederation and the War in Ireland 1641-1649* (Dublin: M. H. Gill and Son, 1879–1880), vol. IV, p.177)

---

139 Wanklyn, *The Army of occupation in Ireland, 1603-43*, p.205; Fissel, *English Warfare*, p.253; Hogan (ed.), *Letters and Papers*, p.125, 'Lords Justices to Speaker of the House of Commons, 12 September 1642'; Tadhg Ó hAnnracháin, 'Conflicting Loyalties, Conflicted Rebels: Political and Religious Allegiance among the Confederate Catholics of Ireland', *English Historical Review*, 119:483 (2004), pp.851–72.

140 Hogan (ed.), *Letters and Papers*, p.151, 'Lords Justices to Parliamentary Commissioners, 29 September 1642'; TNA: *HMC Report on Franciscan Manuscripts in Dublin*, p.154, 'Hugh Bourke to Wadding, Brussels, 12 April 1642'.

141 Anon., 'Owen "Roe" O'Neill', *Ulster Journal of Archaeology*, 1st series, 4 (1856), pp.25–39; Gilbert (ed.), *Contemporary History*, vol. I, p.397; Clive Hollick, *The Battle of Benburb 1646* (Cork: Mercier Press, 2011), p.163.

142 Gilbert (ed.), *Contemporary History*, vol. I, pp.153–54; Hogan (ed.), *History of the Warr of Ireland*, pp.141–42.

143 BoL: Carte MS 3, fol. 508: Ormond to the Speaker of the English parliament, Dublin, 14 September 1642.

to be imported, namely, 'brimstone', or sulphur.[144] Another ingredient was saltpetre (potassium nitrate), which was refined from soil enriched with organic matter, which led to the 'gruesome obscenities' of Protestant corpses being exhumed for that purpose in the cities of Limerick, Kilkenny and Waterford.[145]

By early summer 1642, gunpowder cost the insurgents five shillings a pound in Wexford, 10 in Galway, 20 in Kilkenny, and a whopping 25 in Laois.[146] These were extortionate prices considering that powder could be bought in the Low Countries for a shilling per pound weight and could be got for one shilling and five pence in the Laggan.[147]

The Lords Justices admitted that 'plentiful store' of powder and match had been their 'only advantage' in the fighting.[148] Many clashes across the country testify to this. About a quarter of the men who attacked Baltimore, County Cork, one night in August 1642 carried muskets (an improvement on the one in 20 who mustered at Charlemont that same month), but they carried a pitiful four charges.[149] One hundred reivers from the garrisons of Jamestown and Carrick-on-Shannon waded a deep ford on their return journey, where many 'wet their powder bags and bandoliers'. Seizing the chance, the pursuing Irish charged, killing 16 men and wounding four, while the survivors escaped to a nearby castle.[150] Frederick Hamilton described marching back to Manorhamilton after a foray and being attacked by the enemy throwing stones 'with such dexterity' that his musketeers were hard put to reload after their first volley. The clash ended happily for Hamilton, as they all seem to, with the Irish being 'chased from hill to hill like dogs'.[151] Less happy was a small foraging party set ashore from a ship anchored off Kilmakilloge in the Kenmare Estuary. Ambushers lay concealed in the houses and:

> [attacked] pell mell with stones, the boat being out of sight of the shipps & the stones flying so fast that they could neither discharge musket nor pistol, but at last recovered [reached] the boat, yet having not the power to launch it forth from the shore through the multitude of stones fling upon them until at last they were all stoned to death.[152]

---

144 TCDL: 1641 Depositions, MS 829 (County Clare), fols 101r–02v: Deposition of John Comyne.
145 Canny, *Making Ireland British*, p.515.
146 Corpus of Electronic Texts (CELT) Henry O'Neill, 'An impartial relation of the most memorable transactions of General Owen O'Neill and his party, from the year 1641 to the year 1650', p.198; TCDL: 1641 Depositions, MS 813 (County Kildare), fols 44r: Information of John Woogan, 48v: Walter Hussey and MS 815 (Laois), fols 326v: Deposition of Samuell Franck, 405v: Examination of Robert Doughtie.
147 McCarthy, 'Preserving Donegal', p.371.
148 Gilbert (ed.), *Irish Confederation*, vol. II, pp.57–59, 62, 'Lord Justices to Commissioners for Affairs of Ireland 1 September 1642'.
149 Boyle, *A letter of the Earle of Corke*, p.3; TCDL: 1641 Depositions, MS 825 (County Cork), fols 17r: Deposition of Richard White, 107r: Deposition of Frauncis Sacheverell.
150 TCDL: 1641 Depositions, MS 831 (County Leitrim), fol. 35r: Deposition of Walter Fraser.
151 Anon., *Colonell Sir Frederick Hammiltons return from London-Derry*, p.23.
152 TCDL: 1641 Depositions, MS 823 (County Cork), fol. 173r: Deposition of Therlagh Kelly.

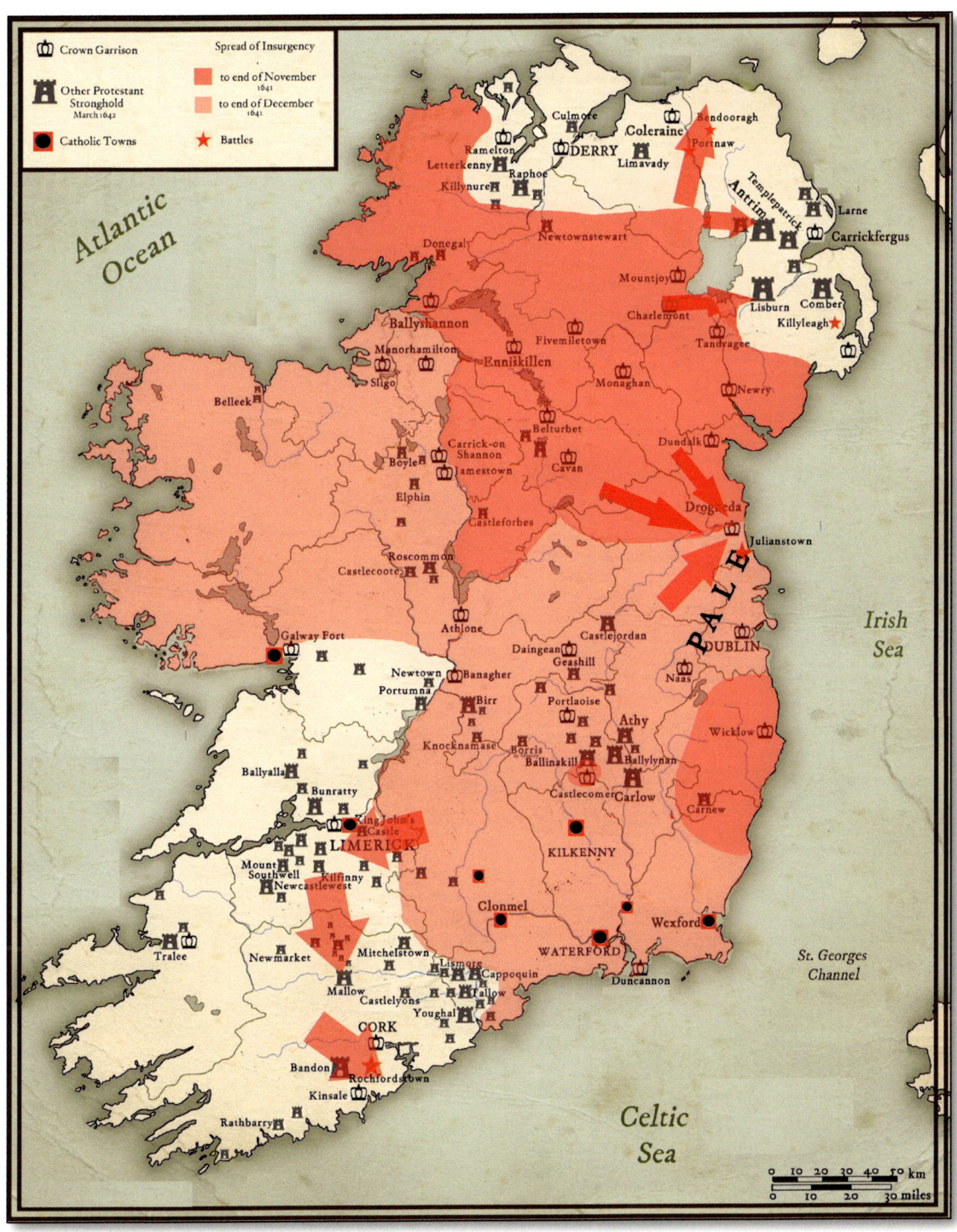

Insurgency, winter 1641–1642. (Tomás Ó Brógáin)

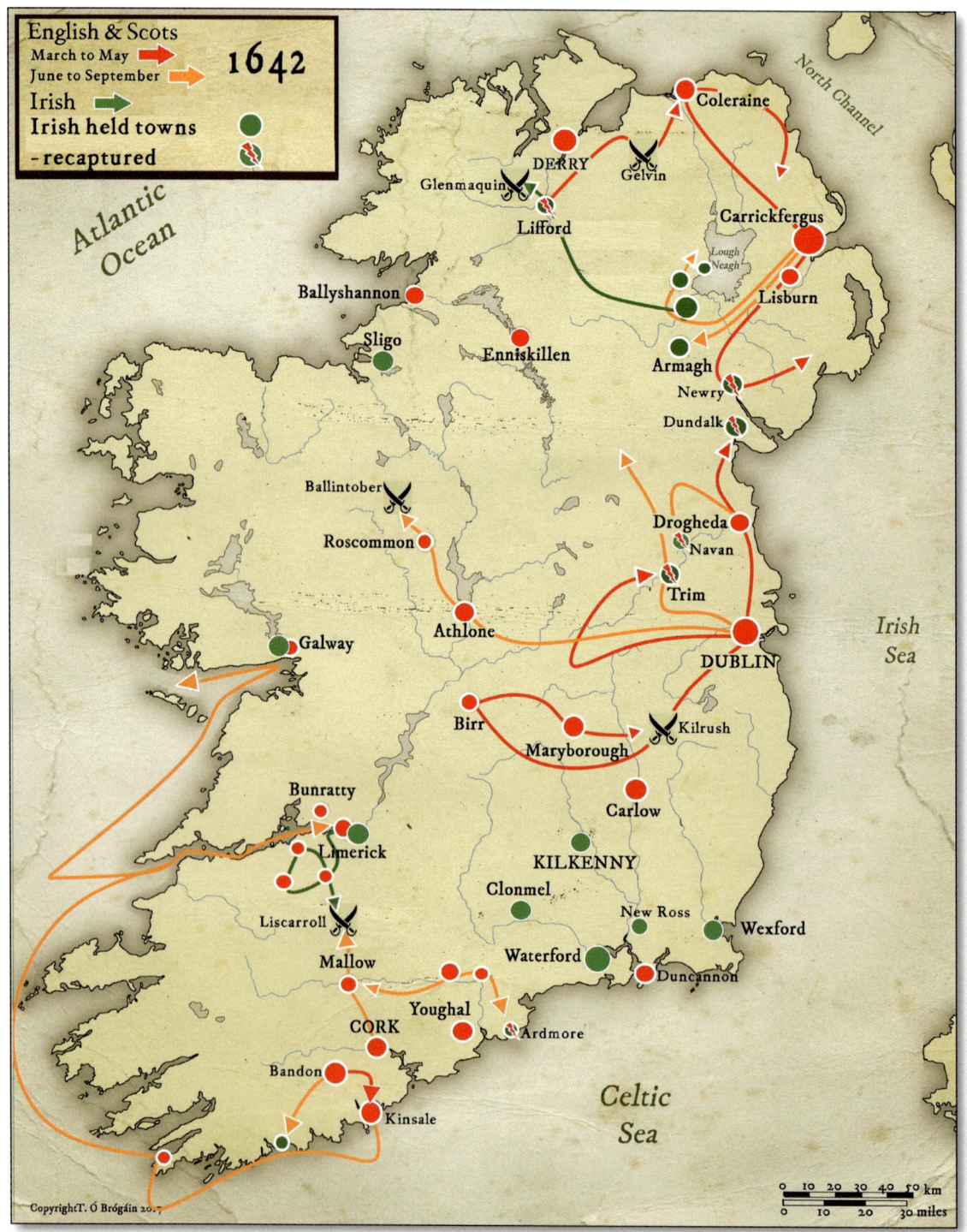

Counterattack, spring and summer 1642. (Author's illustration)

Plate A
Musketeer
(Illustration by Seán Ó Brógain © Helion & Company 2023)
See Colour Plate Commentaries for further information.

Plate B
Pikeman
(Illustration by Seán Ó Brógain © Helion & Company 2023)
See Colour Plate Commentaries for further information.

Plate C
Cavalryman
(Illustration by Seán Ó Brógain © Helion & Company 2023)
See Colour Plate Commentaries for further information.

**Plate D
Officer**
(Illustration by Seán Ó Brógain © Helion & Company 2023)
See Colour Plate Commentaries for further information.

**Plate E
Ensign**
(Illustration by Seán Ó Brógain © Helion & Company 2023)
See Colour Plate Commentaries for further information.

Plate F
Gunner
(Illustration by Seán Ó Brógain © Helion & Company 2023)
See Colour Plate Commentaries for further information.

Plate G
European Officer
(Illustration by Seán Ó Brógain © Helion & Company 2023)
See Colour Plate Commentaries for further information.

Plate H
Highlander
(Illustration by Seán Ó Brógain © Helion & Company 2023)
See Colour Plate Commentaries for further information.

The phase of stone-age warfare passed in September 1642 when 20 ships disgorged a 'vast quantity' of arms and ammunition at Wexford brought from Dunkirk, Saint Malo, Nantes and La Rochelle. Afterwards, gunpowder could be bought for one shilling and seven pence a pound: still pricey but not ruinously so.[153]

'Logistics determined not just when campaigns were fought, the pace of operations and what might be achieved, but how wars were conducted'.[154] For present purposes, logistics may be taken as feeding horses and men, and large-scale campaigns began when the grass started to grow and horses could graze or forage. Campaigns were conducted largely in response to logistical exigencies: 'Campaigns became forays, [and] battles became encounters void of strategic significance'.[155] These remarks concern the closing decade of the Thirty Years' War but might just as easily have been written about contemporaneous warfare in Ireland. Purposeful campaigns were hard to envisage because a field army could not really count on a supply train or magazines. For example, Monro's Scots usually set out from Carrickfergus with 14 days of provender, which meant that Charlemont was at the end of a tight logistical tether: four-days' march there and four back again left less than a week to actually fight.

Holding territory during the Thirty Years' War meant planting garrisons that would dominate a hinterland whence to extort 'contributions'. Villagers would be set a quota of foodstuffs to supply, and, in return, they would be offered protection. In other words, soldiers from the garrison would not kill them, burn their dwellings or steal all their crops and beasts. But no provisions, no protection. English, and latterly British, warfare in Ireland had a colonial nastiness in which hard-man boasting about atrocities against soldiers and civilians alike grew 'numbingly tedious'.[156] The Lords Justices and the Privy Council were waging genocidal war on the whole native population, and they even pleaded with King Charles in March 1643 not to stop the fighting 'before the sword and famine have so abated them in number' that 'English colonies might overtop them'.[157] Frightfulness had a practical utility as well. If the enemy is 'more malicious than valorous' and will not 'show himself' on the field of battle, opined Monck, 'there is no other way, than so to harass and waste the country, that the enemy may be famished out of his holds'.[158] The Lords Justices agreed and were grimly satisfied with how Philip Sidney, Viscount Lisle and lieutenant general of the Horse, swept through Kells to Virginia, County Cavan, 'burning, wasting, spoiling and destroying all the

---

153 Carte, *History of the Life of James Duke of Ormonde*, vol. I, p.367; Peter Edwards, *Dealing in Death: The Arms Trade and the British Civil Wars, 1638–52* (Cheltenham: The History Press, 2000), p.120.
154 Tallett, *War and Society*, pp.54–56.
155 Michael Roberts quoted in Derek Croxton, 'A Territorial Imperative? The Military Revolution, Strategy and Peacemaking in the Thirty Years War', *War in History*, 5:3 (1998), p.253.
156 L., *A true relation of the late expedition of the right honorable*, p.3; Charles Carlton, *This Seat of Mars: War and the British Isles, 1485–1746* (New Haven, CT: Yale University Press, 2011), p.136.
157 Gilbert (ed.), *Irish Confederation*, vol. II, p.xiii.
158 Heath (ed.), *Observations upon military & political affairs*, p.12.

Rapine, detail from Jacques Callot, 'Les Petites Misères de la Guerre'. (*Bibliothèque nationale de France*)

country about him' in September 1642.¹⁵⁹ Moreover, 'none can be spared' because 'the Irish women are most cruel in execution'.¹⁶⁰

O'Neill and Preston, schooled in continental warfare, deplored wanton destructiveness. Preston complained of brutality 'unwarrantable either by the law of God or man' when Colonel Gibson was sent out in January 1643 to march into County Kildare to 'kill, slay and destroy all rebels' on his way.¹⁶¹ O'Neill lamented on the pragmatic grounds that it 'is in no way politic to destroy the land which you hope to occupy'.¹⁶² Their objections missed the point. Massacre could work and had worked before. Viceroy Mountjoy had smothered the embers of Tyrone's War 40 years ago because, as he put it, 'we spoil the corn, burn their houses, and kill so many churls as it grieveth me to think it is necessary to do it'.¹⁶³ Mountjoy's strategy of extermination was rational. He did not have to depend on those same 'churls' to feed his army and could count on a logistical base in the Pale and fairly regular sea-borne provisions from England. The Lords Justices could count on neither.

While lauding Lisle for his destructive foray, the Lords Justices complained in the same breath of their 'extremities of want', as if the two were somehow unrelated. The Lords Justices belatedly offered protection to some inhabitants, but it is hard to discern any consistent policy. Severe orders to carry out 'all possible destruction' of crops and dwellings exempted districts like Moyglare in County Meath or Allen in County Kildare, which lay cheek

---

159 Samuel R. Gardiner, *History of the Great Civil War, 1642-1649* (London: Longmans, Green and Co., 1886), vol. 1, p.134.
160 Verney, *Memoirs*, vol. II, p.51, 'Sir John Leeke to Edmund Verney. Yougal, December 1641'.
161 Bodleian Library (BoL) Carte MS 4, fol. 199: Lords Justices to Colonel Gibson; Meehan, *Confederation of Kilkenny*, p.157.
162 Gilbert (ed.), *Contemporary History*, vol. I, p.45.
163 John McGurk, 'The Pacification of Ulster, 1600–3', in D. Edwards, C. Tait, and P. Lenihan (eds), *Age of Atrocity: Violence and Political Conflict in Early Modern Ireland* (Dublin: Four Courts Press, 2007), pp.122–23.

Plunder, detail from Jacques Callot, 'Les Petites Misères de la Guerre'. (*Bibliothèque nationale de France*)

by jowl with the districts 'around' Kilcock and Maynooth, which were to be ravaged.[164] The Lords Justices exempted places 'very near' English garrisons, but some commanders did the opposite: Tichborne boasted that he set the villages within five miles of Dundalk ablaze. Where an English garrison did grant protections, Irish forces often attacked peasants who accepted them, as had happened around Croghan, County Offaly, for instance, where they 'fired their provisions of corn, driving away their cattle'.[165] The problem for the Lords Justices was that they did not give themselves enough unscorched earth around Dublin to feed so many thousands of troops. Inchiquin, for all his fearsome reputation as 'Murrough Totane', kept the two whole baronies of Imokilly and Barrymore under protection, even though most of the two baronies occupied precisely the sort of debatable land that was ravaged in Leinster and in Ulster.

By late summer 1642, the insurgents were almost routed out of Ulster and pushed out of striking range of Dublin and Cork. Even the most naïve knew that there was no immediate prospect of a negotiated settlement: 'We have no choice but to conquer or be conquered'.[166] In June 1642, a meeting of priests and prominent laymen at Kilkenny agreed on an 'Oath of Association', binding the 'Confederate Catholics of Ireland'. Less than four days later, the interim Confederate Catholic executive decreed that a national army of 4,000 infantry and 500 horse soldiers be raised in the counties of south Leinster and east Munster 'next adjoining' Kilkenny: the territorial core of the Confederate Catholic regime, which was relatively urbanised, fertile and safe from enemy incursions.[167] The infantry was to be commanded by Hugh O'Byrne, and the cavalry by Piers Mac Thomas Fitzgerald, both veterans.[168]

---

164 BoL: Carte MS 4, fols 126, 190: Richard Grenville to Lords Justices, Trim 18 December and Lords Justices to Captain Treswell. 18 December 1642.
165 BoL: Carte MS 3, fol. 316: Gifford to Ormond, Castlejordan, 12 July 1642.
166 Meehan (ed.), *Rise and Fall of the Irish Franciscan Monasteries*, p.329, 'Fr. Anthony Geoghegan, September 1642'.
167 TCDL: 1641 Depositions, MS 813 (Kildare), fol. 48v: Information of Walter Hussey.
168 The National Archives (TNA) SP 63/260, fols 234–35: Elizabeth I to George III, 1558–1782.

This 'running army', as it was called, was to be sent by the Supreme Council 'into such parts of the kingdom, as shall be thought most necessary'. It was precisely such an army that had been so desperately needed to redress the odds against the hard-pressed insurgents in the vicinity of Cork and Dublin and, of course, in Ulster, but the scheme proved to be a dead letter and need not detain us.[169]

The actual germ of the standing army is to be found in the order that each province was to maintain 6,000 foot and 400 horse 'permanently quartered' in the province for 'defence of the country'.[170] Let us examine one of these provincial armies in more detail. Thomas Preston was commissioned 'commander-in-chief of the Catholic Army raised in Leinster' on 14 December 1642 by the Supreme Council, which included his nephew Gormanston. He was instructed to 'govern the army by the methods of military discipline used in England': discipline in this sense meant formations and drills. Spanish influence is apparent in jargon like 'tirone' (*tirón*) for 'recruit', but, in general, English influence predominated, and the building block of a company with a paper strength of 120 to 130 men was closer to the English than the Spanish model.[171] The company was to comprise half shot and half pike.[172] The musketeer also bore a sword or skeane.

A public meeting of 'gentlemen and freeholders' of Ely O'Carroll (in south-west Offaly) was convened in February 1643 to raise a 'standing foot company' or 'trained band' under a captain to be chosen by 'the general vote of that country'. Two 'young gentlemen' vied for the captaincy, and the one elected was a great-grandson of the last O'Carroll chieftain. The purpose of Tadgh O'Carroll's trained band was to guard 'the several straits and passages' of Ely O'Carroll and to campaign elsewhere when called upon by Preston. In mid-Offaly, a meeting of the King's County (Offaly) Council in Tullamore reviewed another trained band. Half of Garrett O'Connor's 120 soldiers were armed with swords, 'skeanes' and muskets; the other half bore pikes.[173] O'Connor's and O'Carroll's trained bands formed part of a 1,400 provincial army quota levied on Counties Laois, Offaly and Kildare. Most companies were associated with baronies, such as the 'trained band company of the Barony of Forth', whose men spent Sunday afternoons being shown how to 'exercise or use their arms'.[174] These companies could be lumped together into regiments based on counties or, in the example just cited, fragments of three

---

169 TCDL: 1641 Depositions, MS 816 (County Meath), fol. 196v: Examination of John Darcy.
170 TNA: *HMC Report on Franciscan Manuscripts in Dublin*, p.217, 'Anthony Geoghegan to Luke Wadding, Kilkenny, 13 November 1642'.
171 Robert P. Mahaffy (ed.), *Calendar of the State Papers Relating to Ireland, Of the Reign of Charles I [and Commonwealth], Preserved in the Public Record Office, 1625-[1660]* (London: HMSO, 1901), vol. 2: 1633–1647, p.374, 'Commission of the Supreme Council of the Confederate Catholics of Ireland'.
172 TCDL: 1641 Depositions, MS 836 (County Armagh), fol. 108r: Deposition of Frauncis Sacheverell; Picouet, *Armies of Philip IV*, pp.139, 142, 144; De Mesa, *The Irish in the Spanish Armies*, p.17.
173 TCDL: 1641 Depositions, MS 814 (County Dublin), fols 248v, 245v, 246r: Deposition of John Holmstead.
174 TCDL: 1641 Depositions, MS 819 (County Wexford), fols 191r, 192v, 277r: Examination of William Synnot.

counties. Leinster had six such regiments of foot and 600 horse in the winter of 1642–1643.

Unofficial companies now began to be stood down, and their self-appointed officers cashiered. The regularisation of provincial armies saw many zealots eclipsed by Johnny-come-latelys who had 'acted nothing', as P. S. sourly observed.[175] Eoghan Rua's clerical sponsors had worried about rivalry with Phelim, but, in the event, Phelim made no fuss about being passed over, settling for a colonelcy and the honorific presidency of Ulster. Rory O'More, in September 1642, could describe himself as general of 'Upper', or north, Leinster, but he faded away some months later, his retirement doubtless sweetened by the grant of the captured enemy lordship of Ballinakill in his ancestral Laois.[176] The young cousins Slane and Gormanston died, as did Slane's cousin Thomas Burke, Viscount Clanmorris, in County Galway.[177] Slane's uncle, Archbishop of Dublin Thomas Fleming took Slane's place and, 'by fine and witty stratagems', destroyed many English strongholds in the barony of Slane.[178] For a fat, old priest, Fleming did not do too badly, but the emergence of clerics as military commanders may testify to a lack of effective laymen ready to step up. Apart from these retirements and deaths from natural causes, some of the original leaders had been killed in action or soon would be: the Kavanaghs (Dermot and Morgan), Stephenson and others. Most of the early activists, however, had their roles regularised. For example, Patrick Purcell of Croagh would enjoy a long and undistinguished career that would finish at the end of a noose thrown over a lantern post after the capitulation of Limerick in 1651.

The provincial armies would grow organically, but, as yet, they proved to be no substitute for a proper 'running' army because, to stay with the Leinster example, most of Preston's men were tied down in garrisons. The rest were necessarily reactive and so usually could not make it to the rendezvous in time to repel English incursions. They were 'like mushrooms', to borrow a description of English Civil War armies, 'shooting up almost overnight and then disappearing almost as quickly'.[179]

---

175 Gilbert (ed.), *Contemporary History*, vol. I, p.41.
176 Meehan (ed.), *Rise and Fall of the Irish Franciscan Monasteries*, p.325, 'Rory O'More to Fr Hugh Burke, Wexford 20 September 1642'; Gilbert (ed.), *Contemporary History*, vol. I, p.229.
177 Duignan, '"All in a Confused Opposition to Each Other"', p.136.
178 Gilbert (ed.), *Contemporary History*, vol. I, pp.52, 75.
179 I. Gentles, 'The Civil Wars in England', in J. Kenyon, J. Ohlmeyer, and J. Morrill (eds), *The Civil Wars: A Military History of England, Scotland, and Ireland 1638–1660* (Oxford: Oxford University Press, 1998), p.104.

3

Winter 1642–1643

The first general assembly dispersed towards the end of November 1642, leaving the Supreme Council to carry on with the day-to-day business of waging war. Let us imagine grave councilmen poring over Speed's 'Kingdome of Irland' laid flat upon a table in Rothe House on Kilkenny's High Street. Such (entirely hypothetical) guiding minds and hands would have grasped certain strategic priorities. It would have been quite beyond their capacity to recover Ulster or even to stabilise Eoghan Rua's position there, but they could have prevented a breakout from Ulster by stopping the Sligo Gap. In Leinster, the corridor from the Pale south-eastwards narrowed between bog and mountain near Carlow. Dublin Castle's writ ran a third of the length of that corridor, stopping close to the Liffey, but for outliers at Athy, Carlow and Portlaoise (Maryborough) and their satellites.[1] Any purposeful strategy should have focused on mopping up these pockets and not just containing but also seizing Duncannon, which dominated the entrance to Waterford Harbour and impeded access to the ports of New Ross and Waterford: 'against the will of those in the Fort without running extreme hazard'.[2] In Munster, there is some evidence of strategic direction. Time and again, the Munstermen moved against Cappoquin and Castlehaven would finally take the town, castle and bridge in 1645, by which time opening the highway from Clonmel to Cork was no longer as relevant as it had been.

Mountgarret, president of the Supreme Council, had interests in south Leinster and east Munster, and while some glimmerings of strategic coordination emerge here, no central body directed and animated provincial or-perish the thought- national strategy. Hostings gathered from neighbouring counties when and where the shoe, so to speak, pinched. They scattered or were scattered by English armies that actively sought battle because they were confident that they could beat any Irish army, even a bigger one, in open battle. For their part, the Irish would contrive to hold their ground (except in Ulster) and nibble at the frayed edges of enemy territory, all the while striving to evade battle.

---

1   N. T., *Very sad newes from Ireland* (London: Publisher unknown, 1646), p.1.
2   Gerard Boate, *The Natural History of Ireland* (London: John Wright, 1652), p.11.

Preston's target in December 1642, Ballinakill, lay just off the Carlow corridor, uncomfortably close to Kilkenny and just a few miles from Ballyragget, one of Mountgarret's houses which meant that Preston could count on provisions, even in deepest midwinter.³ Nevertheless, Monck's relief column of 600 shot and 300 horse broke through, at which Preston shadowed Monck from Ballinakill with 700 musketeers, 500 pikemen and 300 horse, 'all very completely armed'. Monck took his stand near Timahoe Castle, covering his flanks with trenches. Preston obliged with a frontal attack, and his men 'shot abundantly' but from too far away while Monck's soldiers held their fire. Suddenly, they 'gave fire so thick' that they shot down the 'boldest' and 'made the rest begin to give way which the English perceiving made hotly upon them'. Preston's men, 'with more shame than slaughter', slipped into Timahoe Castle and safety.⁴ Timahoe was a setback, though it showed a willingness to confront enemy forays. Preston quickly made good whatever losses (60 men, at most) he sustained and took Borris-in-Ossory, an especially remote outpost that had been relieved only twice. From there, he marched in January 1643 to Birr a strongpoint that had been ringed by four companies for a year and a quarter.⁵ The strategic object was to open secure routes between north and south Leinster, but the promise by local headmen of ample foodstuffs during a siege and money afterwards was probably a bigger lure.⁶

Preston's 'short culverin' probably fired a 14-pound shot capable of knocking a hole in the walls of most tower houses, but it did little damage to Birr. Instead, Preston drove a mine under the castle at a well-chosen spot close to the foundations. By break of day, on 19 January 1643, Preston's men had burrowed their way underground, for all the shot and rocks rained down on them. At that stage, Chidley Coote realised 'how impossible it was' to hold out with only 50 fighting men left from the original 100 foot soldiers and 40 horsemen he had raised from Birr's Protestant inhabitants. Dublin Castle would not send an army of relief 60 miles in the depths of winter through 'passes, and fords, rivers, and strong entrenchments'. The women and children were 'ready to starve', and the cattle gnawed each other's tails 'for want of fodder'. The few soldiers left were worn out by lack of sleep and sick 'with cold they Took, [in] the often rushing through the dirty court to answer Alarms, which was made so noisome by the treading of the Cattle, that each step a man took, he was sunk to the very Knees in mud and filth'.⁷ One gets the impression that it was the mud that finally got to Coote.

On 26 January, Preston summoned Banagher on the Shannon. The fort was held by a strong garrison of regular troops who would have long since been entirely starved out but for timely help from Clanricarde across the

---

3   Gilbert (ed.), *Irish Confederation*, vol. I, p.150.
4   J. B., *A Famous Victory obtained against the Rebels in Ireland, very lately by Colonell Muncke* (London: R. B., 1642), pp.3–4; Borlase, *Irish Rebellion*, p.105.
5   TCDL: 1641 Depositions, MS 815 (Laois), fol. 324r: Deposition of Samuell Franck; Gilbert (ed.), *Irish Confederation*, vol. II, p.147.
6   TCDL: 1641 Depositions, TCD MS 814 (Offaly), fol. 254r: Deposition of Robert Shepley, Thomas Mitchell, George Walter, Laurance Mulhann; Gilbert (ed.), *Contemporary History*, vol. I, p.46.
7   TCDL: 1641 Depositions, MS 814 (Offaly), fols 205v, 215r: Deposition of Chidley Coote. N. T., *Very sad newes from Ireland*, p.1.

river. Reassured by how Preston had punctiliously honoured the surrender terms at Birr, the commander at Banagher capitulated without fuss.

Meanwhile, 16 miles farther up the Shannon, the 'sick and weak' survivors were being pulled out of Athlone Castle and on 4 February, Richard Grenville shepherded them towards Mullingar and Trim in foul weather and over rough ways, 'which … killed divers'.[8] It was a relatively small gathering that stood in Grenville's way because Dillon had prevaricated too long about sending his lieutenant colonel with the County Longford companies to intercept Grenville's column. The Irish hastily threw up a parapet where the road sloughed through a stream and between bogs stretching away on each side. Rathconnell Castle, whence the battle takes its name, did not stand close enough to support the men in the trench.

English accounts claim that 'multitudes' of Irish outnumbered Grenville's 1,700 men, but, in fact, the Irish mobilisation was not yet complete. Most fighting still fell on local militia companies, which could only be mobilised after an incursion, and the response was even slower than usual because of Grenville's feint. The County Cavan militia was nowhere near, and the County Longford militia appeared late on the day of the battle.[9] In short, the Irish army was the smaller of the two.

Irish Forces at Rathconnell[10]

Name	Numbers	Description
James or Diego Preston	700	Infantry
Rory O'More	300	Infantry
Patrick or Richard or George Plunkett[11]	300	Infantry
Andrew Buí Tuite of Rathconnell, County Westmeath	100	Infantry
Francis Nugent of Dardistown, County Westmeath	100	Infantry
Sir Luke Fitzgerald of Ticroghan, County Meath	20	Cavalry
Brien	40	Cavalry
Total	**1,560**	

---

8   Carte, *History of the Life of James Duke of Ormonde*, vol. I, pp.382–83; W. Saintliger, *Joyfull and happy news from Ireland* (London: Edward Blackmore, 1643), pp.2–3; Gilbert (ed.), *Contemporary History*, vol. I, p.56.

9   Ball (ed.), *Calendar of the Manuscripts of the Marquess of Ormonde*, vol. II, p.233, 'Lords Justices to Speaker Lenthall'.

10 Plunkett was either the Patrick who was son of Oliver Baron Louth or Richard, Fingal's brother. Trinity College Dublin Library (TCDL) 1641 Depositions, MS 809 (County Dublin), fols 261r: Deposition of Anne Cappar, 280r: Deposition of Christopher Hewetson; TCDL: 1641 Depositions, MS 813 (County Kildare), fol. 150rv: Examination of Elenor Jepsson, MS 814 (County Offaly), fol. 147r: Examination of Anthony Preston, MS 816 (County Meath), fols 79v: Examination of William Malone, 181r: Deposition of John Prendergasse & Edwin Nash, 196: Examination of John Darcy, and MS 817 (County Westmeath), fol. 82v: Deposition of Thomas O Maghery.

11 The 'Colonel Plunkett' at Kilsallaghan could have been George, brother of the Earl of Fingall. TCDL: 1641 Depositions, MS 834 (County Monaghan), fol. 101r: Deposition of Matthew Browne.

Two regiments of refugee Palesmen formed the nucleus of the emergent Leinster standing army (under Sergeant Major Diego or James Preston, Thomas Preston's son) that had been force-marched from Banagher. His brother Anthony together with Rory O'More commanded the three counties of Kildare, Laois and Offaly, but Anthony came alone ('not being able to gather his men together sufficiently furnished so suddenly'), and O'More brought just 300 men, who manned the breastwork. O'More's band included some hardened fighters like the priest Lawrence Rowan alongside Garret Fitzgerald of nearby Ticroghan, where the south-western salient of County Meath protrudes into the Bog of Allen.[12]

Grenville broke his column into five parts, each of about 300 men, these being a vanguard of shot, three battalions of pike (with 'sleeves', or outer ranks, of musketeers) and a rearguard of shot. Three formations of horse screened the three battalions. For over two hours, the vanguard of shot and the next two battalions of pikemen tried, in turn, to overrun the sconce, with Grenville shouting at them to 'carry it or die'.[13] They suffered 'little loss' in there assaults because the Irish had not fully charged their muskets, so their shots hit home 'but dropped down without doing any hurt'.[14] Edmund Verney, a captain in the vanguard, told of how a ball struck the collar of his doublet, which 'made my neck black and blue' but inflicted 'no further hurt'.[15]

To block the Longford men from reinforcing the Irish, the third of Grenville's battalions was pulled out of the column and rushed forwards and to the left. An Irish cavalry troop made to charge them when the troop captain, one Captain Bryan (a deserter from Ormond's own troop of regulars), was shot and mortally wounded. Bryan's troopers recoiled, which in turn encouraged English horsemen to tread the bog and find, to their surprise, firm footing. With that, the Irish fell apart. More English cavalry followed, and the Longford men took to their heels. The cavalry pursued them for four miles, cutting down over 200 of them. The Irish cavalry, too, were pursued. P. S. told of what happened to one horseman when he was taken prisoner:

> … being disarmed, [he] was left to the keeping of one horse[man], the rest followed the rout, the prisoner having a pocket pistol, thrusting his hand to his pocket, trying if he could open it with that only hand, but being not of that ability, his keeper observing some extraordinary motion by him to be attempted, asked him whether he had a skine, if so to deliver it, answered that he had a meddog and by and by taking the pistol out, pointed therewith at the trooper's breast … and away he galloped.

---

12 TCDL: 1641 Depositions, MS 814 (County Offaly), fol. 147r: Examination of Anthony Preston.
13 Saintliger, *Joyfull and happy news*, p.2.
14 Quoted in Adrian Tinniswood, *The Verneys: A True Story of Love, War and Madness in Seventeenth-Century England* (London: Jonathan Cape, 2007), p.194.
15 Verney, *Memoirs*, vol. II, p.284.

Meanwhile, Rowan, 'gazing about him, saw only the enemy in the field' and his men quickly 'began to show a good pair of heels'.[16] The 'unhappy skirmish' was over.

Grenville had managed to extricate survivors, but Athlone Town was lost, the door to Connacht from Dublin shut, and County Westmeath secured for the Catholic cause. Tactically an English victory, Rathconnell was an admission of strategic defeat in an attritional process of blockades, *chevauchées*, burnings, preys, sieges and reliefs, whereby the belligerents planted garrisons to consume a region's food and deny those provisions to the enemy. A belligerent could destroy an enemy army in a pitched battle, but cutting off his provisions could destroy him 'just as effectively' and 'with less risk'.[17]

Inchiquin's grip was feeblest over his outflung garrisons between the Blackwater and the hill country on the County Limerick border, and, unsurprisingly, the Irish challenged him here. At eight o'clock in the morning, on 14 February 1643, a large raiding party burned Mitchelstown, having marched from the east along the natural corridor formed by the Kilworth Mountains to the south and the Galtee Mountains to the north. They caught their breath in a staging area at Clonodfoy and then set Doneraile ablaze on 25 February.[18] Seventeen companies and three troops of cavalry took part in one or both operations, making between 1,000 and 1,100 foot soldiers and over 100 horsemen. As one would expect from an operation in the corner of County Cork that abuts Limerick and Tipperary, the soldiers came in more or less equal numbers from those two counties, with a sprinkling from Cork, Kerry and Waterford. The table below showing the companies is the closest thing we have to an order of battle for the Catholics in Munster, wherein the hierarchy of two lieutenant generals, colonels and lieutenant colonels reveals the skeletal outline of two regiments in what looks otherwise like an agglomeration of companies.

---

16   Gilbert (ed.), *Contemporary History*, vol. I, p.57.
17   Tallett, *War and Society*, pp.65, 75.
18   Lynch (ed.), *Castlehaven's Memoirs*, p.93.

Burning of Mitchelstown and Doneraile[19]

Rank	Surname	Name	Place	County
Lieutenant General	Purcell	Tibbott	Loghmoe	Tipperary
Sergeant Major General	Butler	Richard	Ikerrin	Tipperary
Lieutenant Colonel	Butler	Edward	Bealadrohid	Tipperary
Captain	Butler	Thomas	Son of Baron Dunboyne	Tipperary
Captain	Butler	Tibbott	Ardmayle	Tipperary
Captain	Butler	James	Kilmoyle	Tipperary
Captain	O'Byrne	James	Cahir	Tipperary
Captain (cavalry)	O'Dwyer	Owny	Kilnamanagh	Tipperary
Lieutenant General	Purcell	Patrick	Croagh	Limerick
Colonel	Burke	William	Baron Castleconnell	Limerick
Captain (cavalry)	Fitzgerald	Edmund Mac Thomas	Clenlis	Limerick
Captain	Herbert	Morris	Rathkeale	Limerick
Captain	Walsh	Walter	Abbeyowney	Limerick
Captain	Baggott	Nicholas	Baggotstown	Limerick
Captain	Mac Sheehy[20]	Rory	Ballylinane	Limerick
Colonel	O'Sullivan Mór[21]	Philip	Dunkerrin	Kerry
Captain (cavalry)	Fennell	Edmund	Dungarvan	Waterford
Captain	Power	Piers	Kilowen or Munsburrow	Waterford
Captain	Barry	William	Lislee	Cork
Captain	Roche	David	Glenanore	Cork

As we have seen, Catholic fighting forces took the field in baronial companies that came together in county regiments for a time and came apart again. Such was the unrelenting pace of combat in 1643; however, these ad hoc regiments coalesced for long enough to reify as institutions rather than occasions.

These emergent regiments were sprinkled unevenly without apparent regard to resources or manpower. Regions that lay closest to the enemy necessarily saw more fighting, raised more regiments and kept them in the field for longer. One can identify five regiments of foot in Leinster –

---

19 TCDL: 1641 Depositions, MS 812 (County Kilkenny), fol. 173r: Deposition of Richard Costalla, MS 829 (County Cork), fols 173r–74v: Deposition of Nicholas Fox, and MS 829 (County Limerick), fol. 173r: Deposition of Dauid Counagh.

20 Of Monagay, Barony of Glenquin, County Limerick, third son of Murrough of Connello. Hubert Gallwey, 'The MacSheehys of Connello in County Limerick', *Irish Genealogist*, 4:6 (1973), p.564.

21 Younger brother of Eoghan O'Sullivan Mór of Dunkerron, County Kerry, 'lately come from Spain'. TCDL: 1641 Depositions, MS 829 (County Limerick), fol. 173r: Deposition of Dauid Counagh.

RAW GENERALS AND GREEN SOLDIERS

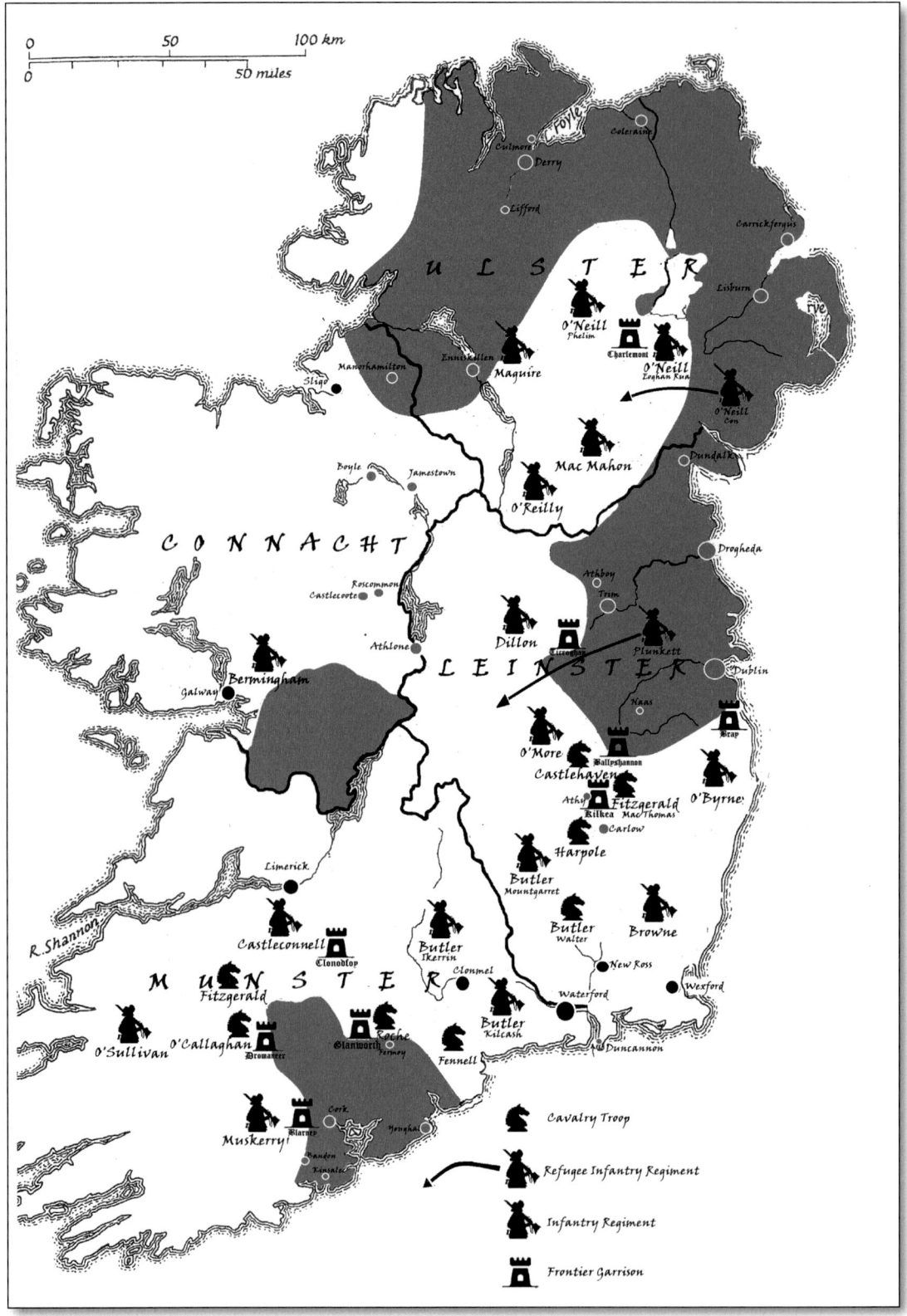

Catholic regiments and troops, 1643. (Author's map)

Dillon's, Plunkett's, Butler's (Mountgarret), O'More's and O'Byrne's – and four troops of horse – Castlehaven's, Mac Thomas's, Harpole's and Walter Butler's. All of them can be associated with a county or pairing of counties, except for Plunkett's, which probably served as home away from home for many fugitives ran out of the Pale. Mobilisation was patchier in Munster. The Claremen hardly took part at all in the war outside the county, Limerick City comported itself as a 'free state', free of such irritants as taxes, and Thomond would be left unmolested in his pile at Bunratty long enough to hand this strategically vital stronghold over to the enemy. Muskerry was not very active beyond his own bailiwick by 1643, and, here, the English would score territorial gains in 1643, quite against the run of play elsewhere in the country. Cavalry troops (O'Callaghan's, Roche's and Fennell's) roamed a porous frontier, whereas, in Leinster, the frontier had hardened on the south and west of the English enclave. We know that three of the five most notable strongholds here were artillery proofed. One was Phelim O'Byrne's 'fort of earth' on a ford over the Bray River, while Ticroghan and Ballyshannon grew a skin of thick earthen ramparts and bastions around the original castle and keep. Comparably important and large castles on the Munster frontier like Blarney, Dromaneen, Kanturk and Glanworth in County Cork, Clonfodnoy in County Limerick and Barnankile in County Waterford were not cladded in ramparts of thick earth but trusted to their natural strength. Blarney, for instance, was 'a strong pile with a flanked bawn standing on a rock'.[22] The reason why the Catholics of Leinster were prepared to invest the considerable time and effort to dig bastioned earthworks must have been their painful memories of Dublin's culverins cracking open tower houses during that awful spring and summer of 1642. We know that 'fortifications did not win wars', but they might avert some of its horrors.[23] Moygara, in the southernmost reaches of County Sligo, probably dates to 1642–1646.[24] It is thoroughly structured to maximise firepower. The shot holes are numerous (there are 10 on the southern curtain and two on each of the adjacent flanks of the corner towers) and so low that a shooter would have to kneel. The field of fire is restricted but angled for very close-range shots at an attacker's midriff. A gun platform made by levelling an older tower house was sited to cover the road from Boyle and Robert King's rampaging troopers.

---

22 Library of Trinity College, Dublin, 'Muskerry', *The Down Survey of Ireland* (2013), <https://downsurvey.tchpc.tcd.ie/down-survey-maps.php#bm=Muskerry&c=Cork>, accessed 10 Sept. 2019.

23 John Childs and John Keegan, *Warfare in the Seventeenth Century* (London: Cassel, 2001), p.113.

24 My thanks to Kieran O'Conor of the Department of Archaeology at the University of Galway for this information.

Catholic Regiments and Troops, 1643

Name	County	Province	Regiment	Troop
Viscount Muskerry[25]	Cork	Munster	✓	
Richard Butler[26]	Tipperary	Munster	✓	
Richard Butler[27]	Tipperary	Munster	✓	
Baron Castleconnell[28]	Limerick[29]	Munster	✓	
Philip O'Sullivan Mór[30]	Cork	Munster	✓	
Edmund Fennell[31]	Waterford	Munster		✓
Edmund Fitzgerald[32]	Limerick[33]	Munster		✓
David Roche[34]	Cork	Munster		✓
Teige O'Callaghan[35]	Cork	Munster		
Edmund Rua Butler	Kilkenny[36]	Leinster	✓	
Sir James Dillon[37]	Westmeath	Leinster	✓	
Hugh O'Byrne	Wicklow[38]	Leinster	✓	

---

25 MacCarthy, Donough (1594–1665), 2nd Viscount Muskerry, 1st Earl of Clancarty. Micheál Ó Siochrú, 'MacCarthy, Donough', *Dictionary of Irish Biography* (2009), <https://www.dib.ie/biography/maccarthy-donough-a5129>, accessed 20 Jan. 2020.

26 Brother of Ormond and 'reputed' general of Waterford and Tipperary – Thomas Butler of Knocktopher was his second-in-command. TCDL: 1641 Depositions, MS 820 (County Waterford), fols 125r: Deposition of John Crockford, 279r: Examination of John Griffin and MS 823 (County Cork), fol. 170r: Deposition of Symon Bridges.

27 Richard, second son of Piers Butler, 1st Viscount Ikerrin.

28 William Burke, Baron of Castleconnell.

29 Nine companies can be identified, all captained by men from east County Limerick: William Burke, Baron Castleconnell; Lieutenant Colonel William Burke, second son of Baron Brittas; Captain Morris Herbert; Captain Walter Walsh of Abbeyowney; Nicholas Baggott of Baggotstown; Maurice Rawley of Rawleystown; John Lacy of Bruff; John Fox of Bulgaden and George Brett of Tulla. TCDL: 1641 Depositions, MS 829 (County Kilkenny), fol. 173r: Deposition of Richard Costalla and MS 829 (County Limerick), fols 173r: Deposition of Dauid Counagh, 258v: Deposition of John Pilkington, 262r: Deposition of John Bradish; Simington and MacLellan, 'Oireachtas Library List', p.354.

30 He was a younger brother of Eoghan O'Sullivan Mór of Dunkerron, County Kerry, 'lately come from Spain'. TCDL: 1641 Depositions, MS 829 (County Limerick), fol. 173r: Deposition of Dauid Counagh.

31 TCDL: 1641 Depositions, MS 820 (County Waterford), fol. 125v: Deposition of John Crockford.

32 Piers Mac Thomas Fitzgerald.

33 TCDL: 1641 Depositions, MS 829 (County Limerick), fols 173r: Deposition of Dauid Counagh, 351r: Deposition of John Welsh.

34 Son of Viscount Roche of Castletownroche, near Fermoy. IMC: Kavanagh (ed.), *Commentarius Rinuccinianus*, vol. I, p.570.

35 TCDL: 1641 Depositions, MS 827 (County Cork), fols 79r: Examination of Phillip Vaughane, 112r: Examination of Dennis Daly.

36 Eldest son of Viscount Mountgarrett. TCDL: 1641 Depositions, MS 812 (County Kilkenny), fols 325r: Examination of Morris Kelly, 327r: Examination of Edward Butler.

37 Of Kilfaughny, Kilkenny West civil parish, barony of Kilkenny West, County Westmeath. Son of Theobald, 1st Viscount Dillon. Terry Clavin, 'Dillon, Theobald', *Dictionary of Irish Biography* (2009), <https://www.dib.ie/biography/dillon-theobald-a2616>, accessed 3 March 2020.

38 Mac Phelim of Ballinacor County Wicklow. Gilbert (ed.), *Contemporary History*, vol. I, p.62.

Richard Plunkett[39]	Dublin	Leinster	✓	
Laoiseach O'More[40]	Kildare	Leinster	✓	
Piers Fitzgerald[41]	Kildare	Leinster		✓
Sir Walter Butler	Kilkenny[42]	Leinster		✓
Earl of Castlehaven	Kildare[43]	Leinster		
Roger Harpole	Laois	Leinster		✓
Phelim O'Neill[44]	Tyrone	Ulster	✓	
Philip O'Reilly[45]	Cavan	Ulster	✓	
Colla Mac Mahon[46]	Monaghan	Ulster	✓	
Eoghan Rua O'Neill[47]	Armagh	Ulster	✓	
Rory Maguire	Fermanagh	Ulster	✓	
Con óg O'Neill[48]	Down	Ulster	✓	
John Bermingham[49]	Galway	Connacht	✓	

---

39   This is Richard Plunkett of Dunsoghly, County Dublin, one of the original conspirators – not to be confused with Thomas Plunkett, brother of Oliver, 6th Baron Louth, and Sergeant Major of the Leinster army cavalry. TCDL: 1641 Depositions, MS 814 (Kings County), fol. 211v: Deposition of Chidley Coote, MS 815 (Queens County), fol. 358v: Deposition of Captain Richard Steele *et al.*, and MS 816 (County Meath), fols 79v: Examination of William Malone, 181r: Deposition of John Prendergasse & Edwin Nash; TNA: *HMC Report on Franciscan Manuscripts in Dublin*, p.178, 'Matthew O'Hartegan to Luke Wadding, Nantes, 22 August 1642'.

40   A younger brother of Rory O'More of Ballina, County Kildare, and Dundalk. Laoiseach was militarily active in the vicinity of Carbury and Birmingham's country, so he was probably domiciled at Ballina.

41   Known as 'Mac Thomas'. TCDL: 1641 Depositions, MS 815 (Queens County), fol. 324r: Deposition of Samuell Franck.

42   Lynch (ed.), *Castlehaven's Memoirs*, p.54.

43   James Touchet, Earl of Castlehaven, but the day-to-day commander of the troops was Garret Garbh Fitzgerald of Tully, County Kildare. Lynch (ed.), *Castlehaven's Memoirs*, p.57.

44   His lieutenant colonel was Shane O'Neill, who was captured at Clones, and subsequently Thomas Sanfort. IMC: Kavanagh (ed.), *Commentarius Rinuccinianus*, vol. II, p.189; Ó Donnchadha, 'Cín lae', pp.19, 21.

45   Philip Mac Hugh Mac Shane O'Reilly of Bellanacargy Castle (near the present-day village of Drung) was a grandson of the Shane Rua (d. 1593) who was the last undisputed chieftain of the O'Reillys. Colm O'Lochlainn (ed.), *Irish Chiefs and Leaders: Studies by Father Paul Walsh* (Dublin: Sign of the Three Candles, 1960), p.369.

46   Colla Mac Brian Mac Mahon of Lisinisky in the barony of Cremorne. Ó Mórdha, 'MacMahons of Monaghan', p.316.

47   His lieutenant colonel was his nephew Hugh Dubh O'Neill, captured at Clones.

48   He was closely associated with the Magennises and was given the title 'Colonel', even as early as February 1641. Trinity College Dublin Library (TCDL) 1641 Depositions, MS 837 (County Down), fols 164r: Examination of Rowland Brown, 165r: Examination of Edward Davis; TCDL: 1641 Depositions, MS 839 (County Tyrone), fol. 40r: Information of John Perkins.

49   TCDL: 1641 Depositions, MS 830 (County Galway), fols 134r–35v: Deposition of William Hamond; Edward Kimber, *The Peerage of Ireland: A Genealogical and Historical Account …* (London: J. Almon, 1768), vol. I, p.99.

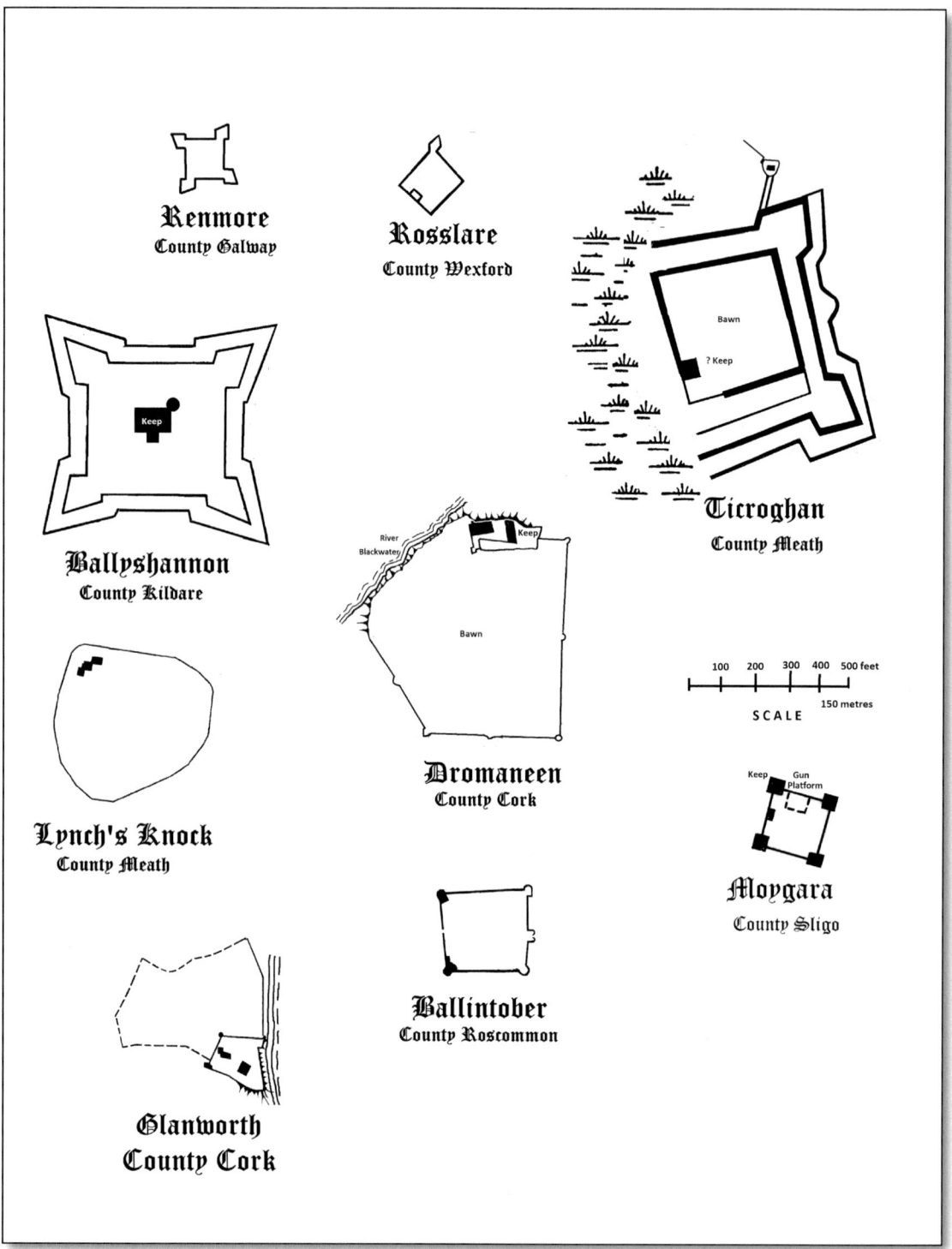

Forts and castles. (Author's map)

Before Clones, O'Neill had only 1,600 men 'fit for service' in his own and Phelim's regiments.[50] Both regiments lacked a secure territorial base, and their captains (and one must assume their followers) were mostly refugees (e.g., O'Dohertys, O'Mullans, Magennises, Mac Donnells and so on) harried from west and east Ulster after those regions had been inundated by Scots and British forces. At Bruse Hill, Eoghan Rua summoned 'all the Ulster gentlemen' who could make up 3,000 men in five or six understrength regiments.[51]

As late as the climactic Battle of Benburb in 1646, the Ulster army looks from the outside like it was organised along clan lines, with three O'Neill regiments of foot apparently representing Tyrone and Armagh, O'Donnell from Donegal, Mac Donnell from Antrim, Maguire from Fermanagh and O'Farrell from County Longford. However, that localism is illusory, and the companies, the building blocks of the regiment, were assembled from whoever could be got. Take Rory Maguire's, for example. At first, nearly all of the captains of the regiment bore the Maguire surname, except for Rory's stepfather, Richard Nugent, and one Phelim Mac Manus. That changed as it evolved into a more or less standing regiment in which the four corners of Ulster would be represented. Rory's uncle Donagh was supplanted in the key sergeant major role by Turlough O'Neill of the Fews, an 'old soldier of Spain'. Rory's captains included Dougal Mac Quillin from the Route in north Antrim, Ever Mac Sweeney of Kilmacrenan in County Donegal and Donagh Carrach Mac Cabe, probably from County Cavan.[52]

The fledgling Connacht army had a duplicate structure of two lieutenant generals, two sergeant majors and two colonels representing Counties Mayo and Galway, respectively. The brittle organization cracked when Mayo, the man and the county, largely withdrew in a sulk from the Catholic cause. The lone Connacht regiment was drawn from County Galway, except for the south-east corner where Clanricarde's fatal shadow lingered.[53]

West of an imaginary line, Cork–Limerick–Athlone–Derry, military mobilisation mostly stalled at the phase of part-time baronial companies fighting locally, reactively and episodically and the core of Catholic military power lay in the Butler heartland of south Leinster and east Munster.

On the face of it, Ormond's campaign of March 1643 looks like an ambitious and purposeful lunge at that core, yet the closer one peers, the less things cohere. The Lords Justices originally envisaged sending the army somewhere, anywhere, 'to spare the provision near the city … and to do what service it should please God to enable them to do'[54] The Lords Justices were

---

50 Ó Fiaich, 'O'Neills of the Fews', pp.1–64.
51 CELT: O'Neill, 'Most memorable transactions of General Owen O'Neill', p.491; TCDL: 1641 Depositions, MS 836 (County Armagh), fol. 14r: Deposition of John Wisdome.
52 TCDL: 1641 Depositions, MS 835 (County Fermanagh), fols 109r: Deposition of Robert French, 131r–32v: Deposition of Thomas Knowles, 241r: Deposition of Edward Erwin, 249r: Deposition of Thomas Wenslowe and MS 839 (County Donegal), fol. 129v: Deposition of Ann Dutton; Ó Donnchadha, 'Cín lae', pp.17, 32, 36, 47; Ó Fiaich, 'O'Neills of the Fews', pp.1–64.
53 Burke, *Memoirs and Letters of Ulick*, p.412; James Hardiman, *The History of the Town and County of the Town of Galway* (Dublin: W. Folds and Sons, 1820), p.120.
54 Gilbert (ed.), *Irish Confederation*, vol. II, p.xviii.

Moygara Castle. (Public domain)

sympathetic to Parliament's cause and to they chose Lisle to lead this food fight but deferred to Ormond, who insisted on the commander-in-chief's right to lead his army on campaign.

Ormond gave orders for a ship to be hired and sent to Duncannon Fort with provisions 'if need should be', which suggests that even at this stage he must have had in mind capturing New Ross.[55] At a stroke, that would have given him Kilkenny's seaport, 24 miles from the open sea on the tidal estuary of the Barrow. It also would have given him another foothold in the Carlow corridor, midway between the latter outpost and Duncannon, and it would have disrupted links between Kilkenny and the ports of Dungarvan, Waterford and especially Wexford, whence the Irish got 'all their Ammunition and assistance from Foreign parts'.[56] Mountgarret had a 10-day warning that Ormond would march south from Dublin, but he had no inkling that New Ross was the target and assumed that Ormond would make for Kilkenny, which is where Preston duly gathered his forces.

---

55 Francis Willoughby, *A relation of the battell fought by the forces of the King and Parliament. The Marquis of Ormond being generall, and the Lord Vicount Lisle lieutenant generall of the horse, against the bloody rebels in Ireland neer Old Rosse, and not far from Doncannon in the year 1642* (London: Fr. Neile, 1648), p.7.

56 Robert Cole, *The true coppies of two letters sent from Ireland: shewing the severall battailes and victories obtained on the rebels there* (London: J.B. and R. Smith, 1643), pp.1–3.

Ormond set off down the Leinster corridor at the head of a large force of up to 3,000 infantry, 700 horsemen and six guns – 'large', that is, by Irish standards, though only about the size of an English regional army like Hopton's Cornishmen.[57] His march was held up by the defenders of a fortified monastic site comprising a castle, church and tower at Timolin in south County Kildare. They did not surrender when summoned, forcing Ormond to plant his two demi-culverins. The guns began battering on Saturday, 7 March, and, at noon two days later, the soldiers broke into the castle and 'slew all', some 500 to 600 'men, and children', even though Ormond had wanted women and children spared. We are told that 'the soldiers were so much incensed' against the women because they 'did much hurt' to them. Another English witness admitted that quarter had been promised and that he was 'heartily sorry' to see the slaughter: the officers were merciful, but the 'soldiers came to be so enraged for the death of Lieutenant Oliver, a very gallant man slain by a stone from the battlements'.[58] Ormond had not intended to attack Timolin in the first place because it was well fortified but let himself be drawn into a siege that gave Preston more time to prepare. In the event, Preston also wasted time because he was wrong-footed and expected a march on Kilkenny, but Ormond unexpectedly turned eastwards through a gap in the Blackstairs Mountains at Clonegal into County Wexford. He did not reveal his final destination to all of the army until he reached the middle of the county, about equidistant from New Ross and Wexford town.

Finally, on the morning of 11 March, Lisle's advance guard of cavalry reached New Ross, where he found one of the town gates open and the citizens unsuspecting. Frustratingly, Lisle missed the fleeting chance to seize the gate, blaming the lack of timely support-infantry backup: Irish cavalry had been harassing Ormond's infantry vanguard and forced it to pull back into the main body.[59]

The circuit of the walls was too ambitious for the town. Indeed, early nineteenth-century maps show extensive voids remaining behind where the walls had been. Moreover, artillery-resistant ramparts had to be low, squat and thick, which demanded an entirely new design philosophy of protruding bastions or bulwarks to eliminate dead ground, not just casting earth against the back of the old masonry walls 'in the manner of a rampart' to thicken them against the impact of artillery.[60] Engineers decried this 'lining of old walls' because 'earth and walls doth never bind together' and 'upon the first storm of the Cannon-shot' the soil would subside forwards into the ditch.[61]

George Monck, in his 1671 *Observations*, claimed that 'man's flesh is the best fortification that belongs to a Town', and Catholic towns invariably

---

57   Gaunt, *English Civil War*, p.97.
58   Anon., *The late prosperous proceedings of the Protestant army against the rebells in Ireland ...* (London: John Wright, 1643), p.3; Cole, *The true coppies of two letters sent from Ireland*, p.3.
59   Saintliger, *Joyfull and happy news from Ireland*, p.3; John Temple, *Ormonds curtain drawn. In a short discourse concerning Ireland; wherein his treasons, and the corruption of his instruments are laid bare to the stroke of justice* (London: Publisher unknown, 1646), p.26.
60   Gilbert (ed.), *Irish Confederation*, vol. I, pp.128–29.
61   David Papillon, *A practicall abstract of the arts of fortification and assailing ...* (London: R. Austin, 1645), p.12.

raised trained bands.[62] Because of these 'warlike and distracted days', Mayor Michael White divided Clonmel into four quarters denominated by four of the five town gates in July 1642 and decreed that 'all and every [adult male] inhabitant' should enroll in one of these companies and present himself with firearms (calivers and snaphances were specified), a 'good sword' or, at least, a 'skeane' and a 'good pike'.[63] The townsmen of Wexford 'made Captains among themselves' for four parish companies of 200 men each 'to command the several Inhabitants within the several parishes'.[64] New Ross had three such companies, and James Duff, military governor of the town, had led them the previous September in a clash with soldiers from Duncannon Fort but was bested and fled 'on horse back with a sword & a case of pistols'.[65]

Luckily, Preston slipped the ubiquitous Arthur Fox into New Ross with 300 soldiers just as Lisle was approaching the gates. Moreover, the Supreme Council hastily called on forces that had been gathering near Waterford City for an attack on Cappoquin, a 'place of great importance'.[66] Ormond planted two demi-culverins that wrecked the tower of the Bunnion Gate in the east wall and knocked a practicable breach four or five yards wide in the wall 'a little' to the south of the gate. Sir Francis Willoughby, the next most senior officer after Ormond and Lisle, blamed the weather:

> … we assaulted [the breach] with certain of our Forces chosen out for that purpose: Sir Fulk Hunks, and Major Morris having the command and full management of that service; Major Morris being there dangerously hurt in the assault, and brought off, and by reason of the multitude of the defenders, who had stopt the breach with wool-packs, and feather-beds, and other provisions, so as we could do no good in it. I had order from the Lord Generall to draw them off, which I accordingly did, in which service we lost some few men; the weather being extreme ill was a great hindrance to our proceedings.[67]

Torrential rain quenched match and soaked powder while Fox's men stood 'within the town' and somehow kept their powder dry: were they in houses firing down from windows and loopholes?[68] This suggests a tentative firefight on either side of the barricade rather than a determined attack. Fox's men shot twenty attackers dead and wounded forty more, but the toll was hardly grievous enough, of itself, to have stopped the storm: Ormond had lost a dozen men at Timolin and 'many hurt', but the storming party had shrugged off the losses and pushed on. Ormond's men had no grenades to lob over the

---

62 Stephen Bull, *The Furie of the Ordnance: Artillery in the English Civil Wars* (Woodbridge: Boydell & Brewer, 2008), p.81.
63 Bríd McGrath (ed.), *The Minute Book of the Corporation of Clonmel, 1608–1649* (Dublin: Irish Manuscripts Commission, 2006), p.288.
64 TCDL: 1641 Depositions, MS 818 (County Wexford), fol. 138v: Examination of Nicholas Rochford.
65 TCDL: 1641 Depositions, MS 819 (County Wexford), fol. 40r: Examination of Peter Hooper.
66 Gilbert (ed.), *Irish Confederation*, vol. I, pp.129, 131.
67 Willoughby, *A relation of the battell*, p.7.
68 Anon., *The late prosperous proceedings*, p.4; Cole, *The true coppies of two letters sent from Ireland*, p.3.

WINTER 1642–1643

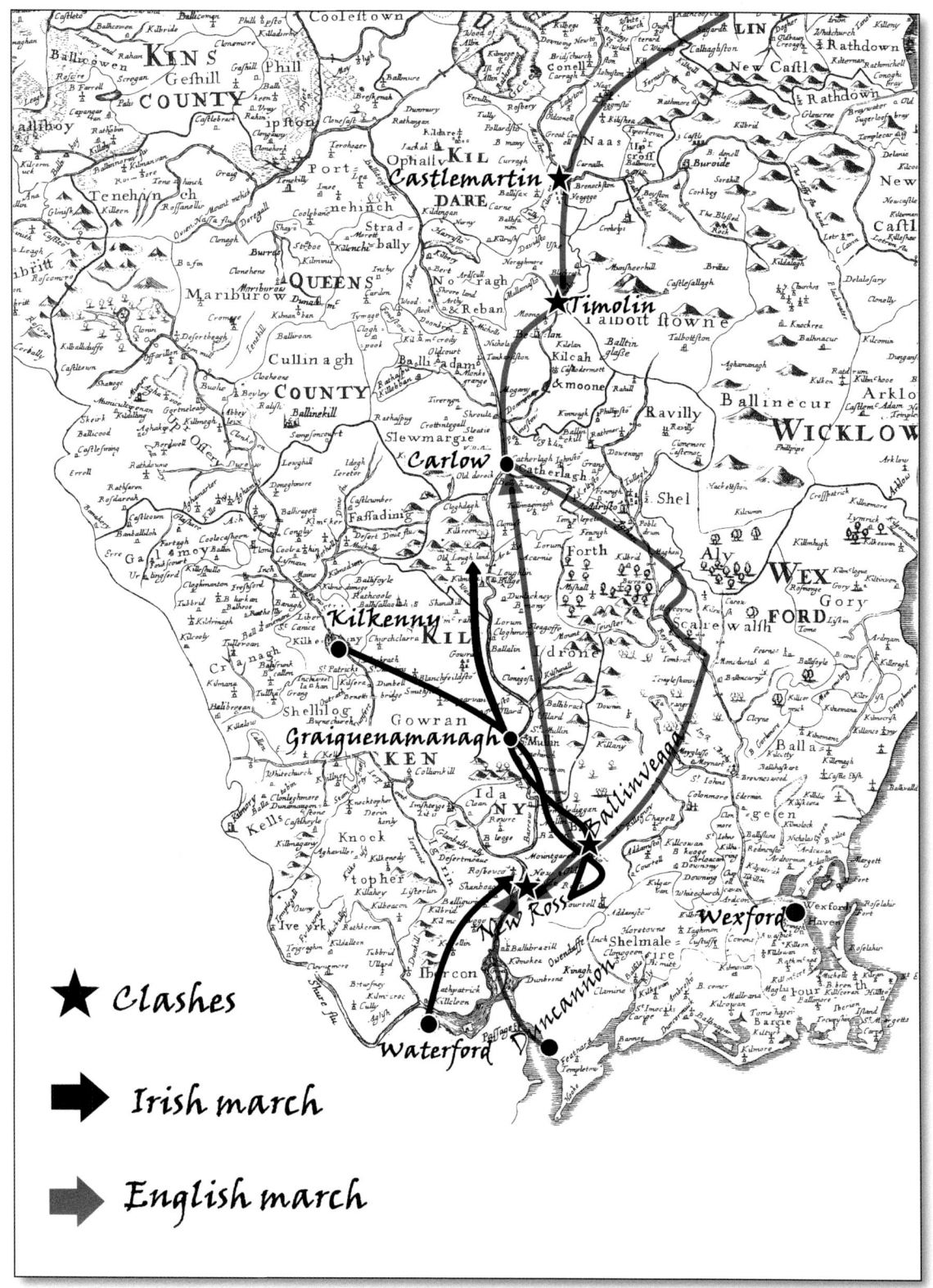

Ormond's march on New Ross. (Author's map)

barricade and they could hear 'the Rebels shout and laugh when any of the army were destroyed' and sense their buoyantly determined mood. Soldiers and civilians alike resisted desperately, and the women 'showed themselves … the best of their sex'.[69] An English soldier in *Colas's Furie* complains of a 'whore' who 'gave me such a damnable thump of a stone, my shoulders feels the weight of it yet'.[70]

Such desperation is not to be wondered at after Timolin: 'from thenceforth it was a common saying not to hope for better quarter at the English hands other than that of Timolin'.[71] Massacres like Timolin were double-edged swords that could cow defenders or terrify them into desperate resistance.[72] Moreover, some of the townsmen had reason to fear payback. James Duff had taken custody of 13 Protestant prisoners being delivered from Gowran, County Kilkenny, early in 1642, and, shortly afterwards, he sent men with 'swords and bats [probably hurleys] in their hands', who hustled the poor wretches away to a wood about a mile away and murdered seven of them, sparing only women and children.[73]

Storming the breach, detail from Jan Luyken, 'Hollandse troepen bestormen de muur van Tienen'. (Rijksmuseum, Amsterdam)

The governor of Duncannon sent supply ships upriver from the promontory fort. One of them, which an English merchantman named the '*Love's Increase*', fired broadsides 'into the heart' of New Ross, raising shouts in the darkness. Daybreak on 16 March revealed to the horrified sailors that the Munstermen had deployed guns at Rosbercon on the western bank of the Barrow.[74] A poem dedicated to Butler of Ikerrin

---

69 Gilbert (ed.), *Contemporary History*, vol. I, p.61.
70 Burkhead, *Cola's furie*, p.51.
71 Gilbert (ed.), *Contemporary History*, vol. I, p.60.
72 Borlase, *Irish Rebellion*, p.112; Kelly (ed.), *Cambrensis Eversus*, vol. III, p.191; Cole, *The true coppies of two letters sent from Ireland*, p.3.
73 TCDL: 1641 Depositions, MS 812 (County Kilkenny), fols 321r: Examination of Ann Bradford, 325r: Examination of Morris Kelly.
74 Elaine Murphy, *Ireland and the War at Sea, 1641-1653* (London: Royal Historical Society, Boydell, 2012), p.30.

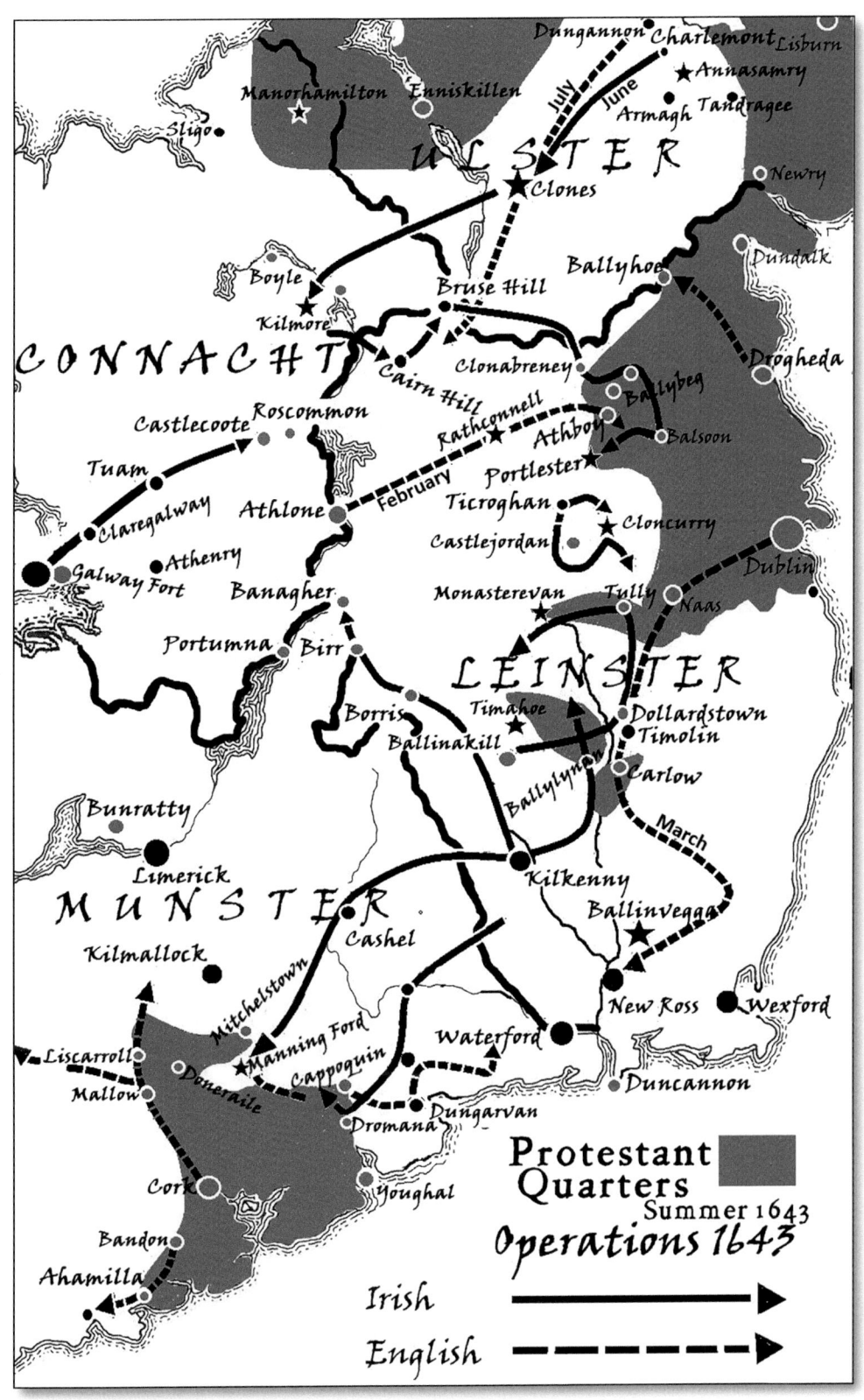

Campaigns of 1643. (Author's map)

brags of how his guns 'left the fleet in a heap in the harbour [*san chuan*]'.[75] Contrary winds had kept the ships at anchor and made them easy marks until the crews abandoned ship and scuttled them, though *Love's Increase* stayed afloat long enough to be seized and repaired.[76]

Soon, Preston set up camp just three miles away from New Ross and hindered Ormond's cavalry from collecting horse fodder, which was what forced Ormond to raise the siege.[77] His men had enough biscuits for three or four more days, but horses needed to eat 20 pounds of dry fodder (there would have been no grass so early in the year) a day: feeding 700 horses, not to mention oxen, demanded as much food as 10 times that many men. Once Ormond began to decamp, Preston pulled back farther to the north-west astride the road to Enniscorthy. If Ormond chose to go back the way he had come, he would have to cut his way through Preston. If he chose to take the shortest route, he would have to negotiate the wooded pass of Poulmounty between the Blackstairs Mountains and the Barrow, and Preston could dog Ormond's army, which was encumbered with heavy guns, sick, wounded, stragglers, loot and prey. Bellings, an armchair general, blamed Preston for not doing just that 'by parties and keeping of passes': 'Carlow, the nearest of their garrisons was twenty miles distance and they must have marched through a country so uneven, so full of bogs, and in other parts so stony that almost at every mile's end there was a pass which they must have forced at great disadvantage'.[78]

Ormond may have worried about squeezing through Poulmounty while leaving Preston's army behind, and so he veered north-west 'to look for him'. More likely, we are giving Ormond too much credit, and he was just doggedly retracing his march to New Ross. Marching through Ballinvegga Townland on St Patrick's Day, Ormond saw his enemy massing beyond the Aughnacrow stream 'in a large field surrounded by ditches', blowing on their match and readying for a fight. Preston had just four regiments of foot and four troops (Morgan Kavanagh's, Mac Thomas's, Edward Butler of Tullow's and Richard Cullen's) of horse, making much less than the 5,600 attributed to him by Bellings.[79]

Drums clattered, and trumpets blew shrill echoes as a narrow column of Irish horsemen, no more than four abreast, wallowed across Aughnacrow's belly-deep mire. By two or three o'clock in the afternoon, they had reached a boreen leading up a gentle incline. 'Why did Preston not have "patience"

---

75 Ní Cheallacháin, *Filíocht Phádraigín Haicéad*, p.54; Michael Hartnett, *Haicéad* (Oldcastle: The Gallery Press, 1993), p.80.
76 BoL: Carte MS 4, fol. 490: Lazarus Haward to Ormond, New Ross 16 March 1643.
77 Willoughby, *A relation of the battell*, p.5.
78 Gilbert (ed.), *Irish Confederation*, vol. I, p.133.
79 Anon., *A full and true relation of the late great victory, obtained by the Protestants against the rebells in Ireland* (London: Henry Overton, 1643), p.2; Amos Miller, 'The Battle of Ross: A Controversial Military Event', *The Irish Sword*, 10:39 (1971), pp.141–58; TNA: *HMC Report on Franciscan Manuscripts in Dublin*, p.239; George Creichtoun, 'A Faithful Account … by G. Creichtoun, chaplain to his Lordship's Regiment', in P. H. Hore (ed.), *History of the Town and County of Wexford: Comprised Principally from the State Papers, the Public Records, and Mss. of the Late Herbert F. Hore, Esq., of Pole Hore, in that County. Old and New Ross* (London: Elliot Stock, 1900), p.297; Gilbert (ed.), *Contemporary History*, vol. I, p.58.

and wait for the English to attack him?' queried Bellings.[80] It was probably because his men stood 'half a musket shot', or 150 yards, from the English, who had six artillery pieces that could topple whole files at that range. A photograph taken from what was then a ford, and is now a bridge, shows a house built close to what was the likely gun position.

View from ford to Ormond's gun position. (Author's photo)

Ormond's guns fired. After the first shots at Preston's cavalry, 'goodly men and horses lay there all torn, and their guts lying on the ground'.[81] The cavaliers 'set up a great cry': some fled back and disordered their own foot soldiers while others burst from the lane into an open field adjoining. The list of the slain in *Good Newes from Ireland* cannot be entirely relied on: it includes two officers, William Browne, colonel of the Wexford regiment, and Edmund Rua Butler, commander of the Kilkenny regiment, who were both alive and well after the battle. As at Kilrush, those cut down were mostly from County Carlow or the adjacent part of County Kildare – notably, Sir Morgan Kavanagh of Clonmullen, 'a brave gentleman', Edward Butler of Tullow, a 'constant, pious and valorous blade', Henry Bagnall, deputy governor of Leighlin Fort, the Ashbolds of unhappy Timolin, father and son, and Tibbot Butler of Tully.[82]

Cavalry on Ormond's right wing, commanded by Lisle and Grenville, cantered towards Cullen's and Mac Thomas's troops, milling about in the

---

80 Gilbert (ed.), *Irish Confederation*, vol. I, p.51.
81 Carte, *History of the Life of James Duke of Ormonde*, vol. I, p.405.
82 Saintliger, *Joyfull and happy news from Ireland*, p.3; TCDL: 1641 Depositions, MS 812 (County Carlow), fols 27r: Deposition of Robert Wadding, 69r: Deposition of Ann Butler, MS 812 (County Kilkenny), fol. 305r: Examination of Ellen Swift, and MS 813 (County Kildare), fol. 10r: Examination of Thomas Ash; Gilbert (ed.), *Contemporary History*, vol. I, p.62.

field near the fatal lane. The front rank of Lisle's horsemen fired a 'caracole' at 'pike length'. It was Liscarroll all over again. As the front rank wheeled about, 'suddenly' Irish horsemen burst among them and 'fell to work with their swords'. One rider struck Sir Thomas Lucas twice with a pollaxe, a sort of long-handled hammer with a head that had a flat bludgeoning face, called a 'poll', on one side and a spike on the other.[83] Each Irish cavalryman wore the usual *súgán* tied about his hat and midriff, but Ormond was nonetheless confused and shouted out when he saw Lucas being bludgeoned, 'Why strike you him, he is one of our men?'[84] A panicked Lisle galloped back to the baggage train and 'carried all the Horse away' from the right wing, calling out (or so we are told by partisans of Ormond), '£10 for a guide to Duncannon. £20 for a guide to Duncannon'. Greenville clapped Lisle on the shoulder, calmed him down – 'Come my Lord we may yet recover it' – and led him back to the fray. Eight Irish horsemen cut their way as far as the artillery before being overwhelmed by foot soldiers to be killed or captured, except for Mac Thomas, who quietly slipped off his *súgán*, shouted, 'Let's follow the rogues', and galloped off in supposed pursuit.[85] The 'rude incensed soldiers' slaughtered Beverley Brittan, 'a valiant English gentleman', while Ormond, 'coming by chance that way', rescued Cullen from their 'violence and fury'.[86]

The main bodies of both armies stood motionless during this scuffle, but, when Lisle's horsemen were coaxed back to their proper positions, the Irish 'broke all to pieces, and they might be seen through the smoke of the gunpowder to run, twinkling like motes in the sunbeams'.[87] 'The Irish lost there the field, arms, lives, and honour.'[88] Yet Ormond did not resume his march, put off by the difficulty of crossing the Aughnacrew or by the menace of Hugh Mac Phelim O'Byrne's rearguard or by both.

The Irish had stopped Ormond's march deeper into County Wexford at the cost of 100 or 200 men, a light body count for a five-hour combat. Those cut down 'had their Gods in their bosoms and in their pockets', gloated one of Lisle's partisans.[89] He may have been mocking the scapular, a holy image contained in a brown cloth that hung under the shirt from the wearer's neck, which certainly did not purport to ward off deadly danger but to come into effect once, and once only, at the very moment of death (*in articulo mortis*). Later that same year, Pope Urban VIII's brief promised soldiers 'absolute remission for all their sins' if they died fighting 'against the

---

83 Margaret Cavendish, *The Life of William Cavendish, Duke of Newcastle: To Which is Added the True Relation of My Birth, Breeding, and Life* (London: John C. Nimmo, 1886), p.285.
84 Martin Doyle, *Notes and Gleanings Relating to the County of Wexford in Its Past and Present Conditions* (Dublin: George Herbert, 1868), pp.164, 166.
85 Gilbert (ed.), *Contemporary History*, vol. I, p.62.
86 Gilbert (ed.), *Irish Confederation*, vol. I, p.132.
87 Gardiner, *Great Civil War*, vol. 1, p.134; Gilbert (ed.), *Irish Confederation*, vol. II, pp.248, 252, 256–67; Carte, *History of the Life of James Duke of Ormonde*, vol. I, p.405; Miller, 'Battle of Ross', pp.148–49.
88 Gilbert (ed.), *Contemporary History*, vol. I, p.62; Gilbert (ed.), *Irish Confederation*, vol. I, pp.131–32 and vol. II, pp.256–58.
89 P. H. Hore (ed.), *History of the Town and County of Wexford: Comprised Principally from the State Papers, the Public Records, and Mss. of the Late Herbert F. Hore, Esq., of Pole Hore, in that County. Old and New Ross* (London: Elliot Stock, 1900), p.308.

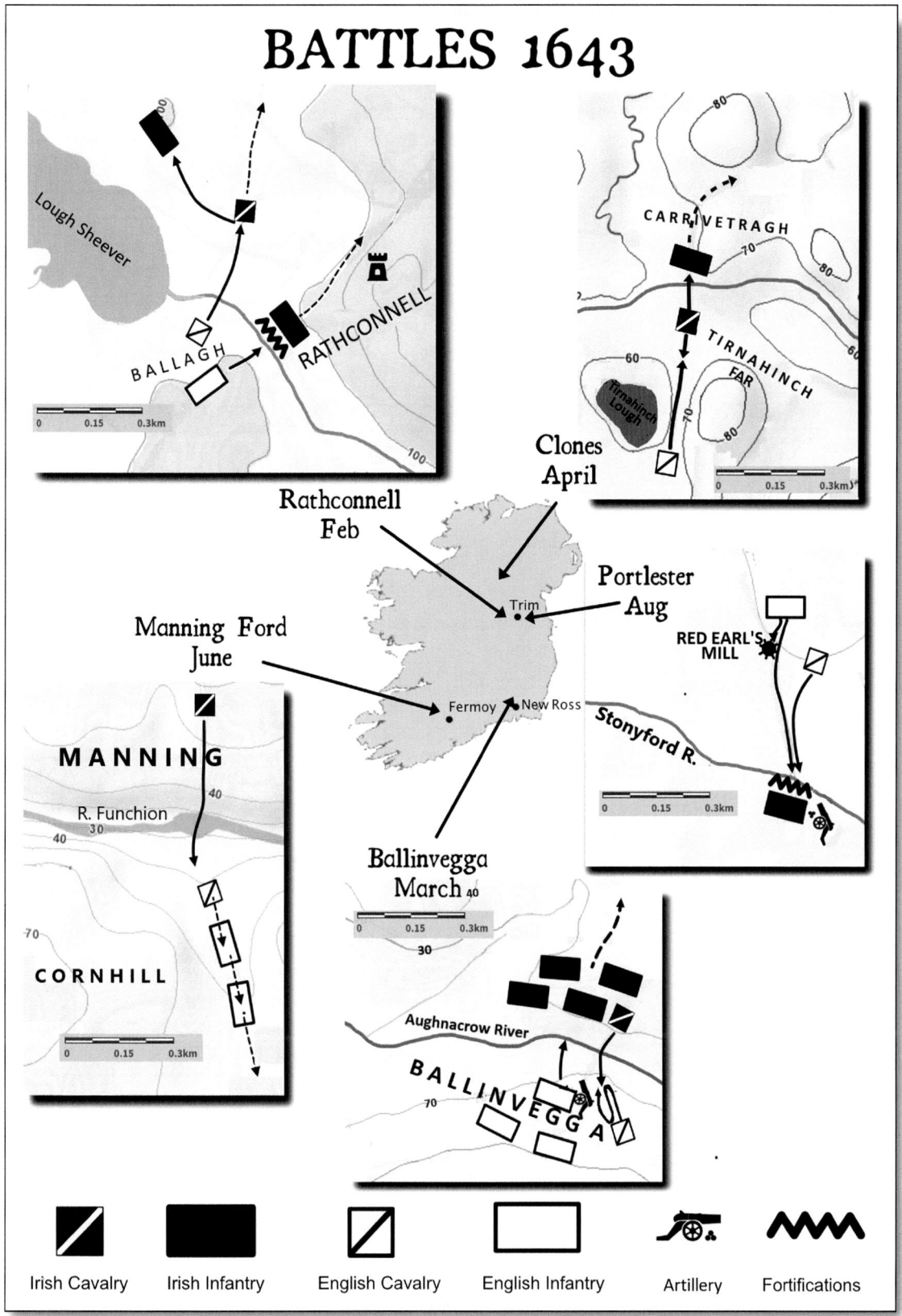

Rathconnell, Ballinvegga, Clones, Manning Ford and Portlester. (Kevin Glynn)

Heretics', provided they had confessed, were 'truly and sincerely penitent' and had received communion.[90]

The dead included 'several brave gentlemen', but 'few of common soldiers as not appearing in the field'.[91] The English admitted to losing 20 at most. But bare numbers do not tell the full story. Those who were killed were 'commanders and gentlemen of very good quality' who would be missed.[92] The common man, so far as we can judge, was not as committed to the Catholic cause as his officer from the gentry, and so, when he was listed in a company and a pike or musket thrust into his hand, he did not suddenly tap into unsuspected depths of zeal or steadiness. He could subsist on poor food, march improbably long distances, shoot from behind a ditch or rampart and throw himself, skeane in hand, into a fast and furious charge. Irish accounts, written of course by members of the gentry class, intimate that the common soldiery lacked the steadiness to stand their ground when plans did not survive contact with the enemy. Consider Ballinvegga. Ormond's centre did not waver even when the right flank was suddenly and unsettlingly exposed. The English foot soldier was no more ideologically driven than his Irish counterpart, but he showed more skill and will and usually held his ground, even in adversity. In contrast, most of the Irish infantry melted away once their own cavalry had been seen to be worsted. These are not racialist generalizations like the 'Celtic' stereotype of the hardy and brave but impulsive and emotional Irish soldier of the Victorian era. Their fragility has another explanation.

Soldiers in battles of pike and shot were peculiarly interdependent. A musketeer who had fired his shot was horribly vulnerable to cavalrymen, and a hedgehog of pikes wielded by steady men was good at keeping horsemen at a respectful distance but little else. A broken square was much less than the sum of its parts. The soldiers had to work together, and their regimental square demanded both internal cohesion within the regiment and external cohesion to the extent of trusting that other regiments would play their part. Ormond's regiments, debilitated and battered as they were, had now messed, drilled and fought side by side for a year. Familiarity and service bred trust, which was only now beginning to shred as their officers began to coalesce into bitterly hostile Royalist and Parliamentary factions. They were an army.

In contrast, the companies that were bundled into Preston's makeshift regiments at Ballinvegga did not yet constitute an army. Castlehaven remarked that, in combat, 'our parties had commonly the better, yet our army had always the worst', by which he meant that Irish armies fared better in the low-intensity fighting called 'war by parties' or 'small war' ('*guerrilla*' in Spanish) rather than battles.[93]

---

90 Anon., *The Whole triall of Connor Lord Macguire* (London: Robert Austin, 1645), p.22.
91 Gilbert (ed.), *Irish Confederation*, vol. I, p.130 and vol. II, p.258; Anon., *The late prosperous proceedings*; Anon., *Truth from Ireland expressed in Two Letters* (London: John Wright, 1643); Miller, 'Battle of Ross', pp.149–50.
92 Verney, *Memoirs*, vol. II, p.139.
93 Gregory Hanlon, *European Military Rivalry, 1500–1750: Fierce Pageant* (Abingdon-on-Thames: Routledge, 2020), p.204; Lynch (ed.), *Castlehaven's Memoirs*, p.67.

Why? 'Of all conduct none is worse than to lose an army without drawing them to fight and to second one another'. The specific criticism here is of Ormond's conduct at the siege of Rathmines (1649), where an advanced guard was defeated while most of his soldiers stood 'gaping on till they were routed without fighting'.[94] But this exact shortcoming arose at Kilrush, Liscarroll and Ballinvegga under three different Catholic generals. Maybe the generals simply could not coordinate actions by different components of an army in conditions of noise, smoke, uncertainty and fear and never launched the opportunistic infantry charge, so successful in smaller actions like Clonakilty. Or maybe winning larger battles demanded a cohesive, articulated corps of men obeying commands: in short, an army.

Musketeer. *(Jacques II de Castlenau, Le Marechal de Bataille* (Paris: Etienne Migon, 1647), p.7) (Author's collection)

Ormond now veered north to Poulmounty. The bulk of Preston's army raced ahead of him, not to block the pass but to cross the Barrow at Graiguenamanagh on a bridge of wooden beams spanning five stone pillars. Preston burned the spans in case Ormond decided to lunge at Kilkenny, and he tracked Ormond's march north from the opposite bank of the Barrow. The operation as a whole – march, sieges and battle – was a strategic defeat for Ormond because his army was 'so enfeebled, as he was not able to make any considerable excursions in half a year after'.[95]

So debilitated was Ormond that, after only a fortnight's pause, Preston could 'raise another army' and sit down unhindered before Ballinakill for the best part of two months.[96] He is credited with having twice as many troops at Ballinakill (up to 4,000 foot soldiers and seven troops of cavalry) as he had at Birr. The regiments of Edmund Rua Butler and Sir James Dillon were there, so too was Preston's own regiment, led by Patrick or Richard Plunkett, who probably replaced Diego Preston, taken prisoner at Rathconnell. Fairly

---

94 Hogan (ed.), *History of the Warr of Ireland*, p.83.
95 Walter Enos, *Second part of the survey of the articles of the late rejected peace* (Kilkenny: Publisher unknown, 1646), p.92.
96 Lynch (ed.), *Castlehaven's Memoirs*, p.51.

continuous service and organizational continuity would knock Butler's and Dillon's into standing regiments by summer's end. Also present was a scattering of militia companies from Laois, brought by Ossory's brother and by Brian O'Dempsey.[97]

Built as an English colony drawn to the backwoods by the abundant supply of wood for iron works, Ballinakill's dwellings and workshops sheltered 900 men, women and children while the keep, manned by about 200 men, was a solid five-storey-high tower surrounded by a 'strong stone wall and that with turrets and flankers' and bastioned rampart and wet ditch deepened and thickened over many months into a place 'impregnable' for a besieger 'without siege guns'.[98]

On 2 April, the besiegers set up camp in the park to the east, unlimbered an eight-pounder on Warren Hill and fired on the brewhouse near the north-east bastion of the outworks. At a range of 300 yards, such light shot could have no impact on solid walls, though one ball punched a hole in the roof and killed an unlucky girl. On 4 April, Preston's men captured a tan house. Ridgeway's men counterattacked, and the Irish 'betook to their heels', leaving 14 dead men, 13 muskets and 30 pikes behind them. The same day, Captain Thomas Tyrrell of County Westmeath led a 'fierce assault' on the outer perimeter. Maybe Tyrrell volunteered so that he could keep his promise to 'sweep all the English out of Ireland as clean as Saint Patrick ever swept the venomous worms', or perhaps he had been chosen by lot for this hazardous service.[99] He was shot dead, and his head was hacked off and displayed on top of the tholsel in an act of calculated barbarity that can only be understood in the brutalizing context of a long leaguer. Some months earlier, a party of Ballinakill's soldiers and civilians sent to gather corn was attacked, and the soldiers were 'forced to leave the women to the cruelty of the enemy where many of them were slain'.[100]

Assault had not worked, and, from 12 April, the besiegers settled down to the more laborious method of cutting trenches towards the castle and town. An old Flanders hand like Preston might be bewildered by the tempo and unpredictability of battle, but this business he knew very well indeed. Every day, his sappers dug 'nearer and nearer' to the outer wall, throwing up trenches and piling up fascines (tightly bound bundles of sticks) as cover from fire. Within a matter of days, they had cut off the main water supply and reached the eastern perimeter before tunnelling under a turret. Meanwhile, however, Ballinakill's defenders had dug a countermine and broken into the gallery. For two hours, they fired muskets and pistols into stygian blackness, broke down the pit props and 'disappointed them of their purpose in blowing us up'. Breaking the props may have actually caused the turret to subside, but

---

97 TCDL: 1641 Depositions, MS 814 (County Offaly), fol. 211v: Deposition of Chidley Coote and MS 815 (County Laois), fols 230r: Deposition of Ellenor Keys, 308r–12v: Deposition of John Carpenter, 319r: Deposition of Roger Comberlidge, 363r: Deposition of John Tucker, 363v: Deposition of Captain Richard Steele *et al.*
98 Gilbert (ed.), *Irish Confederation*, vol. I, pp.149–50.
99 TCDL: 1641 Depositions, MS 814 (County Dublin), fol. 248r: Deposition of John Holmsted and MS 814 (County Offaly), fol. 178v: Deposition of Henrie Aylyffe.
100 TCDL: 1641 Depositions, MS 815 (County Laois), fol. 384r: Examination of James Hobb.

Preston could do no more because he had lost his chief gunner, shot through the eye. The guns fell silent, and the attack stalled for a fortnight.[101]

James Talbot the Irish agent at the court of Philip IV had bought siege guns and mortars which were -by dumb luck- unloaded at Dungarvan during that fortnight's intermission. The Irish could mill small batches of gunpowder but had no skill in gun-founding, such expertise being confined to the settler community, specifically to Boyle's works at Cappoquin and Richard Blacknall's at Ballinakill.[102] Therefore, these guns were a game changer. One of the demi-cannons was hauled by alternating teams of 28 oxen (stolen from Ormond's army in the retreat from Ballinvegga) to Ballinakill. It fired a 25-pounder shot, a huge step up from the eight-pounder. Preston contrived to set up a battery in secret, and it came as a nasty shock when he pounded the staircase of the castle from five o'clock in the morning until two in the afternoon on 4 May and opened a hole in the wall.

'A mortar shooting upon a castle'. (Anon., *The Compleat Gunner* (London: E. Tyler and R. Holt, 1672), p.89)

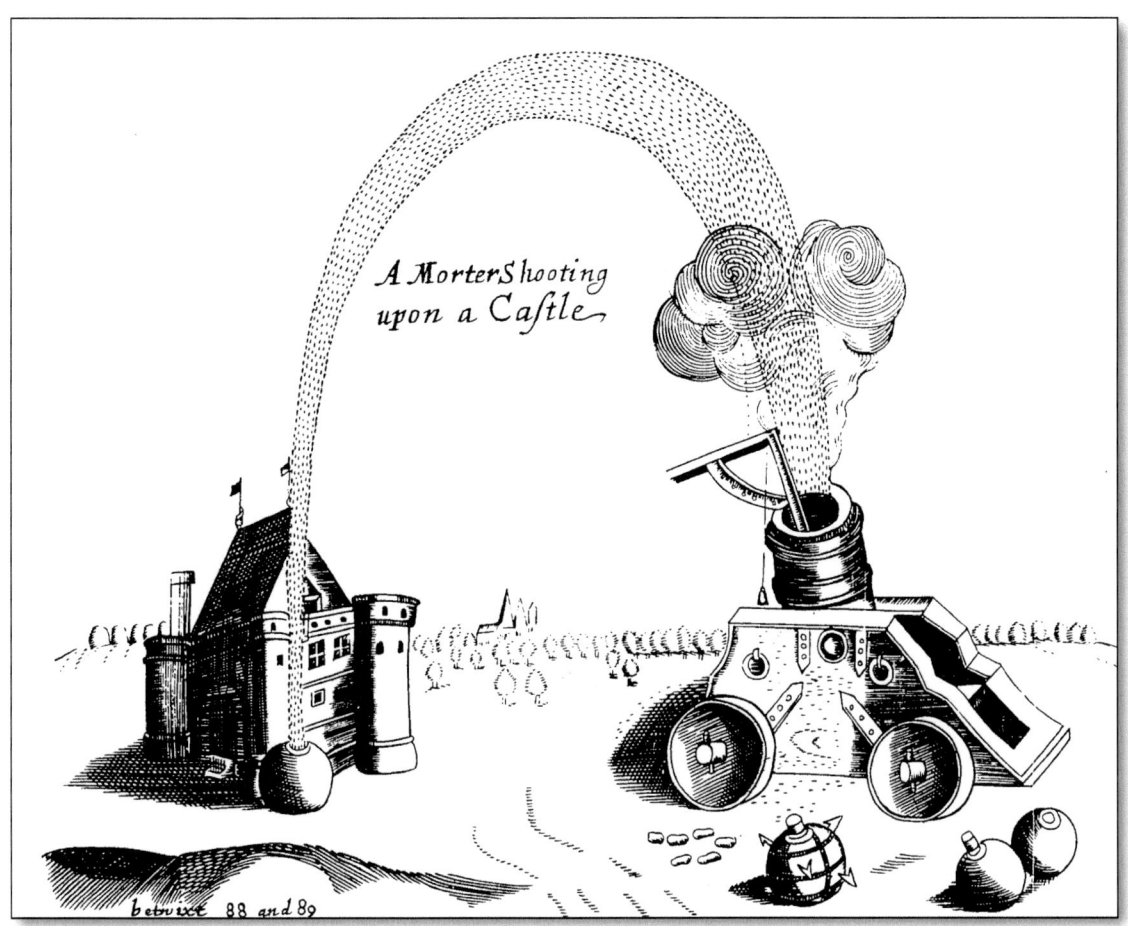

---

101 TCDL: 1641 Depositions, MS 815 (Queens County), fol. 358v: Deposition of Captain Richard Steele *et al*.
102 B. G. Scott, R. R. Brown, A. G. Leacock, and C. J. Salter, *The Great Guns like Thunder: The Cannon from the City of Derry* (Derry: Guildhall Hall Press, 2009), p.31.

Preston's Spanish mortar also lobbed incendiary bombs of the kind described lovingly in Barry's *Discourse* as 'excellent to burn towns'.[103] The mortar was 'a late invention' (this was the first time mortars were fired in Ireland) and threw the projectile in a high parabola: 'Nothing gives greater terror to the Towns-people of a Besieged Town, than Bombes; and the ravage that there they do is so extraordinary, and so gall Men, Women, and Children, that they know not where to be in safety'.[104] The idiomatic phrase to 'drop a bombshell' recalls the shock of this terror weapon. The women of Ballinakill 'cried out with every shot', and with their cries ringing in his ears, Captain Ridgeway turned to worrying about 'the multitude of people which were thronged together' in so little space. With the beat of a drum, Ridgeway offered to parley, 'protesting that he would not have the blood of so many Innocents fall upon his head, and that if he had been as well stored with valiant and Lusty Men as he was with women and children he would not have surrendered the Castle so Long as one stone would have lain upon another'.[105] Preston's officers counted 735 persons coming out, down from an estimated 900 a year earlier, 'the rest being slain and dead by sickness'.[106]

---

103 Gerat Barry, *A discourse of military discipline devided into three boockes* ... (Brussels: John Mommart, 1634), p.196; Brian G. Scott, 'The Deployment of Mortars in Ireland up to the 1689 Siege of Londonderry', *Ulster Journal of Archaeology*, 3rd Series, 73 (2015–2016), pp.205, 209, 215.
104 Anon., *A treatise of the arms and engines of vvar of fire-works, ensigns, and military instruments, both ancient and modern; with the manner they are at present used, as well in French armies, as amongst other nations. Inriched with many figures* (London: Robert Hartford, 1678), p.90.
105 Gilbert (ed.), *Contemporary History*, vol. I, p.122.
106 TCDL: 1641 Depositions, MS 815 (Queens County), fol. 312r: Deposition of John Carpenter.

4

Summer 1643

As late as May 1643, Ormond was still upbeat and marvelling at 'how few places of importance, or great acts have been performed' by the Irish 'notwithstanding the distractions of England'.[1] But the Irish in three provinces were more than holding their own. In the fourth, raids on the Irish quarters in Ulster, from the north, west and east, proved unrelenting. The most notable attack was made by Robert Monro, who set out 'to touch the enemy's pulse' and, on 13 May, reached Tandragee, driving out an Irish garrison. Monro next chose to pay a surprise visit to Eoghan Rua's paternal home at Summer Island, four miles east of Charlemont. Monro's outriders blundered into O'Neill while he was abroad hunting, probably near Loughgall, a name that crops up often in the dismal history of the sectarian cockpit that was County Armagh. Loughgall was the site of the Battle of the Diamond in 1795, birthplace of the Orange Order and scene of a bloody ambush during an IRA (Irish Republican Army) attack on a police barracks in 1987.

But back to 1643. Monro's 'terrified' horsemen were 'shamefully chased back' and ran down Monro's vanguard of foot, led by Major James Turner, which was moving along cautiously on a narrow road in 'very close country'.[2] Turner brandished a pike and reproached the fleeing horsemen, 'Fay, fay, run awa frae awheen rebels', before he began to regroup and:

> … advanced towards the enemy whom I could not see, he having sheltered himself with 1,500 fixed musketeers in enclosures, ditches and hedges; yet he made me quickly know where he was, by a salvo of 4 or 500 shot he made at me, at which some of my men fell. I then made a stand, and lined the hedges on all sides of me, constantly firing from them, and advancing still on the highway, though very leisurely.[3]

---

1 Burke, *Memoirs and Letters of Ulick*, p.399, 'Ormond to Clanricard, Dublin Castle, 11 May 1643'.
2 Stevenson, *Scottish Covenanters and Irish Confederates*, p.131; Turner, *Memoirs of His Own Life*, p.28; Gilbert (ed.), *Contemporary History*, vol. III, part 2, p.199; Ó Donnchadha, 'Cín lae', p.19.
3 Stevenson, *Scottish Covenanters and Irish Confederates*, p.131; Turner, *Memoirs of His Own Life*, p.28.

O'Neill's steady Spanish veterans loosed a well-timed salvo, which held Turner up for an hour before reinforcements came up and Turner's men began to hew and hack gaps in the quickset hedges along the roadside. Seeing his men 'began to look over their shoulders', O'Neill made for Charlemont and swept up 'the country people, with near 3,000 cows'.[4] His delaying action had saved the creaghts and had given Phelim time to carry off stores and weapons just hours before the Scots torched Summer Island. Turner admitted to losing 15 men, while an Irish source insists that Eoghan Rua withdrew his 400 men (a more likely figure than Turner's) 'without the loss of a man'.[5] Eoghan Rua did not pay the price for careless reconnaissance this time. Monro's main body withdrew to Tandragee. If he had planned on attacking Charlemont, he was dissuaded by the usual shortages of food and munitions and by Phelim's lieutenant colonel Tom Sanfort, who cut off upwards of 100 Scottish reivers near the shores of Lough Neagh.

Taking the slightly longer view, however, this no-name 'scuffle' was a setback for Eoghan Rua. Gone were his hopes of holding the sadly misnamed Oneilland as a resource base for his little army. No sooner did Monro retire than Chichester's 'Old British' forces, numbering over 2,000 men, linked up with a party from Dundalk and ranged at will through Counties Armagh, Monaghan and Cavan, 'preying all before them'.[6] Next, it was the Laggan army's turn.

Maestre de campo in the tercio of John O'Neill, Earl of Tyrone, (who had been killed at Barcelona in January 1641) and now lieutenant general to Eoghan Rua, Donal Geimhleach ('of the fetters') O'Cahan was so called because he had been conceived while his father, the last O'Cahan chieftain, was imprisoned in the Tower of London. On 4 May, the Laggan army raided for cattle up the Clogher Valley, and this 'Hector in arms' carried out a solo reconnaissance of the enemy camp near Aughnacloy, 'not trusting any body that day with that office'. He was surprised by five Laggan horsemen:

> Finding himself between two armies, O'Cahan spurred his horse which then fell. The horse would not lift its head and O'Cahan was taken prisoner before he could get it to stand up. The swiftness of their steeds bore the troop of horsemen away. Seeing this, Sir Phelim vowed they would not let O'Cahan be taken from them. They set off in pursuit. A Scots horseman fired a shot through O'Cahan's head and he fell to the ground, dead. They took his mount and weapons.[7]

Around now, we read of outright famine afflicting the natives. As late as 31 May 1643, Eoghan Rua, as general of the field army, solemnly promised President Phelim that he would not abandon the province. But no sooner had Phelim left for Kilkenny two days later than Eoghan Rua ordered the creaghts to make for County Longford with his army as their escort.[8] The symbiosis of army and creaght would be a distinctive feature of the Ulster

---

4 Gilbert (ed.), *Contemporary History*, vol. III, p.199.
5 Gilbert (ed.), *Contemporary History*, vol. III, p.199.
6 Carte, *History of the Life of James Duke of Ormonde*, vol. I, p.432; Ó Donnchadha, 'Cín lae', p.19.
7 Gilbert (ed.), *Contemporary History*, vol. I, p.52; Ó Donnchadha, 'Cín lae', p.18.
8 Ó Donnchadha, 'Cín lae', p.20; Gilbert (ed.), *Contemporary History*, vol. III, p.199.

army from now on. The 'creaght' (*Caoraidheacht* is defined by Dineen as 'cattle and their caretaker') was a horde of civilians – far in excess of the usual number of camp followers – and their cattle herds. These were refugees from that arc of territory from County Armagh right around to County Fermanagh closest to, or in, enemy quarters. They could not or would not buy protection by paying contributions, and constant *chevauchée* forced them to leave their homes and growing crops and to drive their herds to whatever grazing land they could find. At first, the idea was that they would wander for the summer and return home to gather the harvest and shelter for the winter, but, for most of them, wartime wandering would become a way of life. Eoghan Rua's marches from now on would be dictated by the search for pastures green.

The Ulster army and creaght were symbiotic but distinct. O'Mellan spoke of 'lords of the creaghts' (*tighernaidh na gcroidheacht*) as distinct from the colonels and captains of the army. The creaght headman's following was familial and local: Patrick Modarra O'Donnelly explained that 'his own poor [under]tenants and followers' made up his creaght. The headman was older than the typical officer: Tuathail Mac Cann was 40 years old in 1643, for instance, and Phelim O'Quinn was 44. He seldom doubled as an officer. O'Quinn was adamant (admittedly while trying to wriggle out of complicity in war crimes) that 'he never had command of soldiers but of men in his creatts who were under his command by directions from Sir Phelemy O neille, who gave every head of creatts orders to keep their men about them to be upon their guard to prevent stealth and to preserve themselves'.[9]

Hearing of O'Neill's march, Sir Robert Stewart led the Laggan Army and reinforcements from Enniskillen (some 3,000 men all told) to block the route and reached Clones first, on 13 June. The natives in County Fermanagh had not given O'Neill the expected 'timely notice', and he was warned only at the last moment that the enemy fast closing on his straggling herds and hordes 'of men, women and children' where 'nothing could be seen or heard but Cows or running'.[10] Stewart recounted how O'Neill, in person, promptly led 'a party of their best Horse very well mounted, which in a daring insulting way came up and charged some of my Troop, which they received very resolutely'.[11] A running fight erupted along the 800 yards of track running south to Clones, sloughing along the 'Cassey' over a stream and squeezing by Tirnahinch Lough.[12] According to Henry O'Neill:

> At this time O'Neill had not above one thousand six hundred men fit for any service, and many of them dispersed amongst the creaghts; but what of them were to the fore, were drawn up upon the enemy's moving towards them, the foot placed at a pass, the general himself with what horse (being only a couple of new-

---

9 TCDL: 1641 Depositions, MS 836, fol. 238r: Examination of Phelemy O Quin and MS 838 (County Tyrone), fol. 43r: Examination of Patrick Modder ô Donnelly; Ó Donnchadha, 'Cín lae', p.31.
10 Gilbert (ed.), *Contemporary History*, vol. III, pp.200–02; Ó Donnchadha, 'Cín lae', pp.20–25; Hogan (ed.), *History of the Warr of Ireland*, p.29.
11 Anon., *Another extract of more letters sent out of Ireland, informing the condition of the kingdome as it now stands* (London: Publisher unknown, 1643), p.9, 'Robert Stewart to the Earl of Eglington, Culmore, 23 June 1643'.
12 P. B. Ó Mórdha, 'The Battle of Clones, 1643', *Clogher Record*, 4:3 (1962), pp.148–54.

raised troops and some gentlemen) made forwards to take a view of the enemy's strength, and before they could well retire, the enemy charged them in the rear (almost mad drunk with usquebaugh) crying aloud, 'Whar's Mc Art! Whar's Mc Art!' (meaning the general) when one captain Stewart, with that hussa in his mouth, came up before the general, as he was entering on a narrow causeway, where O'Neill himself shot him off his horse …[13]

O'Neill's horsemen had crossed the ford to buy time for Lieutenant Colonel Shane O'Neill to scrape together enough men to block the pass. But the horsemen were forced to turn tail by weight of superior numbers and were overtaken. Eoghan Rua escaped the mêlée because Shane pushed forwards to rescue the hapless riders, yet the old general heaped blame on Shane for the 'disorder and confusion' that followed when Stewart sent 'commanded men', or musketeers, to shoot their way across the causeway. The musketeers drove Shane's vanguard back and harried them so much that 'they broke in upon the second battalia of their own army'.[14] Eoghan Rua was left alone on the battlefield but for his son Henry and four other horsemen. P. S. breathlessly recounted pistol shooting worthy of Rooster Cogburn:

> … four enemy troops followed him, they all as swift as their horse could run the general espied after him, one only horse, the rest a good distance behind, advising his son to draw on turned himself on that enemy horse, passed him through with a brace of bullets, then followed he his own, the next cut was for his son Henry, who turning in the like manner on a single horse, fell him dead to the ground; 5 or 6 did the general and his son kill of the pursuing enemy successively: two or 3 miles they followed in this pastime, at length the enemy turned back, and left those poor men wandering in mountains and bogs that night.[15]

By morning, the fugitives reached the drumlin country around Brantry Friary, where steep hills pressed close like a basket of eggs. O'Neill wrote to Stewart that very day enquiring about prisoner exchange or ransom:

> Sir,
> I Should entreat you to be pleased for to certify unto me by this bearer what prisoners you have taken or have in restraint of ours since the other day, together with your demands, whether you will exchange them for any Prisoners we have, or if for Ransom, how much, wherein you shall do me a curtesy, and to yourself no hurt, for now though Fortune be favourable unto you, it may chance fall out hereafter, that your kindness and favour therein may be requited, if ever it comes in the way of
> Your assured Friend as I find you Owen ô Neale.
> From our Camp the 16 of June, 1643.[16]

---

13   Gilbert (ed.), *Contemporary History*, vol. III, pp.200–02.
14   Gilbert (ed.), *Contemporary History*, vol. III, p.202.
15   Gilbert (ed.), *Contemporary History*, vol. I, p.49.
16   Bodleian Library (BoL) Carte MS 6, fols 99–100: Sir William Stewart to Ormond, Culmore, 19 July 1643.

To describe a handful of riders as a 'Camp' was a stretch, but O'Neill had to keep what shreds of dignity he could. 'It was thought that Ulster would never recover' from such a 'crushing blow', the heaviest suffered by the Ulster army until its annihilation in 1650.[17] Stewart's horsemen were able to harry the fleeing Irish for eight miles, picking up 'great store' of discarded weapons, cutting down at least 150 men and taking half a dozen officers prisoner. Only six of Stewart's men were killed. The normally deadpan O'Mellan concluded his account of Clones with an anguished outburst: '*Och, och, is bocht!*' (Och, Och, for sorrow!)[18] The loss of the veteran officers and soldiers was irreplaceable. Moreover, many of the scattered and unprotected creaghts were killed over the following days. At length, Stewart withdrew to the Laggan, having no interest in maintaining a permanent presence in the middle of the province:

> We have made so many marches this Summer into Donegal, Tyrone and Londonderry, that there is little or no provisions left in the Country, and few or no Rogues to be seen, all either killed or fled into Connought, but great store of women and children, whereof few Cabins in our march was empty, in some 5, in some 10 and in some 20 found dead in a Cabin, part of them eaten by the living …[19]

The debris of Clones clustered at Mohill, County Leitrim, where O'Neill held out against pressure from the gentlemen (*maithibh*) of Ulster to return home and reap what corn they could. His overriding strategic imperative was to keep moving to pastures across the Shannon. A camp near the hostile garrison of Jamestown on the Shannon guarded Brian Maguire's creaght, but the sentinels were caught unawares by a dawn raid, not from Jamestown but from the opposite direction, whence Robert King had drawn men from the many English garrisons scattered thereabouts.

Yet again, O'Neill's intelligence had let him down, and he had not reckoned with the danger posed by enemy riders, who now dominated the maghery that extended from Roscommon Castle to Boyle and bled imperceptibly into County Mayo. Prudently, O'Neill slipped back across the Shannon.

Ceding the maghery of Connacht was one of the many symptoms of a provincial malaise. After Ballintober, Viscount Mayo had evidently chosen to do no more than watch his county's bounds. In August 1642, for instance, he had encamped at Shrule in case Forbes marched into County Mayo and demanded that Lucas Taaffe send his County Sligo troops, all 300 of them, to join his hosting. Taaffe refused because he faced a 'greater danger' on his doorstep from Manorhamilton.[20] Just a month earlier, Frederick Hamilton had sacked Sligo Town, burnt the Dominican abbey, killed two friars as they ran out of the blazing building, thrashed 'all their superstitious trumperies'

---

17 Gilbert (ed.), *Contemporary History*, vol. I, p.49; Ó Donnchadha, 'Cín lae', p.20.
18 Ó Donnchadha, 'Cín lae', p.20.
19 Anon., *Another extract of more letters sent out of Ireland*, p.12, 'Henry Finch, Derry, 20 June 1643'.
20 Anon., *The information of Sir Frederick Hammilton, Knight, and Colonell, given to the Committee of Both Kingdoms, concerning Sir William Cole, Knight, and Colonell; with the scandalous answer of the said Sir William Cole, Knight* … (London: Publisher unknown, 1645), pp.21, 66.

and 'destroyed that night near 300 souls by fire, sword and drowning, to God's everlasting great honour and glory'.[21] However, Mayo was unimpressed by Taaffe's excuses and made good on his threat not to help in the future.[22] As if this were not bad enough, on 12 March 1643, Taaffe sent his lieutenant colonel and brother-in-law Brian Mac Donagh to arrest Tadhg O'Connor Sligo and others because they 'do daily commit several incursions, massacres, robberies, outrages and many other enormities and pillages within the County of Sligo'.[23] Among the outrages listed was the Sligo gaol massacre of 13 January 1642, when two of O'Connor's younger brothers gathered a dozen other 'dissolute villains' and 'Owltaghs', or Ulstermen 'banished and driven out of the north of Ireland upon their rebellion', and murdered 20 Protestant prisoners.[24]

The main fissure in the Confederate Catholics is usually thought to have opened between the Old English and Gaelic Irish, but deeper suspicions were felt by those who had recently owned landed estates towards their countrymen who had been spared expropriation. In most other places, religious solidarity papered over these cracks, but not in Connacht and still less in Sligo, perhaps due to O'Connor's alliance with refugees from Ulster and Leitrim who did not, for one reason or another, trust the Confederate Catholic authorities.[25]

The luckless County Sligo regiment is well documented because it was defeated near Manorhamilton on 1 April 1643 and Mac Donagh was killed. When Hamilton's men went through his pockets, they found a run of correspondence about pay, provisioning and morale.[26] To contain Hamilton's rampages, Taaffe's men had camped at Creevelea Abbey, near Dromahair Castle. On the morning of 29 March, Hamilton's men took 400 cattle from Creevelea, killing two Irishmen and losing no one in the action. Taaffe wrote to Mac Donogh for reinforcements, and a letter from the lieutenant of Mac Donogh's own company reinforces Taaffe's orders:

> … he doth desire your own speedy repair hither; and without you send for all your men upon sight hereof, and give them straight charge to be here this night with us, you will otherwise be ashamed forever, seeing we are called upon speedy service: For my own part, I thought you did regard the loss of me more than thus, to leave me here all this while unappointed with Soldiers and Ammunition; for without Gods great help, I had never come off alive from the last mornings service we had with Manor Hamilton's Soldiers: I pray you as you love your own

---

21 Anon., *Colonell Sir Frederick Hammiltons return from London-Derry*, p.31.
22 Anon., *Colonell Sir Frederick Hammiltons return from London-Derry*, pp.57, 63.
23 TCDL: 1641 Depositions, MS 831 (County Sligo), fol. 135r: Examination of Francis Taaffe.
24 TCDL: 1641 Depositions, MS 831 (County Mayo), fol. 187r: Deposition of Henry Bringhurst and MS 831 (County Sligo), fols 60r: Deposition of Edward Braxton, 65r, 65v: Deposition of William Walsh, 135r: Examination of Francis Taaffe; Hickson, *Ireland in the Seventeenth Century*, vol. I, p.395.
25 Mary O'Dowd, *Power, Politics, and Land: Early Modern Sligo, 1568-1688* (Belfast: Institute of Irish Studies, Queen's University of Belfast, 1991), p.128.
26 TCDL: 1641 Depositions, MS 831 (County Sligo), fols 60r: Deposition of Edward Braxton, 65v: Deposition of William Walsh.

credit and my life, send me the rest of the Soldiers; otherwise, if you will let me go upon service without them, by Christ I will never be an Officer under your command more …²⁷

Cormac Mac Donogh's letter discloses a regiment that was understrength, hungry, short of arms (with just eight shot for a company of 100 men), almost out of gunpowder, truculent and dispirited.

Brian Mac Donagh arrived soon after this mutinous missive was written and set off the very next day to wreak revenge on Manorhamilton. He marched at the head of a column of six companies, two each from three of the county's six baronies, making (if the companies were up to strength) 600 men. In the vanguard was Brian Mac Donagh's company and that of Cormac O'Hara. The second division was led by Sergeant Major Tadgh Reagh O'Dowd and Brian O'Hara, and the rearguard comprised the companies of Brian Mac Sweeney and Roger O'Connor. To extrapolate from Mac Donagh's own company, the whole column would have had less than 50 musketeers. Hamilton spotted the column 'marching in a loose body' two miles from Manorhamilton and pulled his foot soldiers back behind a 'ditch for all out musketeers to play out of'. At the first volley, Mac Donagh's men ran off in a 'disorderly and confused retreat', leaving their commander mortally wounded behind them to 'fight upon his knees'. The runaways bunched up at a ford on a stream, where Hamilton's men cut down 60 of them.[28]

Fortunately for the Sligo men, Hamilton's rampages began to wind down. In May, he took cattle from near Grange Castle, now occupied by Hugh O'Gallagher, who had been 'chased out of Ulster'. On his return march, he fought Manus O'Donnell and 'left stripped upon the Fields, above threescore of naked Bodies', though at the cost of many 'sore wounded'.[29] All the while, Hamilton's numbers were falling from the cumulative attrition of small war, from sickness and, above all, from men running away to William Cole's garrison at Enniskillen: Hamilton was insufferable, to enemy, friend and underling. He persuaded John Cunningham of south Donegal to join the Manorhamilton garrison in a 1,000-strong raiding party into County Sligo. They burnt many 'poor country villages', but Cunningham did not find the booty that Hamilton had promised in this devastated country and returned home.[30]

Mac Donogh's letter leaches despair that must have percolated throughout north Connacht and explains the pitiful Catholic war effort there. In south Connacht, however, things were looking up at last. An uneasy accommodation that Clanricarde had brokered between Galway City and the English garrison on Forthill lasted throughout the latter half of 1642 and the early weeks of 1643. The fort was hardly more than a stone's throw from the town walls, which was too close for comfort when Captain Willoughby,

---

27   Anon., *Colonell Sir Frederick Hammiltons return from London-Derry*, p.45.
28   Anon., *Colonell Sir Frederick Hammiltons return from London-Derry*, p.45.
29   Anon., *Information of Sir Frederick Hammilton*, p.51.
30   Burke, *Memoirs and Letters of Ulick*, p.434, 'Viscount Taaffe to Earl of Clanricard, Glinsk, 19 August 1643'.

commander of the fort, was wont, among other aggravations, to fire off his guns into the town. A renewed siege began on 28 February 1643 with the seizure of Clanricarde's castle at Claregalway, which had served Clanricarde as the base to cut off the beleaguerers of Forthill from their supplies. Such was not the case this time, as the 'principal gentlemen' of the north-eastern half of the county defected.[31] The bishop of Clonfert – in Clanricarde's own backyard – insisted in March 1643 that his flock was 'bound under pain of mortal sin to take the Oath of Association', and, soon after, the citizens of Galway announced their intention to join the 'common cause' of their countrymen and share 'their hazards, losses and dangers'. The general assembly that convened on 24 October 1642 had appointed John Bourke of County Mayo as lieutenant general of Connacht, having left the general's spot open for Clanricarde in case he accepted their invitations to assume command. After 'John of the Hill' (*Seán an tSléibhe*) Burke put men in Claregalway and Athenry, he still had 1,000 soldiers to besiege Forthill 'from afar', digging no approach saps but keeping the fort 'straightly besieged by land'. Willoughby sent 50 men by ship to raid for cattle in Connemara, west of the town, but 'they so dispersed themselves, being greedy of pillage, that the town sent out greater forces, met them in their return, killed eight, and took thirteen prisoners'. Short of provisions, Willoughby promptly sent off his ship to beg for help from Inchiquin.[32] At Inchiquin's urging, Richard Swanley, appointed by Parliament as 'Admiral of the Fleet on the Irish Coast', sent two ships in mid-May 'to lie before Galway, and to render to that fort all the help [they] possibly may'. The captain of the *Providence* reported on 8 June how he had come under fire from three guns that had been dismounted from the walls and redeployed in fortified 'bulwarks' on Mutton Island: '… they all three played upon me, and I was not idle with them; although like a bear in a stake, not able to come under sail, having spent thirty whole culverin of brass on them, I was forced to swing away some further distance'.[33]

After nightfall, the *Providence* sent in her longboats to slip supplies through to Willoughby, but the town's boats were waiting, and they were fired on from fortified promontories at Rintinane to the west and at Renmore ('*Rinn*' in Irish denotes a headland) on the eastern shore.[34] The captain confessed that there was now 'little probability' of relieving Willoughby in his 'great distress'.[35] Willoughby now offered to put his fort in Clanricarde's hands, but Bourke rebuffed the transparent delaying tactic and insisted that Willoughby capitulate, which he finally did on 20 June.

In the end, when Burke got down to it, the whole business took just six weeks. Technically, Bourke's siege was less sophisticated than Barry's at Limerick, in that he made no attempt to attack Forthill directly. Nevertheless, he faced a sea-borne threat and a menacing regional notable behind his back.

---

31 Carte, *History of the Life of James Duke of Ormonde*, vol. I, p.430; TCDL: 1641 Depositions, MS 830 (County Galway), fols 134r–35v: Deposition of William Hamond.
32 Burke, *Memoirs and Letters of Ulick*, pp.387, 389, 391.
33 Burke, *Memoirs and Letters of Ulick*, pp.406–07.
34 Hardiman, *History of Galway*, p.121.
35 Burke, *Memoirs and Letters of Ulick*, pp.406–07.

SUMMER 1643

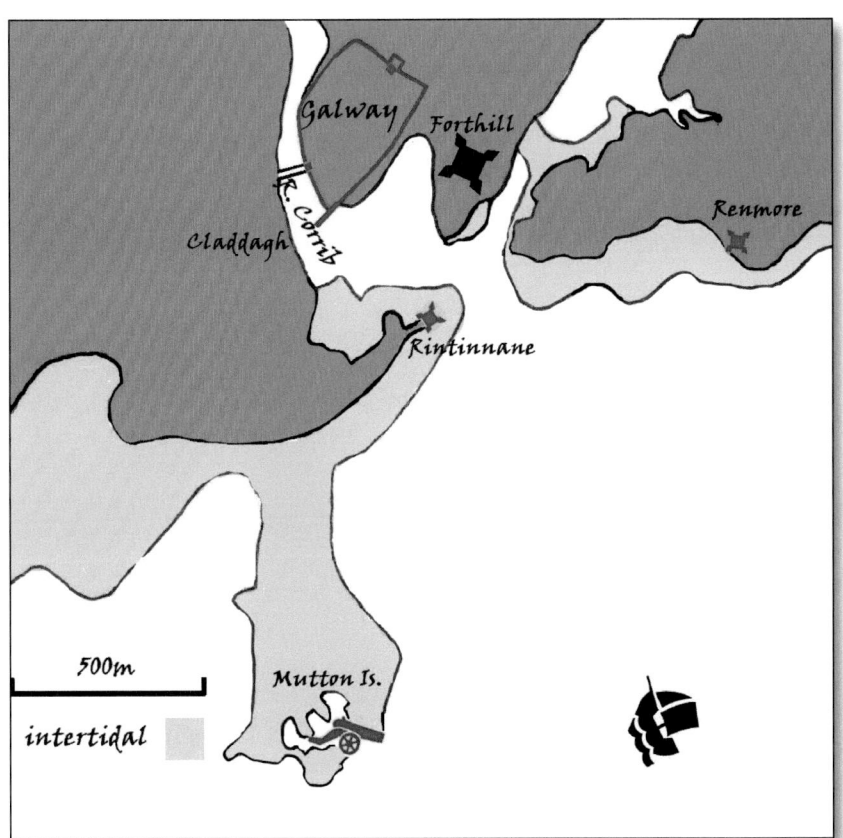

Siege of Galway Fort, May–June 1643. (Tomás Ó Brógáin)

Bourke's guns were properly sited, they hit their targets, and their barrels did not burst, all of which was to be expected from a veteran who knew his trade.

In contrast to Connacht, the Munster Catholics were very much on the back foot. By the summer of 1643, everyone had guessed that a ceasefire was coming and poked each other with sharp elbows for last-minute advantage. At the beginning of May, Inchiquin sent out his army in three columns – each of about 1,400 men, besides civilians, who traipsed along for the plunder – to range across Munster in divergent directions. In hindsight, this looks like overconfidence, but Inchiquin may have had to split his field army to live off the land. One column penetrated as far as Tralee, Inchiquin's own column was stalled at Buttevant, and the third, under Charles Vavasour, pushed through the gap between the Comeragh Mountains and the sea into the fat pasturelands of County Waterford. To check Vavasour, we are told that the Irish had cast up a breast-high barricade running from a wood under 'an exceeding high mountain' to an impassable bog, anchored by two 'courts of guard' to accommodate the shot. This was probably in the townland of Barnankile (*Bearna an Choill*), which might be translated as 'Woody Pass'. The 'barricade' was probably the embankment of a stream that flowed northeast for 1,400 yards from Corraun's shadow into a bog, and the two 'courts of guard' were corner bulwarks of Barnankile's bawn. Unseen in the thick fog, Vavasour's advance guard of dragoons surprised the defenders, and the rest poured through, 'fired the country', rounded up cattle and returned to Castlelyons.[36] But Vavasour pushed his luck too far when he planned to march by a track over the blanket bog and scrub of the Kilworth Mountains to Clogheen in the south-western nook of County Tipperary.

By now, Muskerry had lost confidence in the 'old and unfortunate' General Barry and persuaded the general assembly sitting at Kilkenny to send his 'great friend' Castlehaven to Munster and to hire some of the cavaliers who had come to town for the conviviality of the parliamentary season.[37] Castlehaven scraped together a troop of 80 horsemen under Garret Talbot, the same man who had claimed his band were 'Queen's Soldiers'.[38] Refugee Palesmen like Talbot would be the ones who mostly rode with the Leinster cavalry, the elite troops of the Confederate Catholics. Talbot's troop and a second under Garrett '*Garbh*' (rough, rugged or coarse) Fitzgerald, another Kildare man, together made up 120 riders. By the time Castlehaven reached Cashel and consulted with Barry, he had heard that Vavasour's column now presented an immediate threat because he was assaulting Cloghleagh Castle which stood sentinel by the track over the Kilworth Mountains, the sole link between the Roche–Condon enclave and the rest of Catholic Ireland.

Cloghleagh Castle. (National Museum of Ireland)

The image of a red and green patchwork quilt best describes the ragged boundaries of Catholic and Protestant quarters. Mitchelstown and Doneraile, with their satellite garrisons, were red patches outflung from the Blackwater Valley, which was dominated by a daisy chain of Protestant garrisons, thinly strung between Mallow and Fermoy and more thickly spread along the middle reaches of the river from Barrymore's Castlelyons to the Boyle patrimony around Cappoquin and Lismore at the elbow of the Blackwater. Pressed just south and west of Mitchelstown and Doneraile, respectively, was the bright green patch of Roche–Condon country. Not a few patches were the washed-out green or red hinterlands of gentlemen who bolted their doors, waited for the conflict to blow over and reached

---

36   Carte, *History of the Life of James Duke of Ormonde*, vol. I, p.431; Borlase, *Irish Rebellion*, p.116; Charles Smith, *The Ancient and Present State of the County of Kerry. Containing a Natural, Civil, Ecclesiastical, Historical and Topographical Description Thereof* (Dublin: W. Cater, 1774), p.313.

37   Lynch (ed.), *Castlehaven's Memoirs*, pp.56–57.

38   TCDL: 1641 Depositions, MS 835 (County Fermanagh), fol. 173r: Deposition of Thomas Spraige.

pragmatic accommodations with whoever was dominant locally. Arthur Hyde of Castlehyde was one such who lived and let live in the tongue of flat and fertile country lying between the valleys of the Funshion and the Blackwater, menaced by Roches to the west and harried Condons to the east.

Losing no time, Castlehaven raced to the aid of the Condons, leaving the foot soldiers behind, but arrived too late. Even as his outriders skirmished with Vavasour's men along the mountain trail, Cloghleagh capitulated and thirty-eight men, women and children stripped and slaughtered. This sort of cruelty was going out of fashion, and Vavasour had given orders to spare the prisoners before riding off to dine at Ballyhindon. We do not know if Vavasour got to finish his dinner before he returned to the scene of bloodshed.

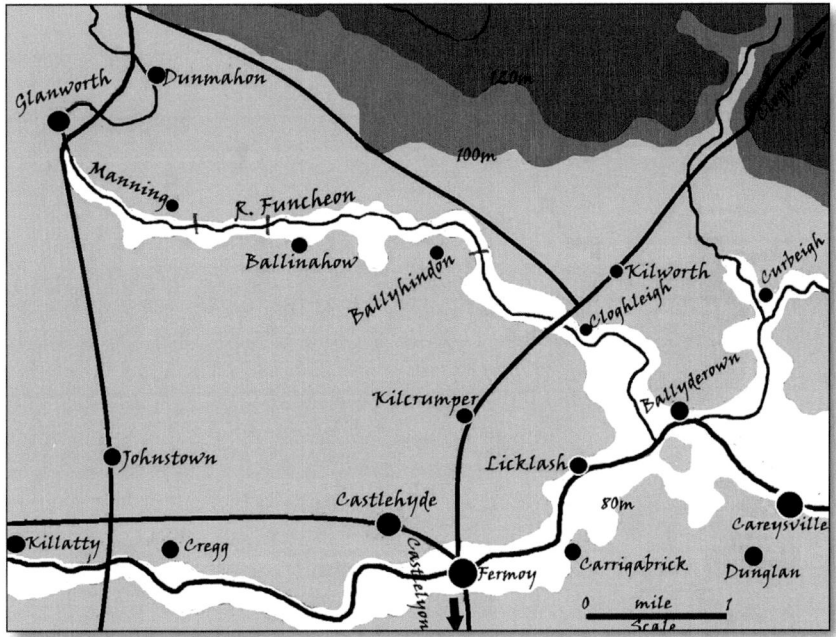

The Blackwater and Funshion Valleys. (Author's map)

Spotting enemy cavalry on the slopes, he nervously assumed that they must be just the visible part of a bigger army and decided to pull back to Fermoy, sending his artillery and baggage off first. Presumably, Vavasour's guns could not cross by the ford nearest Cloghleagh or by the next two upriver. There seems to have been nothing for it but to cross farther upriver at Manning Ford. Castlehaven shadowed as Vavasour straggled along the bank of the Funshion.[39] A nineteenth-century patriotic ballad imagines the 'waving and flaunting of banners', a 'clear shrilly clamour [of trumpets]' and a 'loud rolling drum', but Vavasour was probably not feeling at all exultant.[40] To return in safety to Castlelyons, he had to extricate his army across Manning Ford in the face of a watchful enemy, march up a steep hill and slog for some miles across the plain before descending into another river valley and

---

39 Borlase, *Irish Rebellion*, pp.116–18.
40 Robert D. Joyce, 'The Battle of Manning Ford', *Duffy's Hibernian Magazine*, 1:3 (1860), pp.132–34.

View south towards Manning Ford. (Author's photo)

negotiating yet more shallows at Fermoy. No sooner had he escaped the Funshion Valley than he found Castlehaven's riders nipping at his heels.

To mask his movements, Castlehaven had left his 'boys' (horsemen usually had a remount and a groom, or horseboy, often an adult man) bunched on a hill in view of the retreating English. Folklore identifies the hill as 'Boy Hill' or 'Knockenabohilly' (*Cnocán na mBuachaillí*), which lies about two miles north of Manning Ford.[41] As can happen, folklore misplaces locational clues, and Knockenabohilly is so far away from Manning Ford as to be invisible. Looking north from the road to the south of Manning Ford just as it cleared the crest of a steep slope, the river bottom is out of sight, but the crest overlooking the north bank of the Funshion is visible. We can imagine Castlehaven's horseboys milling about on this crest and his cavaliers bursting from the dead ground, 'not in order and warlike manner but by troops and scattered companies', letting off no more than 20 pistol shots before they 'fell on with their swords'.[42] In their preference for swordplay, Castlehaven's horsemen can be compared to Rupert's cavaliers, although the latter usually kept their ranks as they advanced to contact.[43] Vavasour's rearguard of 120 cavalrymen, supported by 200 detached musketeers, was outmatched because it included too many horsemen who had tagged along 'for the sake of plunder'. The rearguard was soon 'hemmed in' and 'pressed back into that lane amongst the foot', where they trampled and shoved their way through the throng of foot soldiers and threw them into confusion.[44] The battle as a contest was over, and what followed was a one-sided slaughter of 600 foot

---

41 Niall Brunicardi, 'The Battle of Manning Ford, 4 June 1643', *The Irish Sword*, 22:87 (2000), pp.9, 13.
42 Borlase, *Irish Rebellion*, pp.116–18; Lynch (ed.), *Castlehaven's Memoirs*, p.58.
43 Trevor Royle, *Civil War: The Wars of the Three Kingdoms 1638–1660* (New York: Palgrave Macmillan, 2004), p.195.
44 Carte, *History of the Life of James Duke of Ormonde*, vol. I, p.431.

soldiers (Vavasour and many of his officers were spared) by as few as 80 horsemen in the space of two hours. There was really nothing 'supernatural' about the business – it was well known that even a 'small squadron of cavalry acting promptly can wreak great havoc amongst large infantry battle lines'.[45]

It seems so simple when described by Castlehaven with affected aristocratic understatement: a headlong gallop and blades slashing at crouched shoulders and backs. Similes used in the Butler of Ikerrin poem of the wolf bursting into the herd or the hawk swooping (*sidhe seabhaic*) both convey the image of a sudden descent on a stunned prey.[46] But consider what Castlehaven had to do before that descent. He contrived to fool Vavasour and fall on the rearguard at just the right instant. This was not just blind luck but demanded that ineffable quality of *coup d'oeil*, that happy gift of apprehending at a glance the possibilities offered by terrain.

The encounter was important because the Catholics inflicted heavy casualties, exceeding those they had suffered at Liscarroll. After the battle, the native gentry across east County Cork felt it was safe to cease paying protection money to Inchiquin, and, in effect, this large tract of countryside was ceded to the Irish, thereby leaving the elbow of the Blackwater as a stranded and vulnerable Boyle exclave. Early in June, the Earl of Cork's Blackwater army had been defeated while marching to relieve Castlelyons and suffered, in relative terms, the 'huge loss' of 300 soldiers. Over a month later, in mid-July, Patrick Purcell spent four days 'wasting and spoiling' the country around Cappoquin and then turned his attention to Lismore Castle. He pounded the walls with 303 'great shot' and breached Cork's main house in several places. Inchiquin stood well back at Tallow, helplessly unable to intervene.[47] Thus were Purcell and Inchiquin poised when the cessation was announced and the music stopped. In west Cork, Inchiquin's forces showed that they still had fight in them when Colonel Mynne, Vavasour's successor in Bandon, thrust south-westwards taking in the castles of Timoleague and Ahamilla.[48]

We had left Eoghan Rua recoiling back across the Shannon. Things got even worse. In July, up to 6,000 of Monroe's Scots Covenanters raided from Dungannon even deeper into Irish territory as far as Bun in the extreme south-west of County Cavan. From there, a detachment of 700 horse made for Cairn Hill (*Sliabh Cairbre*), the highest hill in County Longford, where the Ulster creaghts were based. O'Mellan was characteristically laconic: the raiders 'returned to Bun because they could not get to them' (*nár rugsat orra*).[49] Early in August, at this low ebb in his fortunes, the Supreme Council

---

45 Empey, 'Diary of Sir James Ware', p.117; Thomas M. Barker (ed.), *The Military Intellectual and Battle: Raimondo Montecuccoli and the Thirty Years' War* (Albany: State University of New York Press, 1975), p.150; Patrick F. Moran (ed.), *Spicilegium Ossoriense: Being a Collection of Original Letters and Papers Illustrative of the History of the Irish Church from the Reformation to the Year 1800* (Dublin: W. B. Kelly, 1874), p.291.
46 Ní Cheallacháin, *Filíocht Phádraigín Haicéad*, p.54; Hartnett, *Haicéad*, p.80.
47 Edwards, 'Holding On', p.35.
48 Charles Smith, *The Antient and Present State of the County and City of Cork* (Dublin: Publisher unknown, 1730), vol. II, p.146.
49 Ó Donnchadha, 'Cín lae', p.23.

ordered Eoghan Rua to gather his forces and join Sir James Dillon. On the way, at Bruse Hill, he was met by Phelim O'Neill and the newly arrived papal envoy Scarampi, who inspected the army and distributed weapons and munitions.

Ormond had not been able to push south-west against a frontier hardened by impregnable strongholds like Ticroghan and Ballyshannon, but the frontier to the north-west of the Boyne was more permeable. In September 1642, only 100 men had held Kells, which had 'no manner of fortifications'.[50] Ormond's army took Kells and threw a ring of strongpoints around the battered town. The strategic purpose of the O'Neill–Dillon campaign was logistical: to recover this recently lost territory and put it 'under contribution'.[51] Boosted by Dillon's field gun, the Irish mopped up the strongpoints in short order, though Ballybeg's 180 soldiers refused when summoned. Two or three shots breached the wall before the garrison surrendered at mercy. Professional soldiers and veterans of the Thirty Years' War like Stewart, Preston and O'Neill were usually more merciful than amateurs like Broghill and Dungarvan. O'Neill disarmed and dismissed the soldiers, and he spared one Major Cadogan: 'notwithstanding the Leinster gentlemen represented him as a very ill man, and deserving death, yet he told them, he would let him live longer, to become better'.[52]

O'Neill's wanderings ended at Portlester, a castle dominating almost 1,000 acres of good grazing land surrounded by the River Boyne to the south, the Stonyford River to the east and bog on the other two sides. This fastness was secure yet spacious enough to shelter thousands of creaghts at need. O'Neill borrowed a gun from Ticroghan, where Preston had left it for safe keeping after he had given up the siege of Castlejordan and drifted towards Maynooth 'for the possessing of the corn thereabouts'.[53] O'Neill planted both his guns against Portlester Castle but to 'to little effect' until he alighted from his horse and ordered the guns to be moved to a better firing position, after which the handful of English troops in the castle slipped away through a sally port.

Charles Viscount Moore had been rampaging in County Monaghan with a large force pulled from the garrisons of Drogheda and Dundalk, but, hearing of O'Neill's movements, he hustled south to winkle the old fox out of his lair. This time, O'Neill had ample forewarning and made careful preparations. The north of the bog island, where the morass was narrowest, presented the only dry-shod access. Moore was approaching from this direction, and so it should have been the obvious place for O'Neill to make a stand. Yet, he chose not to. One may surmise that the pass had dried out or that he was fearful of losing depth in his defence and being pent up with his creaghts, already packed 'as close as cows in a pound'.[54]

---

50 TCDL: 1641 Depositions, MS 816 (County Meath), fol. 196r: Deposition of John Darcy.
51 Gilbert (ed.), *Contemporary History*, vol. I, p.67; Casway, *Struggle for Catholic Ireland*, p.85; Gilbert (ed.), *Irish Confederation*, vol. I, p.152.
52 Gilbert (ed.), *Contemporary History*, vol. III, p.201.
53 BoL: Carte MS 6, fols 87: Michael Jones, Maynooth 17 July 1643, 89: John Gifford to Ormond, Castlejordan 18 July 1643, 168: Moore to Ormond, Monaghan, August 1643.
54 Hogan (ed.), *History of the Warr of Ireland*, p.33.

At any rate, he chose a different pinch point a mile north-east of Portlester, where a ford crossed over the Stonyford River, nowadays little more than a canalised drain but rather wider in those days. That O'Neill's two artillery pieces were placed behind a breastwork 'at the ford' tells us that this was not a delaying position and that he did not have in mind a skirmish of the kind that he was wont to fight in order to wear down an advancing enemy. He could not have dismounted and repositioned his guns quickly enough for that. Here, his main body had to stand. He himself took a squadron of dragoons across the Stonyford River to a 'ruined old building of a mill' (Earl's Mill) 400 or 500 yards to the north. So far, so familiar.[55] O'Neill had likewise brought horsemen forwards at Clones as a 'forlorn hope' in order to disrupt and delay. Seeing Moore advancing in battle array, Eoghan Rua pulled back in a 'leisurely' fashion – too leisurely. The English vanguard cut off some of his dragoons before they reached the ford. 'We beat them from one side of the pass to the other', boasted Monck, Moore's second-in-command, in his after-action report.[56]

O'Neill left a 'Captain Magennis' behind with 60 men to occupy the mill and had some pioneers throw up a breastwork to protect the door. It is harder to fit this action into any recognisable tactical repertoire because Magennis was left too far forwards and too isolated to constitute a proper forlorn hope. Mac Tuathail claims that O'Neill's guns at the ford fired in support ,'often clearing both sides of the mill'. This is a doubtful claim because the location of the ruined mill cannot be seen looking north across the wide open fields from the modern bridge from the Stonyford, and it was unlikely to have been much more visible almost 500 years ago. Three times, Moore's men tried to push across the ford with 'undaunted courage' and assaulted the mill 'very fiercely', coming so close that they 'snatched' muskets by the muzzle from loopholes, but several' were killed by 'thrust of pike', and the rest were 'forced to fall off'.[57] During pauses between the attacks, O'Neill was able to send up ammunition and reinforcements, though the forlorn hope would not accept reinforcements, insisting that 'only they should have the honour of defending that place'.[58]

Moore was inspecting the ground on horseback and barking orders to a huddle of officers when a six-pounder shot knocked him from out of his saddle, and he 'immediately gave up the ghost in the hands of his saviour'.[59] P. S. was sure that Moore's ghost migrated somewhere else entirely: 'the trunk of his body falling down, and some of his members whistling in the air to take possession by flight in some other field, or made such speed to accompany his soul to hell'.[60] Artillery shot was the prime hazard for a commander on the battlefield: Turenne at Salzbach (1675) and Saint-Ruhe at Aughrim (1691),

---

55 Gilbert (ed.), *Contemporary History*, vol. I, p.71.
56 Bodleian Library (BoL) Carte MS 5, fol. 467: Monck to Ormond, camp near Trim, 12 Sept 1643.
57 Gilbert (ed.), *Contemporary History*, vol. III, p.201; Hogan (ed.), *History of the Warr of Ireland*, p.33.
58 Gilbert (ed.), *Contemporary History*, vol. I, p.71.
59 Gilbert (ed.), *Contemporary History*, vol. III, p.202; BoL: Carte MS 5, fol. 467: Monck to Ormond.
60 Gilbert (ed.), *Contemporary History*, vol. I, p.71.

View north from Red Earl's Ford. (Author's photo)

to take two examples. The gunner could not pick out an individual at long range, but, if he discerned a swirl of gaily coloured aides and flunkeys on a hilltop, he could guess that the general must be the still centre. O'Neill had been impatient with his gunner for aiming too high, and, after peering through his spyglass, he had aimed the gun that fired the killer shot with his own hands. By lowering the elevation, O'Neill must have reduced the range, which suggests that Moore must have been close enough to be struck full force by a direct shot that penetrated his body rather than by a glancing blow. Moore's chaplain was clear on the point – 'I saw the cannon bullet taken out of his body'.[61] Besides Moore, the English lost 93 men that day and 17 the next during their retreat.[62]

For O'Neill, it was enough to have protected the creaghts as he challenged his officers who clamoured to pursue and inflict more casualties: 'What need a rich man to be a thief?'.[63] Monck retreated in good order and halted only a short distance away. Had O'Neill pursued, Monck would most likely have beaten him, as he had defeated Preston at Timahoe and again at Cloncurry towards the end of June when he bulled his way home across a defended 'straight passage' and lost 'not one man killed'.[64]

O'Neill was 'solid rather than brilliant', and neither he nor Preston could expect to beat Monck, Moore, Grenville, Crawford or any of the other English commanders in a stand-up fight in open countryside. Indeed, they were hard put to hold defiles against them.[65] What they could do was harass. Writing the night after the action at Portlester, Monck and his officers threatened Ormond that they would march on Dublin if they were not supplied with a 'speedy relief' of 'bread, shoes and cheese'. Crawford's regiment was

---

61 Thomas W. Jones (ed.), *A True Relation of the Life and Death of the Right Reverend Father in God William Bedell, Lord Bishop of Kilmore in Ireland* (London: Camden Society, 1872), p.213.
62 Ó Donnchadha, 'Cín lae', p.25.
63 Casway, *Struggle for Catholic Ireland*, p.88.
64 Anon., *Another extract of more letters sent out of Ireland*, p.2.
65 Hollick, *Battle of Benburb*, p.162.

worst off because their stores were empty and his men depended on what corn they could glean in the fields. An army had to disperse to forage and scavenge, and, consequently, the men and women mowing hay, reaping corn or stealing livestock could be surprised by horsemen from a hostile army hovering nearby, who 'drove' Crawford's foragers away.[66] The Lords Justices bluntly told Ormond that he should keep his army away from the capital, as it was 'not now possibly able to feed so many', and they told him to jostle with Preston for control of north-east County Offaly, which they had been told was 'a place full of corn'.[67] Meanwhile, the marauding garrisons of Carlow and Laois joined together and cheekily plundered to the 'very gates of Kilkenny'. Reacting after the event, as usual, the Supreme Council mandated Castlehaven to 'secure the country', whereupon he got his hands on some guns and about 2,000 men, comprising the County Wexford regiment of foot and some companies of the Kilkenny regiment, together with at least three squadrons of horse, Harpole's, Mac Thomas Fitzgerald's and Sir Walter Butler's, making up to 400 horsemen in all. Castlehaven first captured Cloghrenan and Ballynunnery. Though he was forced to plant his guns and batter Ballynunnery, he nonetheless 'pardoned all the multitude, none of his army upon pain of death durst touch worth a penny of their goods; goods and arms was given them, and a convoy to their choice garrison. This is more mercy than the laws of armes, and specially in a just and lawful war do require'.[68] P. S. may not have been the only one to feel cheated: the County Wexford regiment mutinied, though, once the mutiny was put down and 'some examples made', the regiment 'served well for the future'.[69]

Next up was Ballylynan, a formidable castle that had been beleaguered twice already by Brian O'Dempsey and by Morgan Kavanagh. During the latter operation, one of Kavanagh's captains had hanged seven English women and children, caught while scavenging abroad.[70] Ballylynan's strength lay not in its walls but in the 300-strong garrison that included 80 horsemen under George Graham, one of a family of 'English and Scottish mongrels, the best horsemen in them parts'.[71] The 'mongrels' were from reiver families – Armstrongs, Elliotts, Grahams and so on – deported to Ireland to pacify James I's Anglo–Scottish border and to serve as the cutting edge of plantation and colonisation in Ulster and elsewhere. Other nearby settlers like Bowen of Ballyadams and Thomas Hovenden of Ballylehane (the Hovendens had been Tyrone's foster family) chose to keep their heads down and cooperate when

---

66 Tadhg Ó hAnnracháin, 'The Poet and the Mutinies: Pádraigín Haicéad and the Munster Army in 1647', *Proceedings of the Royal Irish Academy: Archaeology, Culture, History, Literature*, 108C (2008), pp.65–74; Bodleian Library (BoL) Carte MS 2, fol. 467: Monck and Council of War 'Our Camp near Trim' 12 September 1643.
67 Ball (ed.), *Calendar of the Manuscripts of the Marquess of Ormonde*, vol. I, p.58, 'Lords Justices to Ormond, 26 July 1643'.
68 Lynch (ed.), *Castlehaven's Memoirs*, p.52.
69 Lynch (ed.), *Castlehaven's Memoirs*, p.52.
70 TCDL: 1641 Depositions, MS 815 (County Laois), fols 367v: Deposition of John Walcockson, 394r: Examination of Daniell O Dowlen, 411r–11v: Deposition of John Goodman.
71 Gilbert (ed.), *Contemporary History*, vol. I, p.69.

politic with the insurgents.[72] There was no definable front line in Laois but the usual patchwork of green, red, palest pink or washed-out green.

Guns soon opened a 'great breach' but while Castlehaven lay resting in his tent, he got word that a big party of 300 horse and 700 foot soldiers was on the march from Athy, three miles away, and beginning to pick their way across the togher through the bog leading to Ballylynan. Rising from his bed, Castlehaven rode to the mouth of a togher where he had placed a strong guard behind a breastwork. Rather than wait, he led his men along the togher, and the Athy force pulled back and formed up on a 'plain', but, when they saw Castlehaven's cavalry drawing up to charge, they pulled back farther behind the waist-high water of a drain. Two of Castlehaven's squadrons floundered across the fosse one after the other but were beaten back, Sir Walter Butler's thigh being pierced with a pike. But seeing yet another squadron coming on, the Athy force 'took their advantage in the smoke to run away'.[73] Castlehaven pursued the runaways to 'the very street' of Athy: P. S. muttered darkly that Castlehaven should have pursued even farther and entered the town but would 'leave some life in his countrymen, and not banish them altogether'.[74] Castlehaven had risked too much already in leaving behind a depleted besieging force, an active enemy garrison and a narrow togher in between. In the event, Graham was so discouraged to see the relief force chased off that he capitulated.

Castlehaven's follow-up capture of Dollardstown shows a sterner side to his character. Dollardstown lay just a mile from the important Catholic garrison of Kilkea, and Castlehaven quietly brokered a capitulation with the owner, an old acquaintance. Unfortunately, a 'Lieutenant Burrowes' (no doubt a relation of Erasmus Burrowes, who captained one of the five companies in and around Athy) arrived the morning that the surrender was to take place and won over the soldiers to defy Castlehaven.[75] Thwarted, Castlehaven imprisoned the unfortunate owner of the castle and sent to Kilkenny for siege guns. The 20 defenders occupied a breastwork, and, once the guns arrived, Castlehaven called for volunteers to storm the perimeter. The infantry officers demurred, but Garret *Garbh* swore, 'in his Dutch like English, that he would lead them to the very sconces'. He drove the enemy back into the castle in a matter of 15 minutes, and, as a 'bullet whistled at his ear', he ordered the musketeers to 'keep the castle in action' while a siege gun fired nine shots: '… every bullet did pass through the house, wherby the defendants, if otherwise good soldiers could do nothing as not seeing anything, the fresh lime shaken and winded, filled the place with its smoke, and raising up their sight was made not capable of any light'.[76]

Castlehaven let 'the wives of some gentlemen' (one does wonder about the other women) leave before the final storm when his men set fire to the door and smoked Burrowes's men out. He hanged Burrowes and four of his

---

72   TCDL: 1641 Depositions, MS 815 (County Laois), fol. 338v: Deposition of Elizabeth Jay.
73   Lynch (ed.), *Castlehaven's Memoirs*, p.54.
74   Gilbert (ed.), *Contemporary History*, vol. I, p.69.
75   TCDL: 1641 Depositions, MS 813 (County Kildare), fol. 359v: Deposition of Francis Dade.
76   Gilbert (ed.), *Contemporary History*, vol. I, p.69.

men, and a half-dozen civilians were also slain during or after the assault. When Castlehaven remarked that Burrowes and the others had 'suffered as they deserved', he was not referring to the accusations by aggrieved locals of 'misbehaviour and tyranny' but to a grim calculus that the weaker the garrison, and the higher the cost it exacted in time and trouble, the more likely it would be to provoke the besieger 'to make an example' and discourage 'unsoldiery obstinacy'.[77] Garret Garbh was granted a custodium of Dollardstown as a reward for his bravery.

Within the next week or so, eight castles surrendered on promise of quarter, giving Castlehaven a swath of territory 12 miles across and half as much north to south, running from the Barrow to the Liffey and including Monasterevan, Kildare Castle and Lackagh, where Chidley Coote experienced dispossession for the second time. Gifford in Castlejordan and Burrowes in Athy now commanded foreign bodies deeply embedded in a hostile region rather than extrusions from the main English quarters, miniature Gloucesters or Newarks.

O'Neill's operation – taken together with other operations by Preston to the west of the Pale, Castlehaven to the south-west and O'Byrne to the south – pushed the English back to the Boyne and the Liffey in a frenetic burst of campaigning designed to grab as much land as possible before a ceasefire.[78] With the highlands to the south looming threateningly close, Dublin was itself on the front line. One night in late July, a 'great company' set fire to houses in the New Street suburb and came as far as the 'black pool' (the original *dubh linn* of Dublin) that lapped the walls of Dublin Castle. The marauders burned cocks of hay as they retreated to the highlands at their leisure because Ormond's field army was manoeuvring near Castlejordan trying to lure Preston 'to hazard a battle'.[79] A month later, more raiders snatched a prisoner near Baggot Rath (modern Baggot Street) and took him to Hugh Mac Phelim's fortified camp at Bray.[80]

O'Neill left a 'hungry wilderness' in Ulster and a scattering of natives 'so miserable that they eat their children, and one another'.[81] Charlemont was the only remaining Irish garrison in mid-Ulster, and the 'British' (i.e., pre-1641 English and Scots settler regiments) had often chivvied Monro to lay siege to the place and sneered that Monro had secret instructions from Edinburgh not to venture west of the Bann too far or too often. In August 1643, the British and the Covenanters came closer than they ever had, or would, to taking that annoying outpost.[82] Having captured Mountjoy and Dungannon, Chichester's British pressed Charlemont from the north while a strong detachment (*iomad slua*) from Monro's field army occupied

---

77 James Turner, *Pallas Armata. Military Essayes of the Ancient Grecian, Roman and Modern Art of War. Written in the Years 1670 and 1671* (London: M. W., 1683), p.319; Gilbert (ed.), *Irish Confederation*, vol. IV, p.8.
78 Gilbert (ed.), *Irish Confederation*, vol. I, p.161.
79 Anon., *Another extract of more letters sent out of Ireland*, pp.15, 59; Carte, *History of the Life of James Duke of Ormonde*, vol. I, p.440.
80 TCDL: 1641 Depositions, MS 810 (County Dublin), fol. 371r: Examination of Katherin Cary.
81 Anon., *Another extract of more letters sent out of Ireland*, p.3.
82 Stevenson, *Scottish Covenanters and Irish Confederates*, pp.137–38.

Dunavally, planted four artillery pieces, probably on Legar Hill, and pressed the fort 'at distance' as 'the growing corn ripened'.[83] Monro kept most of his men back in a fortified camp at Armagh, whence he reaped the harvest sown by the Irish and ranged far and wide for cattle, once penetrating as far as Virginia, County Cavan, over 30 miles away.

Charlemont Fort was more mansion than castle, and it protruded three storeys proud over the ramparts atop a hill overlooking a bridge on the Blackwater. No doubt, Monro's shot sailed over the ramparts to chip stonework and break glass in some of the 24 mullioned windows that graced the front, but he simply could not breach the double stone-faced ramparts and four corner bastions at such extreme range.[84] It may be that Monro was not serious about taking Charlemont at all but instead used the operation as an excuse to ignore appeals from Dublin to come south.

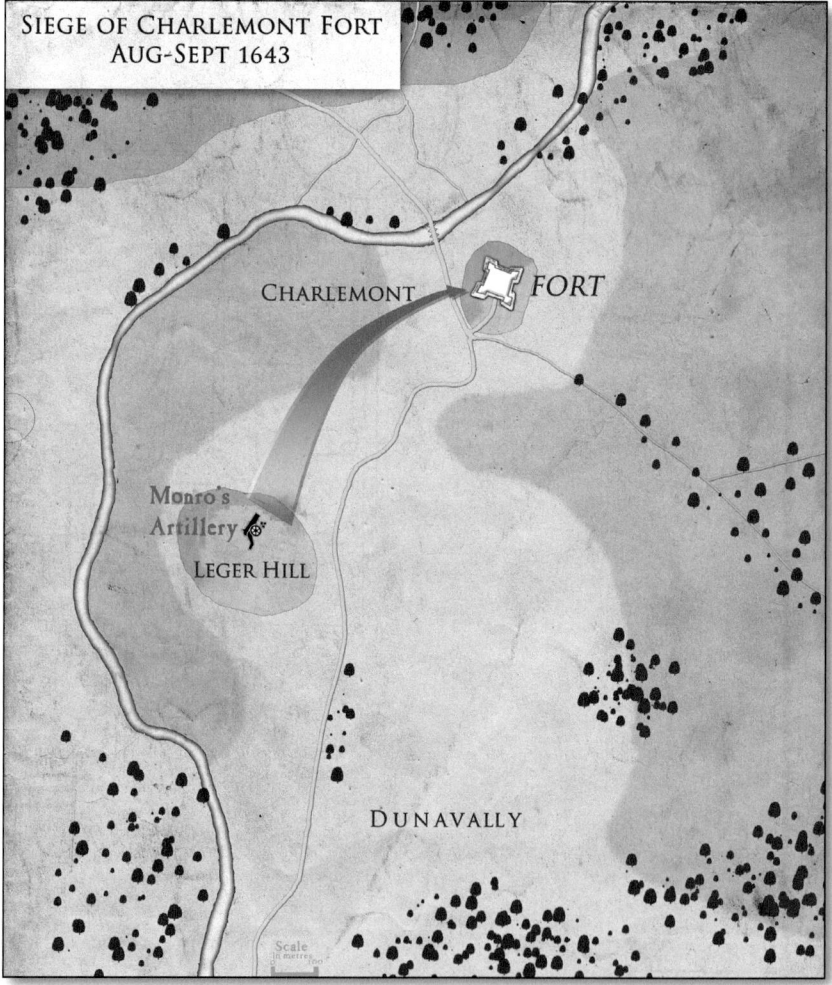

Siege of Charlemont, August–September 1643. (Tomás Ó Brógáin)

---

83 Ó Donnchadha, 'Cín lae', pp.22, 25–26; Hogan (ed.), *History of the Warr of Ireland*, p.34.
84 British Museum (BM) Add.MSS, 24200, fols 38v–39: Nicholas Pynnar, 'The fort and castle of Charlemont'.

The governor Niall O'Neill, a second cousin of Red Phelim, had but a paltry 120 soldiers, yet they showed spirit and resourcefulness.[85] Niall ambushed a supply train coming from Mountjoy (presumably, supplies were ferried there across Lough Neagh from Clandeboye), killed eight of the escort and took 'wine, beer, vinegar, whiskey, two tents, spades, picks, as much as two horses would draw; also two carts full of meal, butter, cheese, and of linen and woollen clothes'. Chastened, the besiegers set up camps surrounding Charlemont but 'lost many of their men in the night time', notably when Niall's men crossed the Blackwater in boats and slew 14 sentries 'before a word was said'.[86]

According to O'Mellan (none of the British or Scots mention this), 300 handpicked Scots storm troopers made to assault the fort, but they got no farther than digging a sconce within a nearby orchard. Perhaps they were an advance party, and the orchard was to be a jump-off point for a full-scale assault. A crowd of locals from Moy, who paid Monro contributions, gathered on a hill to the north, across the Blackwater to watch the show, until O'Neill loaded his artillery with musket balls and fired on them. Shortly afterwards, men of the ward (O'Mullan refugees from County Derry) counterattacked. They fired their muskets, drew swords and skeanes and fell on the Scots, stabbing and scattering them into the wetlands. An attempt by Monro's men to fire a volley came unstuck: 'One of them made to raise his musket but before he brought the butt off the ground he was shot in the shoulder by the man behind him and tumbled head first into the bog.'[87]

When the cessation was announced, three sieges were in train in three provinces: Cappoquin, Charlemont and, not least, Castlecoote, County Roscommon. Sir Charles Coote Sr, victim of an accidental shooting at Trim, had been nominated to a commission for confirmation of land titles in 1615 and used his office to 'discover' defects in native land and pick up estates in Counties Leitrim, Sligo and Roscommon, which last he rebranded as 'Castlecoote'.[88] By 1643, his youngest son, Richard, was responsible for Castlecoote and had rather better luck than his brother Chidley at Birr, where the Irish came calling in July 1643. The grateful citizenry of Galway City had bestowed £300 on *Seán an tSléibhe*, and he could raise enough troops for the operation, but it is doubtful if he brought any heavy guns dismounted from the ramparts of Galway. Had Bourke brought guns, he would have made short work of Castlecoote's walls. Castlecoote sat in a loop of the River Suck, which gave it defensive strength, so Bourke ensconced himself in and around the bridge or ford just south of the castle. This would have been a good place to tie off the river loop and starve Coote into submission, but Burke ran out of time. At first, Burke ignored Clanricarde's messages that claimed a countrywide ceasefire was now in effect, replying that he would

---

85 Ó Donnchadha, 'Cín lae', pp.22, 25–26.
86 Hogan (ed.), *History of the Warr of Ireland*, p.34.
87 Ó Donnchadha, 'Cín lae', p.26.
88 Armstrong, 'Coote, Sir Charles'; Clarke, *Old English*, p.53; Treadwell, *Buckingham and Ireland*, pp.59, 144, 200–02, 266; Burke, *Memoirs and Letters of Ulick*, pp.439–40; Gilbert (ed.), *Contemporary History*, vol. I, p.82.

neither observe a ceasefire nor do his lordship's bidding until he heard from his superiors.

'Not to go forward is to go backward', complained papal envoy Scarampi, and nowhere does this hold truer than in Connacht.[89] Bourke resigned or was dismissed, his troops went home, and with them went any hope of concerted action by the Confederate Catholics in Connacht.

In the winter of 1642–1643, Charles had come to the view that his chances of a decisive victory were 'bleak' without thousands of more foot soldiers, and, on 23 April, he told Ormond to embark in earnest on secret talks towards a truce.[90] Ormond temporised so that he could dictate the terms of a ceasefire from a position of military strength, and, latterly, the Irish delayed signing off on a ceasefire while they mopped up Protestant outliers.[91] Only on 15 September 1643 did the Catholics and Ormond sign the cessation at Ormond's tent near Jigginstown, County Kildare. The year's ceasefire with Ormond, to whom nearly all the British armies in Ireland still owed nominal allegiance, left him with two blocks of territory, the inner Pale and a long tongue of land stretching from the city of Cork almost to the Limerick county line, with some straggling outliers. Ormond would downsize his army and ship reinforcements to Charles. The Irish would pay a subsidy of £30,000 to pay for the shipping costs and to support those soldiers holding Ormond's remaining enclaves. That was a hefty sum, not enough to keep the Irish army going for half a year, as critics claimed, but enough to keep one of the four provincial armies of over 6,000 men, as envisaged, in the field for three months. By way of putting this in context, the English Parliament sent £76,000 in money to support the English armies in Ireland in 1642.[92] The symbolism was no less important: losers paid tribute, and potential backers were likely to react with puzzled surprise. The English Parliament did not recognise the cessation, the Scots in Ulster were not party to it, and the Laggan army was a reluctant party, so the agreement made little difference in the north.[93]

War was being waged with unprecedented intensity across four provinces in late summer when, on a sudden, the guns fell silent. The story wants a natural ending. What would have happened if the fighting had gone on?

For the parties and factions within parties, strategic analysis served political prejudice and preconception. Royalists knew that the perception of being soft on Irish papists damaged them in England and insisted that nothing less than a ceasefire could have saved the English interest in Ireland because the King's 'Protestant subjects could not defend the little they had

---

89 Gilbert (ed.), *Irish Confederation*, vol. II, p.323.
90 Joyce L. Malcolm, 'All the King's Men: The Impact of the Crown's Irish Soldiers on the English Civil War', *Irish Historical Studies*, 22:83 (1979), pp.254, 246.
91 TNA: *HMC Report on the Manuscripts of the Earl of Egmont*, vol. I, p.195, 'Philip Percival to Thomas Bettesworth, 17 November 1643'.
92 In April 1647, it cost just over £10,000 to pay the Leinster army of 6,000 foot and 800 horse for six weeks. The National Archives (TNA) SP 63/264, pp.25–26; Carte, *History of the Life of James Duke of Ormonde*, vol. I, pp.447, 465.
93 Robert Armstrong, 'The Long Parliament Goes to War: The Irish Campaigns, 1641–3', *Historical Research*, 80:207 (2007), p.96.

left'.[94] Roundhead sympathisers decried the cessation as shameful and needless because, with 'a little subsistence out of England' and a large pinch of optimism, Ormond's army could yet win.[95]

A debate between Supreme Council Secretary Bellings and papal envoy Scarampi exemplifies opposing Catholic views of the cessation. Bellings and the Butler–Muskerry faction, for which he spoke, would settle for a nod-and-wink connivance of Catholicism from Charles because 'more than which he could not do, in the present state of his affairs in England'.[96] The overriding political and strategic objective was to 'be serviceable to the King, and prevent any disaster to him which might eventually lead to our destruction'. Castlehaven insisted that the Irish 'could subsist no longer than the war lasted between king and parliament'.[97] Irish aspirations, or military prospects, were less urgent than helping Charles further by reaching a definitive treaty and even embarking Catholic troops to England and Scotland as a counterweight to Covenanter troops in England. As against this, Scarampi saw that a completely decisive victory by Charles I was the least likely outcome and that the Confederates should, realistically speaking, plan for a less happy scenario of Parliamentary victory or a compromise peace:

> … if we now adopt proper measures the party eventually triumphing in England will find us in arms, well provided, with increased territories, and stronger in foreign succours. Thus, they could not so readily invade us nor swallow us up, so as to leave us without the free exercise of our faith or some share in the administration of the Kingdom.[98]

Charles would throw over his Catholic allies to clear the ground for a negotiated settlement in Britain, Scarampi was sure. His was a lone voice, for now, but others of the Irish gentry and clergy ('Clericalists', as they came to be called) soon came to doubt the King's good faith and agreed that stopping had been a mistake when they should have surged on what they now saw as the swelling tide to victory.

Treaty talks between the Confederate Catholics and Charles would drag on, except for brief intervals, from September 1643 until a fortnight before the King's beheading, during which time 'mutual jealousies, distinctions, temporizing expediency and wily diplomacy broke their compact awry and left them victims to the horrors which subsequently desolated the land'.[99] Oliver Cromwell cast a long shadow, and, with the benefit of hindsight, we can see that the Clericalists were right and the Ormondists wrong. The question was how far could Charles I's promises on religious freedom or

---

94 Edward Hyde, *The History of the Rebellion and Civil Wars in England* (Oxford: Printed at Theater, 1707), vol. II, p.419.
95 Anon., *Another extract of more letters sent out of Ireland*, p.6.
96 Ó Siochrú, *Confederate Ireland*, p.62.
97 Lynch (ed.), *Castlehaven's Memoirs*, p.64.
98 Piero Scarampi, 'Reasons against a Cessation with the English', in J. T. Gilbert (ed.), *History of the Irish Confederation and the War in Ireland 1641-1649* (Dublin: M. H. Gill and Son, 1879–1880), vol. II, p.xciii.
99 Lowe, 'Charles I and the Confederation', pp.1–19; Meehan, *Confederation of Kilkenny*, p.66.

toleration be trusted?[100] The more successful the King was, the less likely he was to grant significant concessions to the Confederate Catholics. The more desperate, the more likely he was to make promises he could not keep.[101] For all that, it is unhistorical to blame the Confederate Catholics for giving Charles the benefit of the doubt and for straining to show their loyalty: their Oath of Association demanded no less.[102]

---

100 Ó Siochrú, *Confederate Ireland*, p.244; Lowe, 'Charles I and the Confederation', pp.2, 4; Jane Ohlmeyer, 'A Failed Revolution? The Irish Confederate War in Its European Context', *History Ireland*, 3:1 (1995), p.28.

101 Ó Siochrú, *Confederate Ireland*, p.62; Pádraig Lenihan, 'Confederate Military Strategy, 1643-7', in M. Ó Siochrú (ed.), *Kingdoms in Crisis: Ireland in the 1640s, Essays in Honor of Dónal Cregan* (Dublin: Four Courts Press, 2001), p.159.

102 Ó hAnnracháin, 'Conflicting Loyalties', p.851; Cregan, 'Confederate Catholics of Ireland', p.509.

Conclusion

The Ulster plotters smarted at wrongs suffered and dreaded wrongs to come. Their resentments or fears – or both – resonated across Catholic Ireland. That was why most of the baronial dominoes fell, the Pale, the Butler domain of south Leinster and east Munster and the MacCarthy country of west Cork, though not Upper and Lower Connacht of the Burkes, where bishops, burghers and blow-ins (e.g., Luke Taaffe and Luke Dillon) had to step up. The usual thing was for a handful of Catholics (or a single man, in the case of Muskerry) in a barony – be they wealthier landowners, bearers of distinguished noble pedigree or the most eligible of the derbfine – to use the nexus of dependency and deference at their fingertips to gather servants, tenants and poor relations into a company or two. Where gentry, smaller landowners and middling tenants were more numerous, there were likely to be more gentlemen rankers than dependents, and the companies were all the better for it. These captains (colonels and regiments would remain abstractions for some time to come) usually did not have experience of soldiering.

If accounts of the horde that swelled Mountgarret's circuitous progress across Munster are at all accurate, this must have been far and away the biggest mobilisation of the war for years to come. But the mountain heaved and brought forth a mouse.

The Palesmen faced the especially tough task alone but for Phelim O'Neill's Ulstermen and without siege guns. They had to contain Dublin long enough to first take Drogheda and then take the capital, all before English reinforcements disembarked. It was clear by 20 February 1642 that they had failed when a relief fleet broke the blockade of Drogheda and almost 2,000 English soldiers disembarked at Dublin. The winter war saw many Droghedas writ small. Usually, the insurgents camped near a Protestant-held castle, set guards and sat down to wait. Fortifications in baroque warfare bought time for the weaker side, and most of these strongholds had enough men to hold the walls and wait for relief. If they ventured out from the walls, they usually came off worst. The Irish charge was so successful because it was a rational response to two tactical exigencies. One, the Irish had few muskets and little gunpowder, and the charge was a case of parallel evolution comparable to the French *á prest* or the Swedish *Gå–På* attack. Two, the settler soldiers had plenty powder, but, at first, they were too jumpy to use the firepower properly: the countermarch was worse than useless when practiced by half-trained men.

In extenuation of the Irish for leaving the men of the Pale to bear the brunt of the fighting, the scale of Catholic wintertime mobilisation from a standing start was awesome, and men were needed almost everywhere. The 7,000 men blockading Drogheda was the largest single operation (exceeded perhaps by Mountgarret's march into County Cork), but, at any one time, the Irish had to blockade dozens of Protestant wards sprinkled across almost every county in Ireland. In County Limerick, as many as 15 sieges rumbled on that winter, and just one of them – the biggest, admittedly – at Newcastle West absorbed the attention of 500 men. Feeding and sheltering so many men out of season was no small matter.

Scene Two of Act One followed with a massive English and Scottish counterattack that gathered pace in the spring of 1642 and came within a hair's breadth of crushing the insurgency. English and Scottish musters return an impressive number of soldiers, more than double the 'monstrous' strength Elizabeth's army had reached in 1599 and unprecedented, unsurpassed and unmatched until the armies of William of Orange in 1690, the year of the Boyne.[1] English armies usually beat the Irish in battle. And battles mattered: 'He that is master of the field may dispose of his affairs as he chooses he may spoil the enemy's country at his pleasure he may march where he thinks best he may lay siege to what towns he is disposed'.[2]

Protestant armies were generously supplied with munitions and developed effective countermeasures to blunt the Irish signature tactic. Rather than fumble with the fire-by-ranks procedure or start shooting once the Irish came within musket range, they took cover. The prelude to Rochfordstown saw St Leger's musketeers shelter behind a ditch in the face of a headlong but ragged charge. As well as firing from behind cover, they fired from very close range: Stewart's soldiers at Glenmaquin held their fire until the Irish came to within a pike length or two, and only then did they loose their volleys.

Another reason why the Catholics lost so many battles may be that their generals were not up to the job: 'An army of sheep led by a lion is better than an army of lions led by a sheep'.[3] Time and again, they gave battle when they need not have. Once battle was joined, they showed a fatal preference for the attack. Whoever was in command of the Irish at Ballintober should have stood fast on a gentle ridge almost surrounded by bog, with a bawn to his back, and let Ranelagh come at him. Even when they stood on the defensive, they did not always deploy in a manner that let all the army's components, pike, shot and horse act in mutual support. To take the most egregious example, leaving battle squares on Bull Hill and at Kilrush three-quarters of a mile apart halved the effective size of the whole army. In the smoke and din of combat, there was little enough for the commander to do after he deployed except hold a body of foot or horse in reserve, recognise the 'crisis' or tipping

---

1 Ruth A. Canning, *The Old English in Early Modern Ireland: The Palesmen and the Nine Years' War, 1594-1603* (Woodbridge: Boydell & Brewer, 2019), p.139.
2 John Bingham, 'Epistle Dedicatory', in *The Art of Embattailing an Army. Or, The Second Part of Aelians Tacticks: Containing the Practice of the Best Generals of all Antiquitie, Concerning the Formes of Battailes* (London: John Beale and Thomas Brudenell, 1629).
3 Gilbert (ed.), *Contemporary History*, vol. I, p.18.

CONCLUSION

point for what it was and intervene decisively. Barry did nothing of the sort at Liscarroll. When Stephenson was cut down, the Munster horsemen scattered, and the three battle squares disintegrated. O'Neill was different to the extent that he was capable of learning from his mistakes and 'thereafter shun those errors'.[4]

A final reason for lost battles may be that the Irish armies were not regimented until quite late in the day. In other words, the horizon for the soldier was his company. He did not know, still less, trust in anything bigger.

Sieges mattered, too. Want of skill and resources in siegework had spoiled Irish chances of a quick win, which was where a plodder like Barry could come into his own. He proved to be a competent practitioner of a methodical form of warfare that followed slow and predictable rhythms before the walls of King John's Castle or the half-dozen tower houses that followed. Consider the technical challenges he surmounted, like driving mines underground and in the right direction, given that the settlers had a near monopoly of the requisite mining skills, or dismounting the giant gun from its block carriage on the walls of King John's Castle, transporting it on a sled and remounting it on a gun carriage when it came time to batter. Had Barry not cleared these hostile nests from the fat grasslands of the Golden Vale, then west Munster would have been even more cut off from Catholic Ireland than it would prove to be.

Catholic soldiers were driven from the Pale and most of Ulster in that summer's onslaught, but they hung on elsewhere until the season of longer nights and sodden ways. They survived because they began to import enough gunpowder to fight a modern war and because they enjoyed some respite from attacks while newly landed English and Scottish lay sick: 'the hazards of bringing over English men bred … to endure the hardships of war in Ireland is very great'.[5]

The argument that the Catholic war effort persisted only because the King and Parliament in England were distracted by civil war spirals into an endless causal loop because it is not possible to hold one thing, Irish insurgency, constant and allow something else to be a variable, namely, the English Civil War. There would have been no war between the King and Parliament but for the rising in Ireland, there would have been no rising but for the sharpening religious conflict between the King and Covenanters, and so on. In the longer term, though, the outbreak of civil war muddied the Irish waters of what had been a straight 'us or them' fight for survival, and the Catholics would never recover that invigorating clarity of purpose.

The second winter of the war brings us to Scene Three, when the Catholics began to recover. The sanguinary glamour of battles should not overshadow war as a process and the uncounted food fights in which castles dominating a patchwork quilt of green and red (and every shade in between) hinterlands jostled with hostile neighbours. It was a war that the English would lose in Leinster, and, as early as September, the Lords Justices were grumbling that

---

4   Turner, *Pallas Armata*, p.258.
5   Richard Lawrence, *The Interest of England in the Irish transplantation, stated …* (Dublin: William Bladen, 1655), p.25.

they had not 'the quiet use of any land in the kingdom, but what we fight for'.[6] One reason for their plight was that they were niggardly and inconsistent in granting protections even compared to, say, Murrough Totane, who granted protections and burned when contributions were not forthcoming.

Throughout the winter, Ormond kept the strategic initiative, in that he could choose whether, when and whither to march his army. It took time to mobilise a militia army, so the Irish reacted rather than acted, disputing homeward marches at defiles. The English fought their way home at Timahoe, Rathconnell and Ballinvegga and 'won' according to war's grim calculus, whereby they killed more of the enemy than they lost to the enemy. They lost ground, however: Ballinakill fell, and Athlone was all but abandoned. With the longer days and better ways of summer, one would expect the English position to recover, but, outside of Ulster (and here Clones was a serious blow to the Irish), it all but imploded.

If the cessation was to the short-term advantage of the Confederate Catholics, 'in the long term it may have proved their undoing'.[7] Perhaps, but counterfactual speculation about the future twists and turns of war and politics in the three Stuart kingdoms is hazardous, and, in the short term, the deal removed at least 8,000 seasoned veterans, most of them English, from enemy ranks.[8] There would be plenty of enemies left to fight: Monro's Scots, Charles Coote's Parliamentarians in west Ulster and Inchiquin after he defected to Parliament. If it is a legitimate exercise of historical imagination to speculate 'what if' the cessation had not been agreed, historical rigour demands we do not pursue the enquiry too far beyond 15 September 1643 into the unknown and unknowable. Still, let us peer into the fog just a little.

The Boyle position in the Blackwater and Bride Valleys was 'on the brink of collapse'.[9] Purcell would have forced Cappoquin and Lismore to surrender because Inchiquin could not have broken through to relieve the siege. Securing the elbow of the Blackwater would have firmly affixed the baronies of Imokilly and Barrymore to the Confederate Catholic heartland. Bourke would have starved Coote out of Castlecoote in another month or six weeks. There was no one to stop him because the King was not going to make any forays from Boyle without reinforcements from the Laggan army. The capture of Castlecoote would have shut Clanricarde up within a landlocked enclave and curtailed his mischief-making. Remaining Protestant garrisons in south Leinster like Carlow and Athy were low-hanging fruits, and their capture that autumn or winter by Preston or Castlehaven would have opened the highways from Munster and south Leinster towards Dublin and securely affixed Counties Kildare and Laois to the core of the Catholic proto-state.

It is best not to get carried away any further. The suggestion that O'Neill could have marched on Dublin but for the cessation is not sustainable.[10]

---

6 Gardiner, *Great Civil War*, vol. 1, p.134.
7 Scott, *Politics and War*, p.78.
8 John Barratt, *The King's Irish: The Royalist Anglo-Irish Foot of the English Civil War* (Warwick: Helion & Company, 2019), pp.177–78.
9 Edwards, 'Holding On', p.21.
10 Coonan, *Irish Catholic Confederacy*, p.168.

CONCLUSION

Ormond had not enough provisions and carriage to send an army into the field, but he could have fed his troops and hung on grimly to Dublin and its surrounds for the coming autumn and winter.[11]

That leaves Ulster. A year after the cessation, O'Neill would not manage to re-establish his army in mid-Ulster, even with the backing of a national army, the first and only one of its kind, recruited from the other three provinces. He could hardly have done so, unaided, in autumn 1643. That said, Ulster was less important than Leinster and Munster. If the Confederates had not agreed to a cessation, they might have extended their control in those two provinces and taken Cork and Dublin over the next two years. Controlling a more cohesive and integrated proto-state, they might then have been able to deter or contain an eventual full-scale Parliamentarian attack.

So much for the 'might have beens'. What actually happened was that, in 1642, the Irish were attacked by enemy armies that were bigger, cumulatively, than anything before or subsequently. And that includes the armies of Oliver Cromwell and William of Orange. Lacking munitions, forced to disperse their strength and outfought in open battle, the Confederate Catholics contained the onslaught and even pushed back. In the circumstances, it was no small thing just to hang on.

---

11 Anon., *Another extract of more letters sent out of Ireland*, p.3.

Colour Plate Commentaries
by Seán Ó Brógáin

Plate A, Musketeer

The musketeer has reversed his matchlock and is preparing to attack or defend himself with 'clubbed musket'. He is wearing a basic woollen *baraid* (hat), but a lappeted bonnet, wide brimmed hat or a Monmouth cap depending on what was available or could be liberated along the way. He has thrown off his *brat* (cloak) as have the other figures here. As the French adventurer in Ireland, François de La Boullaye-Le Gouz, states in 1644:

> 'For cloaks they have five or six yards of frize drawn round the neck, the body, and over the head, and they never quit this mantle, either in sleeping, working, or eating.'

Our man is armed with a *muscaed* (musket) and *scían* (knife) which was a long knife with a 21-inch blade, one edge. This was used by the Irish up until the late seventeenth century. Most famously shown in John Derricke's *Images of Ireland*, *c*. 1571 and Gareth Morphy's portrait of Sir Neill O'Neill in 1688.

He wears a short, loose, grey-blue lined woollen *íonar* (jacket) similar to a English soldier's coat.

On his legs he wears the characteristic long tight-legged 'trews' commented on by non-Irish sources. These practical leg coverings were made in two pieces and sometimes of two different fabrics. The trunk was very full at the rear and cut straight, while the legs were cut on the bias, giving some stretch and tightness.

On his feet he wears the ubiquitous Irish *broga* (brogues), made of sturdy flexible leather and tied with a thong, these were issued to English soldiers during the Elizabethan wars as a practical alternative to English shoes. A recent shoe of this type was found with straw padding covered by a piece of material, as an insole or to cover the hole in the heel.

The *brat*, hat, short jacket, brogues and trews were worn by the native Irish from the late sixteenth century, as described in 1588 by Francisco de Cuéllar, shown by Tilsch's watercolour *c*. 1600, of an 'Irish lackey' with his long hair, large dart, blue *íonar*, brogues and tight red trews. Le Gouz says of the Irish:

> 'The Irish carry a scquine skein or Turkish dagger, which they dart very adroitly at fifteen paces'

'The Irish, whom the English call savages, have for their head-dress, a little blue bonnet, raised two fingers breadth in front, and behind covering their head and ears. Their doublet has a long body and four skirts; and their breeches are a pantaloon of white frize which they call trowsers. Their shoes which are pointed, they call brogues with a single sole.'

'For cloaks they have five or six yards of frize drawn round the neck, the body, and over the head, and they never quit this mantle, either in sleeping, working, or eating. The generality of them have no shirts'

Plate B, Pikeman
This pikeman again is preparing to attack or defend, is again is dressed as a native in the *ionar* (jacket based on the Dungiven jacket), *baraid* (hat), *broga* (shoes) and armed with the pike and *scian* (knife). From the Elizabethan wars to the Wars of the Three Kingdoms the Irish fighting man was essentially dressed as above.

Plate C, Cavalryman
We see a dismounted native cavalryman, again he wears typical native clothing, but is armed with a sword and a lance. He is inspecting a cavalry helmet hit by a musket ball. His trews are slightly different in that they are of a plaid cloth. Plaid was more expensive and suggests he is of a slightly higher social status than the other soldiers. He wears a *baraid caol* (bonnet) of which a number have been found in Ireland and are mentioned in literary sources, as sometimes having lappets.

Plate D, NCO or Officer
This NCO/officer is using his partizan to parry or defend himself; he wears a broad-brimmed felt hat, an *ionar*, trews, brogues, with the addition of a sash in red. His clothing is covered by a long coat, based on the Killery bog body found in the 1820s, this coat had a buttoned split sleeve from wrist to shoulder.

Plate E, Ensign
The ensign is dressed in an early war style of breeches and split sleeved jacket, sash, wide-brimmed felt hat, shirt, falling band and cavalry boots. He would be from a higher social status than the men and probably connected to the proprietor or others in the higher echelons of the regiment. He carries the Irish Confederate colours.

The colour is reconstructed from a number of sources but based on Hayes-McCoy's reconstruction of the Confederacy of Kilkenny colours. The cross potent is based on the coinage, an illumination from 1646 and a Latin description.

Plate F, Gunner
The gunner is of a more European type, either an Anglo-Irish soldier or an Irish veteran from the Continent. He is dressed in breeches, hose, soldier's shoes of an English type, shirt, collar and tall, wide-brimmed felt hat, such as

we see in contemporary images from the Continent by artists such as Pieter Snayers. He is checking the angle of a gun. He also wears a large powder horn and carries a leather bag for his utensils.

Plate G, European Officer

This is a European veteran, taking time to catch up with correspondence, his paperwork resting on a folio on top of armour. He is dressed in the style of contemporaries of his rank in this period.

Plate H, Highlander

This Highlander is depicted in the classic 'Highland charge' with his broadsword and targe. He is of a better sort, having shoes and hose, and under his belted plaid he wears a loose shirt and a blue bonnet. There are references to Highlanders in trews, stripping down to fight in only their shirt and/or bare legged.

Bibliography

Archival Sources

Bodleian Library (BoL)
Carte MS 2–6, 64

British History Online (BHO)
Rushworth, John, 'Historical Collections: Passages relating to Ireland 1642-43', in *Historical Collections of Private Passages of State: Volume 5, 1642-45* (London: D. Browne, 1721), pp.504–59

British Library (BrL)
Sloane MS 190 (12): 'A collection of letters and papers formerly belonging to Edmund Borlase'

British Museum (BM)
Add.MSS, 24200, fols 38v–39: Nicholas Pynnar, 'The fort and castle of Charlemont'

Corpus of Electronic Texts (CELT)
O'Neill, Henry, 'An impartial relation of the most memorable transactions of General Owen O'Neill and his party, from the year 1641 to the year 1650'
T100076: 'The tour of the French traveller M. de La Boullaye Le Gouz in Ireland, A.D. 1644'

Irish Manuscripts Commission (IMC)
Kavanagh, Stanislaus (ed.), *Commentarius Rinuccinianus, de sedis apostolicae legatione ad foederatos Hiberniae Catholicos per annos 1645–1649* (Dublin: Publisher unknown, 1944), vols I–II

Lennon Wylie (LW)
Anon., 'A brief Relation of the miraculous Victory gained there that day over the first formed Army of the Irish, soon after their Rebellion, which broke out the 23rd October, 1641', in *Historical Account of the Town of Lisburn*

The National Archives (TNA)
A Treatise or Account of the War and Rebellion in Ireland since the Year 1641 (London: Publisher unknown, n.d.)

HMC 2nd Report (London: HMC, 1871)
HMC 7th Report, Manuscripts of Sir Harry Verney (London: HMC, 1879)
HMC Report on Franciscan Manuscripts in Dublin (London: HMC, 1906)
HMC Report on the Manuscripts of the Earl of Egmont (London: Mackie & Co., 1905–1909), vol. I
SP 63/237, fol. 36
SP 63/260, fol. 160
SP 63/260, fol. 190
SP 63/260, fol. 210
SP 63/260, fols 234–35
SP 63/264
SP 63/277, fol. 121

Trinity College Dublin Library (TCDL): 1641 Depositions
MS 809–40

Primary Sources

Anon., *A Briefe relation of the proceedings of our army in Ireland, since the tenth of June to this present July 1642 together with the petition of the Parliament there assembled, to the lords, iustices, and counsell* (London: R. Oulton and G. Dexter, 1642)

Anon., *A continued iournall of all the proceedings of the Duke of Buckingham his Grace, in the Isle of Ree, since the last of Iuly …* (London: Augustine Mathewes, 1627)

Anon., *A full and true relation of the late great victory, obtained by the Protestants against the rebells in Ireland* (London: Henry Overton, 1643)

Anon., *A Full relation, not only of our good successe in generall, but how, and in what manner God hath fought his own cause miraculously* (London: G. Miller, 1642)

Anon., *A iournall of the most memorable passages in Ireland. Especially that victorious battell at Munster, beginning the 25. of August 1642. and continued. Wherein is related the siege of Ardmore Castle; together with a true and perfect description of the famous battell of Liscarroll* (London: T. S., 1642)

Anon., *A treatise of the arms and engines of vvar of fire-works, ensigns, and military instruments, both ancient and modern; with the manner they are at present used, as well in French armies, as amongst other nations. Inriched with many figures* (London: Robert Hartford, 1678)

Anon., *A true and perfect diurnall: of the most remarkeable passages in Ireland …* (London: Edward Blackmore, 1652)

Anon., *A True relation of the latest occurrences in Ireland. Sent from the postmaster there, to a friend of his in London. Dated in Ireland, August 17. 1642* (London: Benjamin Allen, 1642)

BIBLIOGRAPHY

Anon., *A true relation of the manner of our Colonell Sir Frederick Hammiltons return from London-Derry in Ireland* (London: Publisher unknown, 1645)

Anon., *A True Relation of the Taking of Mountjoy in the County of Tyrone by Collonell Clotworthy …* (London: R. Oulton and G. Dexter, 1642)

Anon., *Admirable, good, true and joyfull newes from Ireland …* (London: John Wright, 1642)

Anon., *Another extract of more letters sent out of Ireland, informing the condition of the kingdome as it now stands* (London: Publisher unknown, 1643)

Anon., *Severall passages of the late proceedings in Ireland* (London: Henry Overton, 1642)

Anon., *The Compleat Gunner* (London: E. Tyler and R. Holt, 1672)

Anon., *The information of Sir Frederick Hammilton, Knight, and Colonell, given to the Committee of Both Kingdoms, concerning Sir William Cole, Knight, and Colonell; with the scandalous answer of the said Sir William Cole, Knight …* (London: Publisher unknown, 1645)

Anon., *The last joyfull newes from Ireland being the copies of two severall letters sent from Dublin the 28 of Aprill, 1642 to a noble person in this city …* (London: T. Fawcet, 1642)

Anon., *The late prosperous proceedings of the Protestant army against the rebells in Ireland …* (London: John Wright, 1643)

Anon., *The Military discipline wherein is martially showne the order for driling the musket and pike : set forth in postures with ye words of comand and brief instructions for the right use of the same* (London: Tho. Jenner, 1642)

Anon., *The Whole triall of Connor Lord Macguire* (London: Robert Austin, 1645)

Anon., *True intelligence from Ireland. Relating many passages of great consequence …* (London: John Sweeting, 1642)

Anon., *Truth from Ireland expressed in Two Letters* (London: John Wright, 1643)

B., J., *A Famous Victory obtained against the Rebels in Ireland, very lately by Colonell Muncke* (London: R. B., 1642)

Ball, F. E. (ed.), *Calendar of the Manuscripts of the Marquess of Ormonde, K. P., Preserved at Kilkenny Castle* (London: HMSO, 1902–1920), vols I–II

Barriffe, William, *Military Discipline: or, the yong artillery man …* (London: Thomas Harper, 1635)

Barry, Gerat, *A discourse of military discipline devided into three boockes …* (Brussels: John Mommart, 1634)

Bernard, Nicholas, *The whole proceedings of the siege of Drogheda in Ireland, vvith a thankfull remembrance for its wonderfull delivery. Raised with Gods speciall assistance by the prayers, and sole valour of the besieged, with a relation of such memorable passages as have falne out there, and in the parts neer adjoyning since this late rebellion* (London: VVilliam Bladen, 1642)

Bingham, John, 'Epistle Dedicatory', in *The Art of Embattailing an Army. Or, The Second Part of Aelians Tacticks: Containing the Practice of the Best Generals of all Antiquitie, Concerning the Formes of Battailes* (London: John Beale and Thomas Brudenell, 1629)

Boate, Gerard, *The Natural History of Ireland* (London: John Wright, 1652)

Borlase, Edmund, *The History of the Execrable Irish Rebellion Trac'd from Many Preceding Acts, to the Grand Eruption the 23. of October, 1641. And Thence Pursued to the Act of Settlement, MDCLXII* (London: Robert Clavel, 1680)

Boyle, Richard, *A letter of the Earle of Corke to the state at Dublin …* (London: Edward Blackmore, 1642)

Brocket, William, *Good newes from Ireland. Or, A true relation of a great victory obtained by the Protestants in the province of Munster in Ireland …* (London: I. Thomas, 1642)

Burke, Ulick, *The Memoirs and Letters of Ulick, Marquis of Clanricarde, and Earl of Saint Albans …* (London: J. Hughs, 1757)

Burkhead, Henry, *A tragedy of Cola's furie, or, Lirenda's miserie* (Kilkenny: Publisher unknown, 1646)

Castlenau, Jacques II de, *Le Marechal de Bataille* (Paris: Etienne Migon, 1647)

Caulfield, Richard (ed.), *The Council Book of the Corporation of Kinsale, from 1652 to 1800* (Guildford: J. Billing and Sons, 1879)

Chappell, Richard, *A true and good Relation of the Valliant Exploits, and Victorious Enterprises of Sir Simon Harcourt, and Sir Charles Coote …* (London: F. Coules and W. Ley, 1642)

Coates, Willson H., Young, Anne S., and Snow, Vernon F. (eds), *The Private Journals of the Long Parliament: 7 March to 1 June 1642* (New Haven, CT: Yale University Press, 1987)

Cole, Robert, *More good and true news from Ireland sent from Dublin by Master Robert Cole merchant, to his brother Iohn Cole here resident in London …* (London: F. Coules, 1642)

Cole, Robert, *The true coppies of two letters sent from Ireland: shewing the severall battailes and victories obtained on the rebels there* (London: J.B. and R. Smith, 1643)

Creichtoun, George, 'A Faithful Account … by G. Creichtoun, chaplain to his Lordship's Regiment', in P. H. Hore (ed.), *History of the Town and County of Wexford: Comprised Principally from the State Papers, the Public Records, and Mss. of the Late Herbert F. Hore, Esq., of Pole Hore, in that County. Old and New Ross* (London: Elliot Stock, 1900), pp.302–03

D., B., *Tvvo letters from tvvo chief officers under the command of the Earle of Ormond Particularly relating their good and happy successe in their late expedition* (London: H. Blunden, 1642)

De Chastenet, Jacques François, *Art de la guerre, par principes et par règles* (Paris: C. A. Jombert, 1748)

De Pas, Antoine, *Memoirs of the late Marquis de Feuquieres: Lieutenant-General of the French army. Written for the instruction of his son. Being *an account of all the wars in Europe, from the year 1672, to the year 1710 …* (London: T. Woodward and C. Davis, 1737), vols 1–2

Dryden, John, *The Works of that Famous English Poet, Mr. Edmond Spenser* (London: Henry Hills, 1679)

Elton, Richard, *The Compleat Body of the Art Military: Exactly Compiled, and Gradually Composed for the Foot, in the Best Refined Manner, According to the Practice of the Modern Times …* (London: Robert Leybourne, 1650)

Enos, Walter, *Second part of the survey of the articles of the late rejected peace* (Kilkenny: Publisher unknown, 1646)

Eustace, Maurice, *A letter from Sir Maurice Eustace Knight, His Maiesties serjeant at law in the kingome of Ireland, and speaker of the House of Commons, in Parliament there being a perfect relation of the last true newes from Ireland* (London: E. G, 1642)

Gething, Richard, *Digitus dei, or, A miraculous victory gained by the English upon the rebels in Munster express in two letters written to Lievtenant Colonell St.Leger, sonne and heire to the Right Honourable Sir William St. Leger, knight, late Lord president of Munster* (London: Thomas Bates, 1642)

Heath, John (ed.), *Observations upon military & political affairs written by the Most Honourable George, Duke of Albemarle* (London: R. White, 1796)

Hill, George (ed.), *The Montgomery Manuscripts: (1603–1706)* (Belfast: James Cleeland and Thomas Dargan, 1869)

Hogan, Edmund (ed.), *The History of the Warr of Ireland from 1641 to 1653. By a British Officer, of the Regiment of Sir John Clottworthy* (Dublin: McGlashan and Gill, 1873)

Hogan, James (ed.), *Letters and Papers Relating to the Irish Rebellion between 1642–46* (Dublin: Stationary Office, 1936)

House of Commons, *A relation touching the present state and condition of Ireland. Collected by a committee of the house of Commons, out of severall letters, lately come from the Lords Justices of Ireland and others, and printed by order of the said house. And also the examination of Hubert Petit, taken the 19. of February, 1641. by the direction of the Lords Justices, and counsell of Ireland* (London: E. G., 1642)

Hyde, Edward, *The History of the Rebellion and Civil Wars in England* (Oxford: Printed at Theater, 1707), vols I–III

Johnson, Thomas, *A true relation of Gods providence in the province of Munster in delivering them from the hands of ther enemies and giving them a great victory : related in a letter / sent from a gentleman, a voluntier in the Lord Dungarvans troope to a worthy friend of his in London* (London: L. N., 1642)

Jones, Thomas W. (ed.), *A True Relation of the Life and Death of the Right Reverend Father in God William Bedell, Lord Bishop of Kilmore in Ireland* (London: Camden Society, 1872)

Kelly, Matthew (ed.), *Cambrensis Eversus. The History of Ancient Ireland Vindicated : The Religion, Laws and Civilization of Her People Exhibited in the Lives and Actions of Her Kings, Princes, Saints, Bishops, Bards, and Other Learned Men …* (Dublin: Celtic Society, 1848–1852), vols I–III

L., A., *A true relation of the late expedition of the right honorable, the Earl of Ormond, and Sir Charles Coote Knight, and Baronet, into the severall counties of Kildare, Queens county, Kings county, and the county of Catherlagh …* (London: Joseph Hunscott, 1642)

Lawrence, Richard, *The Interest of England in the Irish transplantation, stated …* (Dublin: William Bladen, 1655)

Lynch, P. (ed.), *The Earl of Castlehaven's Memoirs Or, His Review of the Civil Wars in Ireland* (Dublin: Espy and Cross, 1815)

MacLysaght, Edward, and Berry, H. F., 'Report on Documents Relating to the Wardenship of Galway', *Analecta Hibernica*, 14 (1944), pp.1–3, 5, 7–141, 143–87, 189–250

Mahaffy, Robert P. (ed.), *Calendar of the State Papers Relating to Ireland, Of the Reign of Charles I [and Commonwealth], Preserved in the Public Record Office, 1625-[1660]* (London: HMSO, 1901), vol. 2: 1633–1647

Meehan, Charles P. (ed.), *The Rise and Fall of the Irish Franciscan Monasteries, and Memoirs of the Irish Hierarchy, in the Seventeenth Century. With Appendices Containing Documents from the Rinuccini Manuscripts, Public Records, and Archives of the Franciscan Convent, Dublin* (Dublin: James Duffy and Sons, 1872)

Mercer, William, *The moderate cavalier, or, The soldiers description of Ireland and of the country disease, with receipts for the same* (Cork: Publisher unknown, 1675)

Moran, Patrick F. (ed.), *Spicilegium Ossoriense: Being a Collection of Original Letters and Papers Illustrative of the History of the Irish Church from the Reformation to the Year 1800* (Dublin: W. B. Kelly, 1874)

O'Rahilly, Cecile (ed.), *Five Seventeenth-Century Political Poems* (Dublin: Dublin Institute for Advanced Studies, 1952)

Ó Donnchadha, Tadhg, 'Cín lae Uí Mhealláin', *Analecta Hibernica, 3 (1931)*, pp.1–61

Papillon, David, *A practicall abstract of the arts of fortification and assailing …* (London: R. Austin, 1645)

Peters, Hugh, *A true relation of the passages of Gods providence in a voyage for Ireland …* (London: Luke Norton, 1642)

Pringle, John, *Observations on the Diseases of the Army, in Camp and Garrison. In Three Parts. With an Appendix, Containing Some Papers of*

Experiments, Read at Several Meetings of the Royal Society (London: A. Millar, D. Wilson, T. Durham, and T. Payne, 1753)

Russell, Charles W., and Prendergast, John P. (eds), *The Carte manuscripts in the Bodleian Library, Oxford. A report presented to the Right Honourable Lord Romilly, master of the rolls* (London: G.E. Eyre and W. Spottiswoode, 1871)

Saintliger, W., *Joyfull and happy news from Ireland* (London: Edward Blackmore, 1643)

Scott, Brendan (ed.), *Dr Henry Jones' Account of the 1641 Rising: Plantation and War in County Cavan* (Newtownards: Ulster Historical Foundation, 2021)

Simington, R. C., and MacLellan, John, 'Oireachtas Library List of Outlaws, 1641-1647', *Analecta Hibernica*, 23 (1966), pp.319–67

Smith, Charles, *The Ancient and Present State of the County of Kerry. Containing a Natural, Civil, Ecclesiastical, Historical and Topographical Description Thereof* (Dublin: W. Cater, 1774)

T., N., *Very sad newes from Ireland* (London: Publisher unknown, 1646)

Temple, John, *Ormonds curtain drawn. In a short discourse concerning Ireland; wherein his treasons, and the corruption of his instruments are laid bare to the stroke of justice* (London: Publisher unknown, 1646)

Temple, John, *The History of the General Rebellion in Ireland. Raised Upon the Three and Twentieth Day of October, 1641. Together with the Barbarous Cruelties and Bloody Massacres which Ensued Thereupon* (Cork: Phineas and George Bagnell, 1766)

Turner, James, *Memoirs of His Own Life and Times* (Edinburgh: Bannatyne Club, 1829)

Turner, James, *Pallas Armata. Military Essayes of the Ancient Grecian, Roman and Modern Art of War. Written in the Years 1670 and 1671* (London: M. W., 1683)

Verney, Margaret M., *Memoirs of the Verney Family during the Seventeenth Century* (London: Longmans, Green and Co., 1892), vols I–II

Willoughby, Francis, *A relation of the battell fought by the forces of the King and Parliament. The Marquis of Ormond being generall, and the Lord Vicount Lisle lieutenant generall of the horse, against the bloody rebels in Ireland neer Old Rosse, and not far from Doncannon in the year 1642* (London: Fr. Neile, 1648)

Yarner, Abraham, *Relation of the battaile fought at Kilrush …* (London: F. Coules, and G. Badger, 1642)

Secondary Sources

Anon., 'Owen "Roe" O'Neill', *Ulster Journal of Archaeology*, 1st series, 4 (1856), pp.25–39

Ardant du Picq, Charles, *Études sur le combat* (Paris: Librairie Hachette, 1880)

Armstrong, Robert, 'Coote, Sir Charles', *Dictionary of Irish Biography* (2009), <https://www.dib.ie/biography/coote-sir-charles-a2027>, accessed 2 April 2020

Armstrong, Robert, *Protestant War: The 'British' of Ireland and the Wars of the Three Kingdoms* (Manchester: Manchester University Press, 2005)

Armstrong, Robert, 'The Long Parliament Goes to War: The Irish Campaigns, 1641–3', *Historical Research*, 80:207 (2007), pp.73–99

Arnold, Thomas F., *The Renaissance at War* (London: Cassell, 2006)

Bagwell, Richard, *Ireland Under the Stuarts and during the Interregnum* (London: Longmans, Green and Co., 1909), vol. II: 1642–1660

Bamford, Andrew, *Sickness, Suffering, and the Sword: The British Regiment on Campaign, 1808–1815* (Norman: University of Oklahoma Press, 2021)

Barker, Thomas M. (ed.), *The Military Intellectual and Battle: Raimondo Montecuccoli and the Thirty Years' War* (Albany: State University of New York Press, 1975)

Barratt, John, *Sieges of the English Civil Wars* (Barnsley: Pen and Sword, 2008)

Barratt, John, *The King's Irish: The Royalist Anglo-Irish Foot of the English Civil War* (Warwick: Helion & Company, 2019)

Bartlett, Thomas, *'The Academy of Warre': Military Affairs in Ireland, 1600 to 1800* (Dublin: National University of Ireland, 2002)

Beer, Jeanette M. A., *A Medieval Caesar* (Geneva: Librairie Droz, 1976)

Begley, John, *The Diocese of Limerick in the Sixteenth and Seventeenth Centuries* (Dublin: Browne and Nolan, 1927)

Bennett, George, *The History of Bandon* (Cork: Henry and Coghlan, 1862)

Black, Jeremy, *European Warfare, 1494-1660* (London: Routledge, 2002)

Black, Jeremy, 'The Thirty Years' War', *Teaching History*, 63 (1991), pp.44–46

Blackmore, David J., *'Destructive and Formidable': British Infantry Firepower, 1642-1765*. 2012. Nottingham Trent University, PhD

Bottigheimer, Karl S., 'English Money and Irish Land: The "Adventurers" in the Cromwellian Settlement of Ireland', *Journal of British Studies*, 7:1 (1967), pp.12–27

Bradbury, Jim, *The Medieval Siege* (Woodbridge: Boydell & Brewer, 1994)

Brunicardi, Niall, 'The Battle of Manning Ford, 4 June 1643', *The Irish Sword*, 22:87 (2000), pp.3–14

Buckley, James, 'The Battle of Liscarroll, 1642', *Journal of the Cork Archaeological and Historical Society*, 2nd series, 4:38 (1898), pp.83–100

Buckley, James, 'The Siege of Ardmore Castle, 1642', *Journal of the Waterford and South-East of Ireland Archaeological Society*, 4:1 (1898), pp.54–59

Bull, Stephen, *The Furie of the Ordnance: Artillery in the English Civil Wars* (Woodbridge: Boydell & Brewer, 2008)
Burne, Alfred H., and Young, Peter, *The Great Civil War: A Military History of the First Civil War, 1642-1646* (London: Eyre and Spottiswoode, 1959)
Butler, William F. T., *Gleanings from Irish History* (London: Longmans, Green and Co., 1925)

Caball, John, 'The Siege of Tralee, 1642', *The Irish Sword*, 2:9 (1956), pp.315–17
Camilo, Francisco, 'The Holy Family or Trinity on Earth', *Museo del Prado*, <https://www.museodelprado.es/en/the-collection/art-work/the-holy-family-or-trinity-on-earth/caf18f44-eb03-4f68-bd7f-139f6b304372>, accessed 13 May 2023
Cannadine, David (ed.), *Oxford Dictionary of National Biography*, <https://www.oxforddnb.com/>, accessed 16 Sept. 2020
Canning, Ruth A., *The Old English in Early Modern Ireland: The Palesmen and the Nine Years' War, 1594-1603* (Woodbridge: Boydell & Brewer, 2019)
Canny, Nicholas, *Making Ireland British, 1580–1650* (Oxford: Oxford University Press, 2001)
Carlton, Charles, *Going to the Wars: The Experience of the British Civil Wars, 1638–1651* (London: Routledge, 1992)
Carlton, Charles, *This Seat of Mars: War and the British Isles, 1485–1746* (New Haven, CT: Yale University Press, 2011)
Carte, Thomas, *An History of the Life of James Duke of Ormonde* (London: J. J. and P. Knapton, 1736), vol. I
Casway, Jerrold I., *Owen Roe O'Neill and the Struggle for Catholic Ireland* (Philadelphia: University of Pennsylvania Press, 1984)
Casway, Jerrold I., 'Owen Roe O'Neill's Return to Ireland in 1642: The Diplomatic Background', *Studia Hibernica*, 9 (1969), pp.48–64
Cavendish, Margaret, *The Life of William Cavendish, Duke of Newcastle: To Which is Added the True Relation of My Birth, Breeding, and Life* (London: John C. Nimmo, 1886)
Childs, John, and Keegan, John, *Warfare in the Seventeenth Century* (London: Cassel, 2001)
Clarke, Aidan, 'The Genesis of the Ulster Rising of 1641', in P. Roebuck (ed.), *Plantation to Partition: Essays in Ulster History in Honour of J. L. McCracken* (Belfast: Blackstaff Press, 1981), pp.32–40
Clarke, Aidan, *The Old English in Ireland, 1625-42* (London: MacGibbon and Kee, 1966)
Clavin, Terry, 'Dillon, Theobald', *Dictionary of Irish Biography* (2009), <https://www.dib.ie/biography/dillon-theobald-a2616>, accessed 3 March 2020
Clavin, Terry, 'Maguire, Rory (Roger)', *Dictionary of Irish Biography* (2009), <https://www.dib.ie/biography/maguire-rory-roger-a5364>, accessed 24 Jan. 2020
Coonan, Thomas L., *The Irish Catholic Confederacy and the Puritan Revolution* (Dublin: Clonmore and Reynolds, 1954)

Cregan, Donal F., 'The Confederate Catholics of Ireland: The Personnel of the Confederation, 1642–9', *Irish Historical Studies*, 29:116 (1995), pp.490–512

Croxton, Derek, 'A Territorial Imperative? The Military Revolution, Strategy and Peacemaking in the Thirty Years War', *War in History*, 5:3 (1998), pp.253–79

Cunningham, Bernadette, and Gillespie, Raymond, '"The Most Adaptable of Saints": The Cult of St Patrick in the Seventeenth Century', *Archivium Hibernicum*, 49 (1995), pp.82–104

Cunningham, John, 'Sickness, Disease and Medical Practitioners in 1640s Ireland', in J. Cunningham (ed.), *Early Modern Ireland and the World of Medicine, Practitioners, Collectors, and Contexts* (Manchester: Manchester University Press, 2019), pp.61–83

Cuthbert, Mhág Craith, 'Toirdhealbhach Ó Conchubhair (floruit circa 1645)', in Franciscan Fathers (eds), *Father Luke Wadding: Commemorative Volume* (Dublin: Clonmore and Reynolds, 1957), pp.414–37

Darcy, Eamon, *The Irish Rebellion of 1641 and the Wars of the Three Kingdoms* (Woodbridge: Boydell & Brewer, 2013)

Davies, John, 'A Discovery of the True Causes Why Ireland Was Never Entirely Subdued nor Brought under Obedience of the Crown of England until the Beginning of His Majesty's Happy Reign', in H. Morley (ed.), *Ireland under Elizabeth and James the First* (London: George Routledge and Sons, 1890), pp.213–342

Debe, Demetri D., 'The Fifth Earl of Clanricarde and the Founding of the Confederate Catholic Government 1641–3', *Irish Historical Studies*, 36:143 (2009), pp.315–31

De Brún, Pádraig, and Pierse, John H., 'Lament for Garret Pierse of Aghamore, Slain at Liscarroll, 1642', *Journal of the Kerry Archaeological and Historical Society*, 20 (1987), pp.5–27

De Mesa, Eduardo, 'The Career of Owen Roe O'Neill in the Spanish Army of Flanders (1606–42): Documentation Held in Spanish Archives', *Archivium Hibernicum*, 67 (2014), pp.7–24

De Mesa, Eduardo, *The Irish in the Spanish Armies in the Seventeenth Century* (Woodbridge: Boydell & Brewer, 2014)

Dinneen, Patrick S. (ed.), *Foclóir Gaedhilge agus Béarla. An Irish-English Dictionary, Being a Thesaurus of the Words, Phrases and Idioms of the Modern Irish Language, with Explanations in English* (Dublin: Irish Texts Society, 1904)

Dorney, John, '"Deceived as Hereafter to the Destruction of Both" – Stories from the 1641 Rebellion', *Irish History Online* (2015), <https://www.theirishstory.com/2015/12/03/deceived-as-hereafter-to-the-destruction-of-both-stories-from-the-1641-rebellion/#.ZF0xjXbMJD8>, accessed 23 Jan. 2021

Dowen, Keith, 'The Seventeenth Century Buff-Coat', *Journal of the Arms and Armour Society*, 21:5 (2015), pp.157–88

BIBLIOGRAPHY

Doyle, Martin, *Notes and Gleanings Relating to the County of Wexford in Its Past and Present Conditions* (Dublin: George Herbert, 1868)

Duffy, Christopher, *Siege Warfare: The Fortress in the Early Modern World 1494-1660* (Abingdon-on-Thames: Routledge, 2013)

Duignan, Aoife, '"All in a Confused Opposition to Each Other": Politics and War in Connacht, 1641–9: PhD. Thesis, University College Dublin, 2005', *Irish Economic and Social History*, 33:1 (2006), pp.72–73

Edwards, David, 'A Haven of Popery: English Catholic Migration to Ireland in the Age of Plantations', A. Ford and J. McCafferty (eds), *The Origins of Sectarianism in Early Modern Ireland* (Cambridge: Cambridge University Press, 2005), pp.95–126

Edwards, David, 'Holding On: The Earl of Cork's Blackwater Army and the Defence of Protestant Munster, 1641–43', in P. Little (ed.), *Ireland in Crisis: War, Politics and Religion, 1641–50* (Manchester: Manchester University Press, 2020), pp.20–42

Edwards, David, '"The Poisoned Chalice": The Ormond Inheritance, Sectarian Division and the Emergence of James Butler, 1614-1642', in T. C. Barnard and J. Fenlon (eds), *The Dukes of Ormonde, 1610-1745* (Woodbridge: Boydell & Brewer, 2000), pp.55–82

Edwards, Peter, *Dealing in Death: The Arms Trade and the British Civil Wars, 1638-52* (Cheltenham: The History Press, 2000)

Empey, Mark, 'The Diary of Sir James Ware, 1623–66', *Analecta Hibernica*, 45 (2014), pp.53, 55–146

Farrell, Gerard, *The 'Mere Irish' and the Colonisation of Ulster, 1570-1641* (London: Palgrave Macmillan, 2017)

Finnegan, David, 'What Do the Depositions Say about the Outbreak of the 1641 Rising', in E. Darcy, A. Margey, and E. Murphy (eds), *The 1641 Depositions and the Irish Rebellion* (London: Pickering & Chatto, 2014), pp.21–34

Fischer-Kattner, Anke, 'Colchester's Plight in European Perspective: Printed Representations of Seventeenth-Century Siege Warfare', in A. Fischer-Kattner and J. Ostwald (eds), *The World of the Siege: Representations of Early Modern Positional Warfare* (Leiden: Brill, 2019), pp.44–84

Fissel, Mark C., *English Warfare, 1511–1642* (London: Routledge, 2001)

Fitzgerald, Frederick, 'Lettice, Baroness of Offaly, and the Siege of Her Castle of Geashill, 1642', *Journal of the County Kildare Archaeological Society and Surrounding Districts*, 3 (1899–1902), pp.419–24

Fitzpatrick, Brendan, *Seventeenth-Century Ireland: The War of Religions* (Dublin: Gill and Macmillan, 1988)

Fitzpatrick, Thomas, *Waterford during the Civil War (1641-1653)* (Waterford: Downey and Co. Publishers, 1912)

Forkan, Kevin, 'Inventing an Irish Protestant Icon: The Strange Death of Sir Charles Coote, 1642', in D. Edwards, C. Tait, and P. Lenihan (eds), *Age of Atrocity: Violence and Political Conflict in Early Modern Ireland* (Dublin: Four Courts Press, 2007), pp.204–18

Furgol, Edward M., *A Regimental History of the Covenanting Armies, 1639–1651* (Edinburgh: John Donald, 1990)

Gallwey, Hubert, 'The MacSheehys of Connello in County Limerick', *Irish Genealogist*, 4:6 (1973), pp.564–77

Gardiner, Samuel R., *History of the Great Civil War, 1642-1649* (London: Longmans, Green and Co., 1886), vol. 1

Gaunt, Peter, *The English Civil War: A Military History* (London: Bloomsbury, 2019)

Gentles, I., 'The Civil Wars in England', in J. Kenyon, J. Ohlmeyer, and J. Morrill (eds), *The Civil Wars: A Military History of England, Scotland, and Ireland 1638–1660* (Oxford: Oxford University Press, 1998), p.104

Gilbert, John T. (ed.), *A Contemporary History of Affairs in Ireland from 1641 to 1652. Now for the First Time Published. With an Appendix of Original Letters and Documents* (Dublin: Irish Archaeological and Celtic Society, 1879–1880), vols I–III

Gilbert, John T. (ed.), *History of the Irish Confederation and the War in Ireland 1641-1649* (Dublin: M. H. Gill and Son, 1879–1880), vols I–VII

Gillespie, Raymond, *Conspiracy: Ulster Plots and Plotters in 1615* (Belfast: Ulster Society for Irish Historical Studies, 1987)

Gillespie, Raymond, 'The Murder of Arthur Champion and the 1641 Rising in Fermanagh', *Clogher Record*, 14:3 (1993), pp.52–66

Gillman, Herbert W., 'Siege of Rathbarry Castle, 1642', *Journal of the Cork Historical and Archaeological Society*, 2nd series, 1:1 (1895), pp.1–20

Gillman, Herbert W., 'The Rise and Progress in Munster of the Rebellion, 1642', *Journal of the Cork Historical & Archaeological Society*, 2nd series, 2:13 (1896), pp.11–63

Gleeson, Dermot F., 'The Silver Mines of Ormond', *Journal of the Royal Society of Antiquaries of Ireland*, 7th series, 7:1 (1937), pp.101–16

Goldsworthy, Adrian K., 'The Othismos, Myths and Heresies: The Nature of Hoplite Battle', *War in History*, 4:1 (1997), pp.1–26

Gouhier, Pierre, 'Mercenaires irlandais au service de la France (1635-1664)', *Revue d'histoire moderne et contemporaine*, 15:4 (1968), pp.672–90

Gravett, Christopher, *Medieval Siege Warfare* (Oxford: Osprey, 1990)

Grosart, Alexander (ed.), *The Lismore Papers (Second Series)* (London: Chiswick Press, 1888), vol. V

Hagan, John, 'Miscellanea Vaticano-Hibernica', *Archivium Hibernicum*, 6 (1917), pp.94–155

Hall, Bert S., *Weapons and Warfare in Renaissance Europe: Gunpowder, Technology, and Tactics* (London: Johns Hopkins University Press, 1997)

Hanlon, Gregory, *European Military Rivalry, 1500–1750: Fierce Pageant* (Abingdon-on-Thames: Routledge, 2020)

Hardiman, James, *The History of the Town and County of the Town of Galway* (Dublin: W. Folds and Sons, 1820)

Hartnett, Michael, *Haicéad* (Oldcastle: The Gallery Press, 1993)

Hayes-McCoy, G. A., 'Strategy and Tactics in Irish Warfare, 1593-1601', *Irish Historical Studies*, 2:7 (1941), pp.255–79

Hayes-McCoy, G. A., 'The Tide of Victory and Defeat: II. The Battle of Kinsale, 1601', *Studies: An Irish Quarterly Review*, 38:151 (1949), pp.307–17

Hazlett, Hugh, *A History of the Military Forces Operating in Ireland 1641-49*. 1938. Queen's University of Belfast, PhD

Hickson, Mary, *Ireland in the Seventeenth Century, or, The Irish Massacres of 1641-2: Their Causes and Results* (London: Longmans, Green and Co., 1884), vol. I

Hill, George, 'The Stewarts of Ballintoy: With Notices of Other Families of the District in the Seventeenth Century', *Ulster Journal of Archaeology*, 2nd series, 6:1 (1900), pp.17–23

Hoffman, Philip T., *Why Did Europe Conquer the World?* (Princeton: Princeton University Press, 2015)

Hollick, Clive, *The Battle of Benburb 1646* (Cork: Mercier Press, 2011)

Holmes, Richard, *Firing Line* (Harmondsworth: Penguin, 1986)

Hore, P. H. (ed.), *History of the Town and County of Wexford: Comprised Principally from the State Papers, the Public Records, and Mss. of the Late Herbert F. Hore, Esq., of Pole Hore, in that County. Old and New Ross* (London: Elliot Stock, 1900)

Hughes, B. P., *Firepower: Weapons Effectiveness on the Battlefield, 1630-1850* (London: Arms and Armour Press, 1974)

Jennings, Brendan (ed.), *Wild Geese in Spanish Flanders 1582-1700* (Dublin: Irish Manuscripts Commission, 1964)

Jones, Inga, 'A Sea of Blood? Massacres during the Wars of the Three Kingdoms, 1641-53', in P. Dwyer and L. Ryan (eds), *Theatres of Violence: Massacre, Mass Killing and Atrocity throughout History* (New York: Berghahn, 2012), pp.63–78

Jones, Inga, '"Holy War"? Religion, Ethnicity and Massacre during the Irish Rebellion 1641-2', in E. Darcy, A. Margey, and E. Murphy (eds), *The 1641 Depositions and the Irish Rebellion* (London: Pickering & Chatto, 2014), pp.129–42

Joyce, Robert D., 'The Battle of Manning Ford', *Duffy's Hibernian Magazine*, 1:3 (1860), pp.132–34

Kelsey, Sean, 'Butler, Richard, Third Viscount Mountgarret (1578–1651)', *Oxford Dictionary of National Biography* (2004), <https://doi.org/10.1093/ref:odnb/4202>, accessed 13 May 2023

Kerrigan, Paul M., 'Castles and Fortifications of County Offaly c. 1500-1815', in W. Nolan and T. P. O'Neill (eds), *Offaly: History & Society* (Dublin: Geography Publications, 1998), pp.393–438

Kimber, Edward, *The Peerage of Ireland: A Genealogical and Historical Account ...* (London: J. Almon, 1768), vol. I

Lecky, W. E. H., *A History of England in the Eighteenth Century* (London: Longmans, Green and Co., 1878), vol. II

Lenihan, Pádraig, *Confederate Catholics at War, 1641-49* (Cork: Cork University Press, 2001)

Lenihan, Pádraig, 'Confederate Military Strategy, 1643-7', in M. Ó Siochrú (ed.), *Kingdoms in Crisis: Ireland in the 1640s, Essays in Honor of Dónal Cregan* (Dublin: Four Courts Press, 2001), p.159–63

Lenihan, Pádraig, *Fluxes, Fevers and Fighting Men: War and Disease in Ancien Régime Europe 1648-1789* (Warwick: Helion & Company, 2019)

Lenihan, Pádraig, 'Siege Massacres in Ireland: Drogheda in Context', in M. Bennett, R. Gillespie, and R. S. Spurlock (eds), *Cromwell and Ireland; New Perspectives* (Liverpool: Liverpool University Press, 2021), pp.19–50

Library of Trinity College, Dublin, 'Muskerry', *The Down Survey of Ireland* (2013), <https://downsurvey.tchpc.tcd.ie/down-survey-maps.php#bm=Muskerry&c=Cork>, accessed 10 Sept. 2019

Little, Patrick, *Lord Broghill and the Cromwellian Union with Ireland and Scotland* (Woodbridge: Boydell & Brewer, 2004)

Loeber, Rolf, 'Warfare and Architecture in County Laois through Seventeenth Century Eyes', in P. G. Lane and W. Nolan (eds), *Laois: History & Society: Interdisciplinary Essays on the History of an Irish County* (Dublin: Geography Publications, 1999), pp.377–414

Loeber, Rolf, and Parker, Geoffrey, 'The Military Revolution in Seventeenth-Century Ireland', in J. Ohlmeyer (ed.), *Independence to Occupation: Ireland 1641–1660* (Cambridge: Cambridge University Press, 1995), pp.66–88

Lowe, John, 'Charles I and the Confederation of Kilkenny, 1643-9', *Irish Historical Studies*, 14:53 (1964), pp.1–19

López, Ignacio and Iván Notario, *The Spanish Tercios 1536-1704* (Oxford: Osprey, 2012)

Mac Cuarta, Brian, 'Religious Violence against Settlers in South Ulster, 1641-2', in D. Edwards, C. Tait, and P. Lenihan (eds), *Age of Atrocity: Violence and Political Conflict in Early Modern Ireland* (Dublin: Four Courts Press, 2007), pp.154–75

Malcolm, Joyce L., 'All the King's Men: The Impact of the Crown's Irish Soldiers on the English Civil War', *Irish Historical Studies*, 22:83 (1979), pp.239–64

Margey, Annaleigh, '1641 and the Ulster Plantation Towns', in E. Darcy, A. Margey, and E. Murphy (eds), *The 1641 Depositions and the Irish Rebellion* (London: Pickering & Chatto, 2014), pp.79–96

McCarthy, Patrick, 'Preserving Donegal - The Battle of Glenmaquin, 16 June 1642', *The Irish Sword*, 23:94 (2003), pp.361–82

McCarthy, Patrick, 'The 1641 Rebellion in Cork to the Battle of Liscarroll, 3 September 1642', *The Irish Sword*, 22:90 (2001), pp.369–90

McCarthy, S. T., 'The Clann Carthaigh (Continued)', *Kerry Archaeological Magazine*, 3:13 (1914), pp.55–72

McGrath, Bríd, 'Mount Taragh's Triumph: Commitment and Organisation in the Early Stages of the 1641 Rebellion in Meath', in E. Darcy, A. Margey, and E. Murphy (eds), *The 1641 Depositions and the Irish Rebellion* (London: Pickering & Chatto, 2014), pp.51–64

McGrath, Bríd (ed.), *The Minute Book of the Corporation of Clonmel, 1608-1649* (Dublin: Irish Manuscripts Commission, 2006)

McGurk, John, 'The Pacification of Ulster, 1600–3', in D. Edwards, C. Tait, and P. Lenihan (eds), *Age of Atrocity: Violence and Political Conflict in Early Modern Ireland* (Dublin: Four Courts Press, 2007), pp.119–29

McHugh, Jason, 'The North Wexford Gentry and the Rebellion of 1641', *The Past: The Organ of the Uí Cinsealaigh Historical Society,* 24 (2003), pp.28–42

Meehan, Charles P., *The Confederation of Kilkenny* (Dublin: James Duffy, 1846)

Miller, Amos, 'The Battle of Ross: A Controversial Military Event', *The Irish Sword*, 10:39 (1971), pp.141–58

Morrill, John, *Revolt in the Provinces: The People of England and the Tragedies of War, 1630-1648* (Harlow: Longman, 1999)

Morrill, John, 'The Rule of Saints and Soldiers: The Wars of Religion in Britain and Ireland, 1638-1660', in J. Wormald (ed.), *Short Oxford History of the British Isles: The Seventeenth Century* (Oxford: Oxford University Press, 2008), pp.83–115

Morrill, John, 'Three Kingdoms and One Commonwealth? The Enigma of Mid-Seventeenth Century Britain and Ireland', in A. Grant and K. Stringer (eds), *Uniting the Kingdom? The Making of British History* (London: Routledge, 1995), pp.170–90

Murphy, Elaine, *Ireland and the War at Sea, 1641-1653* (London: Royal Historical Society, Boydell, 2012)

Murphy, Elaine, 'Siege of Duncannon Fort in 1641 and 1642', in E. Darcy, A. Margey, and E. Murphy (eds), *The 1641 Depositions and the Irish Rebellion* (London: Pickering & Chatto, 2014), pp.143–54

Nicholls, Kenneth (ed.), *The Irish Fiants of the Tudor Sovereigns: During the Reigns of Henry VIII, Edward VI, Philip & Mary, and Elizabeth I* (Dublin: Éamonn de Búrca, 1994), vols I–III

Ní Cheallacháin, Máire, *Filíocht Phádraigín Haicéad* (Dublin: An Clóchomhar, 2003)

Ní Mhurchadha, Maighréad, *Fingal, 1603–60: Contending Neighbours in North Dublin* (Dublin: Four Courts Press, 2005)

Ní Mhurchadha, Maighréad, 'War in Winter: The 1641 Rising in the Balbriggan Area', *Dublin Historical Record*, 68:2 (2015), pp.164–79

Nolan, Cathal J., *Wars of the Age of Louis XIV, 1650-1715: An Encyclopedia of Global Warfare and Civilization* (Westport, CT: Greenwood Press, 2008)

Oakeshott, Ewart, *European Weapons and Armour: From the Renaissance to the Industrial Revolution* (Rochester, NY: Boydell & Brewer, 2012)

O'Brien, Barry, *Munster at War* (Cork: Mercier Press, 1971)

O'Brien, Barry, 'The Battle of Liscarroll – 3 September 1642', *The Irish Sword*, 22:90 (2001), pp.391–402

O'Byrne, Emmet, O'Byrne, Aodh', *Dictionary of Irish Biography* (2009), <https://www.dib.ie/biography/obyrne-aodh-a6527>, accessed 13 April 2021

O'Byrne, Emmet, 'O'Toole, Fiach (Luke)', *Dictionary of Irish Biography* (2009), <https://www.dib.ie/biography/otoole-fiach-luke-a7091>, accessed 9 March 2021

O'Dowd, Mary, *Power, Politics, and Land: Early Modern Sligo, 1568-1688* (Belfast: Institute of Irish Studies, Queen's University of Belfast, 1991)

O'Driscoll, Alan, and Hodkinson, Brian, 'Who Was Who in Early Modern Limerick', <https://www.limerick.ie/sites/default/files/atoms/files/who_was_who_in_early_modern_limerick_1.pdf>, accessed 22 May 2021

O'Hanlon, John, and O'Leary, Edward (eds), *History of the Queen's County* (Dublin: Sealy, Bryers & Walker, 1914), vols I–II

Ohlmeyer, Jane, 'A Failed Revolution? The Irish Confederate War in Its European Context', *History Ireland*, 3:1 (1995), pp.24–28

Ohlmeyer, Jane, 'Ireland Independent: Confederate Foreign Policy and International Relations during the Mid-Seventeenth Century', in J. Ohlmeyer (ed.), *Independence to Occupation: Ireland 1641–1660* (Cambridge: Cambridge University Press, 1995), pp.89–111

O'Lochlainn, Colm (ed.), *Irish Chiefs and Leaders: Studies by Father Paul Walsh* (Dublin: Sign of the Three Candles, 1960)

O'Riordan, Michelle, *Poetics and Polemics: Reading Seventeenth-Century Irish Political Verse* (Cork: Cork University Press, 2021)

Ó Dálaigh, Brian, 'Mícheál Coimín: Jacobite, Protestant and Gaelic Poet 1676-1760', *Studia Hibernica*, 34 (2006–2007), pp.123–50

Ó Doibhlin, Éamon, 'Domhnach Mór: Part IV: The Insurrection of 1641 and Its Background', *Seanchas Ard Mhacha: Journal of the Armagh Diocesan Historical Society*, 3:2 (1959), pp.401–29

Ó Drisceoil, Cóilín, 'Excavation of a Seventeenth Century Bastioned Fort at High Street, Castlecomer, Co. Kilkenny', *Old Kilkenny Review*, 70 (2018), pp.46–77

Ó Fiaich, Tomás, 'The O'Neills of the Fews', *Seanchas Ard Mhacha: Journal of the Armagh Diocesan Historical Society*, 7:1 (1973), pp.1–64

Ó hAnnracháin, Tadhg, 'Conflicting Loyalties, Conflicted Rebels: Political and Religious Allegiance among the Confederate Catholics of Ireland', *English Historical Review*, 119:483 (2004), pp.851–72

Ó hAnnracháin, Tadhg, 'The Poet and the Mutinies: Pádraigín Haicéad and the Munster Army in 1647', *Proceedings of the Royal Irish Academy: Archaeology, Culture, History, Literature*, 108C (2008), pp.65–74

Ó hAnnracháin, Tadhg, 'Vatican Diplomacy and the Mission of Rinuccini to Ireland', *Archivium Hibernicum*, 47 (1993), pp.77–88. <http://hdl.handle.net/10197/7900>

Ó Mórdha, P. B., 'The Battle of Clones, 1643', *Clogher Record, 4:3 (1962), pp.148–54*

Ó Mórdha, Pilib, 'The MacMahons of Monaghan (1600 — 1640)', *Clogher Record*, 2:2 (1958), pp.311–27

Ó Mórdha, Séamus P., 'Heber Mac Mahon, Soldier-Bishop of the Confederation of Kilkenny', *Clogher Record*, 3 (1975), pp.41–62

Ó Siochrú, Mícheál, *Confederate Ireland, 1642–1649: A Constitutional and Political Analysis* (Dublin: Four Courts Press, 1999)

Ó Siochrú, Micheál, 'MacCarthy, Donough', *Dictionary of Irish Biography* (2009), <https://www.dib.ie/biography/maccarthy-donough-a5129>, accessed 20 Jan. 2020

Ó Siochrú, Micheál, 'Martin, Richard', *Dictionary of Irish Biography* (2009), <https://www.dib.ie/biography/martin-richard-a5486>, accessed 18 Nov. 2020

Ó Siochrú, Micheál, 'Nugent, Sir Richard', *Dictionary of Irish Biography* (2009), <https://www.dib.ie/biography/nugent-sir-richard-a6258>, accessed 18 Nov. 2020

Ó Siochrú, Micheál, 'Roche, David', *Dictionary of Irish Biography* (2009), <https://www.dib.ie/biography/roche-david-a7742>, accessed 18 Nov. 2020

Ó Siochrú, Micheál, and Sweetnam, Mark S., 'The 1641 Depositions and Portadown Bridge', *Seanchas Ard Mhacha: Journal of the Armagh Diocesan Historical Society*, 24:1 (2012), pp.72–103

Paradowski, Michał, 'Aston, Butler and Murray – British Officers in the Service of Polish Vasa Kings 1621-1634', in S. Jones (ed.), *Britain Turned Germany: The Thirty Years' War and Its Impact on the British Isles 1638-1660* (Warwick: Helion & Company, 2019), pp.64–65

Perceval-Maxwell, Michael, *The Outbreak of the Irish Rebellion of 1641* (Dublin: Gill and Macmillan, 1994)

Perceval-Maxwell, Michael, 'The Ulster Rising of 1641, and the Depositions', *Irish Historical Studies*, 21:82 (1978), pp.144–67

Peterson, Gary D., *Warrior Kings of Sweden: The Rise of an Empire in the Sixteenth and Seventeenth Centuries* (Jefferson, NC: McFarland & Company, 2007)

Picouet, Pierre, *The Armies of Philip IV of Spain 1621-1665: The Fight for European Supremacy* (Warwick: Helion & Company, 2019)

Plant, David, *British Civil Wars, Commonwealth & Protectorate 1638-1660*, <http://bcw-project.org/>, accessed 20 May 2021

Roberts, Keith, *Cromwell's War Machine: The New Model Army 1645-1660* (Barnsley: Pen and Sword, 2005)

Roberts, Keith, *Pike and Shot Tactics 1590–1660* (Oxford: Osprey, 2010)

Royle, Trevor, *Civil War: The Wars of the Three Kingdoms 1638–1660* (New York: Palgrave Macmillan, 2004)

Russell, Conrad, *The Causes of the English Civil War* (Oxford: Clarendon Press, 1990)

Russell, Conrad, *The Fall of the British Monarchies, 1637-1642* (Oxford: Clarendon Press, 1990)

Ryder, Ian, *An English Army for Ireland* (Leigh-on-Sea: Partizan Press, 1987)

Scarampi, Piero, 'Reasons against a Cessation with the English', in J. T. Gilbert (ed.), *History of the Irish Confederation and the War in Ireland 1641-1649* (Dublin: M. H. Gill and Son, 1879–1880), vol. II

Schlegel, Donald M., 'A Clogher Chronology: October, 1641 to July, 1642', *Clogher Record*, 16:1 (1997), pp.79–94

Schlegel, Donald M., 'An Index to the Rebels of 1641 in the County Monaghan Depositions', *Clogher Record*, 15:2 (1995), pp.69–89

Scott, B. G., Brown, R. R., Leacock, A. G., and Salter, C. J., *The Great Guns like Thunder: The Cannon from the City of Derry* (Derry: Guildhall Hall Press, 2009)

Scott, Brendan, and Nicholls, Kenneth, 'The Landowners of the Late Elizabethan Pale: "The Generall Hosting Appointed to Meet at Ye Hill of Tarrah on the 24 of September 1593"', *Analecta Hibernica*, 43 (2012), pp.1–15

Scott, Brian G., 'The Deployment of Mortars in Ireland up to the 1689 Siege of Londonderry', *Ulster Journal of Archaeology*, 3rd Series, 73 (2015–2016), pp.204–18

Scott, David, *Politics and War in the Three Stuart Kingdoms, 1637-49* (London: Palgrave Macmillan, 2003)

Shiels, Damian, 'Siege, Storm and Slaughter: 17th Century Mass Graves', *Archaeology Ireland*, 33:4 (2019), pp.35–38

Smith, Charles, *The Antient and Present State of the County and City of Cork* (Dublin: Publisher unknown, 1730), vol. II

Smyth, W. J., 'Property, Patronage and Population – Reconstructing the Human Geography of *Mid Seventeenth-Century County* Tipperary', in W. Nolan and T. G. McGrath (eds), *Tipperary: History and Society* (Dublin: Geography Publications, 1985), pp.104–38

Smyth, William J., 'Towards a Cultural Geography of the 1641 Rising/Rebellion', in M. Ó Siochrú and J. Ohlmeyer (eds), *Ireland: 1641: Contexts and Reactions* (Manchester: Manchester University Press, 2013), pp.71–94

Stevenson, David, *Scottish Covenanters and Irish Confederates: Scottish-Irish Relations in the Mid-Seventeenth Century* (Newtownards: Ulster Historical Foundation, 1981)

Stradling, R. A., *The Spanish Monarchy and Irish Mercenaries: The Wild Geese in Spain, 1618-68* (Blackrock: Irish Academic Press, 1994)

Talbott, Siobhan, '"Causing Misery and Suffering Miserably": Representations of the Thirty Years' War in Literature and History', *Literature & History*, 30:1 (2021), pp.3–25

Tallett, Frank, *War and Society in Early Modern Europe 1495-1715* (London: Routledge, 1992)

Tallett, Frank, and Trim, D. J. B. (ed.), *European Warfare, 1350–1750* (Cambridge: Cambridge University Press, 2010)

Tinniswood, Adrian, *The Verneys: A True Story of Love, War and Madness in Seventeenth-Century England* (London: Jonathan Cape, 2007)

Treadwell, Victor, *Buckingham and Ireland 1616-1628: A Study in Anglo-Irish Politics* (Dublin: Four Courts Press, 1998)

Valladares Ramírez, Rafael, 'Un reino más para la monarquía? Felipe IV, Irlanda y la guerra civil inglesa, 1641-1649', *Studia historica. Historia moderna*, 15 (1996), pp.259–76

Vigors, Urban, 'Urban Vigors' Relation', *Journal of the Waterford and South-East of Ireland Archaeological Society*, 15 (1912), pp.82–96

Wanklyn, Malcolm, *The Army of Occupation in Ireland 1603-42: Defending the Protestant Hegemony* (Warwick: Helion & Company, 2022)

Westropp, Thomas J., 'Notes on the Sheriffs of County Clare, 1570-1700', *Journal of the Royal Society of Antiquaries of Ireland*, 5th series, 1, part 1 (1890), pp.68–80

Westropp, Thomas J., 'The Principal Ancient Castles of the County Limerick', *Journal of the Royal Society of Antiquaries of Ireland*, 5th series, 37:2 (1907), pp.153–64

Wheeler, James S., *The Irish and British Wars, 1637–1654: Triumph, Tragedy, and Failure* (London: Routledge, 2002)

Wheeler, Scott, 'Four Armies in Ireland', in J. Ohlmeyer (ed.), *Independence to Occupation: Ireland 1641–1660* (Cambridge: Cambridge University Press, 1995), pp.43–65

Wiggins, Kenneth, *Anatomy of a Siege: King John's Castle, Limerick, 1642* (Woodbridge: Boydell & Brewer, 2001)

Wilson, Peter H., *Europe's Tragedy: A New History of the Thirty Years War* (London: Allen Lane, 2009)

Wright, John W., 'Sieges and Customs of War at the Opening of the Eighteenth Century', *American Historical Review*, 39:4 (1934), pp.629–44

Other titles in the Century of the Soldier series

No 1 **'Famous by my Sword'**: The Army of Montrose and the Military Revolution

No 2 **Marlborough's Other Army**: The British Army and the Campaigns of the First Peninsular War, 1702–1712

No 3 **Cavalier Capital**: Oxford in the English Civil War 1642–1646

No 4 **Reconstructing the New Model Army**: Vol 1: Regimental Lists April 1645 to May 1649

No 5 **To Settle the Crown**: Waging Civil War in Shropshire, 1642–1648

No 6 **The First British Army, 1624–1628**: The Army of the Duke of Buckingham

No 7 **Better Begging Than Fighting**: The Royalist Army in Exile in the War against Cromwell 1656–1660

No 8 **Reconstructing the New Model Army**: Vol 2: Regimental Lists April 1649 to May 1663

No 9 **The Battle of Montgomery 1644**: The English Civil War in the Welsh Borderlands

No 10 **The Arte Militaire**: The Application of 17th Century Military Manuals to Conflict Archaeology

No 11 **No Armour But Courage**: Colonel Sir George Lisle, 1615–1648

No 12 **Cromwell's Buffoon**: The Life and Career of the Regicide, Thomas Pride

No 14 **Hey for Old Robin!** The Campaigns and Armies of the Earl of Essex During the First Civil War, 1642–44

No 15 **The Bavarian Army during the Thirty Years War**

No 16 **The Army of James II, 1685-1688**: The Birth of the British Army

No 17 **Civil War London**: A Military History of London under Charles I and Oliver Cromwell

No 18 **The Other Norfolk Admirals**: Myngs, Narbrough and Shovell

No 19 **A New Way of Fighting**: Professionalism in the English Civil War

No 20 **Crucible of the Jacobite '15**: The Battle of Sheriffmuir 1715

No 21 **'A Rabble of Gentility'**: The Royalist Northern Horse, 1644–45

No 22 **Peter the Great Humbled**: The Russo-Ottoman War of 1711

No 23 **The Russian Army In The Great Northern War 1700–21**: Organisation, Matériel, Training, Combat Experience and Uniforms

No 24 **The Last Army**: The Battle of Stow-on-the-Wold and the End of the Civil War in the Welsh Marches, 1646

No 25 **The Battle of the White Mountain 1620 and the Bohemian Revolt, 1618–22**

No 26 **The Swedish Army in the Great Northern War 1700–21**: Organisation, Equipment, Campaigns and Uniforms

No 27 **St. Ruth's Fatal Gamble**: The Battle of Aughrim 1691 and the Fall Of Jacobite Ireland

No 28 **Muscovy's Soldiers**: The Emergence of the Russian Army 1462–1689

No 29 **Home and Away**: The British Experience of War 1618–1721

No 30 **From Solebay to the Texel**: The Third Anglo-Dutch War, 1672–1674

No 31 **The Battle of Killiecrankie**: The First Jacobite Campaign, 1689–1691

No 32 **The Most Heavy Stroke**: The Battle of Roundway Down 1643

No 33 **The Cretan War (1645–1671)**: The Venetian-Ottoman Struggle in the Mediterranean

No 34 **Peter the Great's Revenge**: The Russian Siege of Narva in 1704

No 35 **The Battle Of Glenshiel**: The Jacobite Rising in 1719

No 36 **Armies And Enemies Of Louis XIV**: Volume 1 - Western Europe 1688-1714: France, Britain, Holland

No 37 **William III's Italian Ally**: Piedmont and the War of the League of Augsburg 1683–1697

No 38 **Wars and Soldiers in the Early Reign of Louis XIV**: Volume 1 - The Army of the United Provinces of the Netherlands, 1660–1687

No 39 **In The Emperor's Service**: Wallenstein's Army, 1625–1634

No 40 **Charles XI's War**: The Scanian War Between Sweden and Denmark, 1675–1679

No 41 **The Armies and Wars of The Sun King 1643–1715**: Volume 1: The Guard of Louis XIV

No 42 **The Armies Of Philip IV Of Spain 1621–1665**: The Fight For European Supremacy

No 43 **Marlborough's Other Army**: The British Army and the Campaigns of the First Peninsular War, 1702–1712

No 44 **The Last Spanish Armada**: Britain And The War Of The Quadruple Alliance, 1718–1720

No 45 **Essential Agony**: The Battle of Dunbar 1650

No 46 **The Campaigns of Sir William Waller**

No 47 **Wars and Soldiers in the Early Reign of Louis XIV**: Volume 2 - The Imperial Army, 1660–1689

No 48 **The Saxon Mars and His Force**: The Saxon Army During The Reign Of John George III 1680–1691

No 49 **The King's Irish**: The Royalist Anglo-Irish Foot of the English Civil War

No 50 **The Armies and Wars of the Sun King 1643-1715**: Volume 2: The Infantry of Louis XIV

No 51 **More Like Lions Than Men**: Sir William Brereton and the Cheshire Army of Parliament, 1642–46

No 52 **I Am Minded to Rise**: The Clothing, Weapons and Accoutrements of the Jacobites from 1689 to 1719

No 53 **The Perfection of Military Discipline**: The Plug Bayonet and the English Army 1660–1705

No 54 **The Lion From the North**: The Swedish Army During the Thirty Years War: Volume 1, 1618–1632

No 55 **Wars and Soldiers in the Early Reign of Louis XIV**: Volume 3 - The Armies of the Ottoman Empire 1645–1718

No 56 **St. Ruth's Fatal Gamble**: The Battle of Aughrim 1691 and the Fall Of Jacobite Ireland

No 57 **Fighting for Liberty**: Argyll & Monmouth's Military Campaigns against the Government of King James, 1685

No 58 **The Armies and Wars of the Sun King 1643-1715**: Volume 3: The Cavalry of Louis XIV

No 59 **The Lion From the North**: The Swedish Army During the Thirty Years War: Volume 2, 1632–1648

No 60 **By Defeating My Enemies:** Charles XII of Sweden and the Great Northern War 1682–1721

No 61 **Despite Destruction, Misery and Privations..:** The Polish Army in Prussia during the war against Sweden 1626–1629

No 62 **The Armies of Sir Ralph Hopton:** The Royalist Armies of the West 1642–46

No 63 **Italy, Piedmont, and the War of the Spanish Succession 1701–1712**

No 64 **'Cannon played from the great fort':** Sieges in the Severn Valley during the English Civil War 1642–1646

No 65 **Carl Gustav Armfelt** and the Struggle for Finland During the Great Northern War

No 66 **In the Midst of the Kingdom:** The Royalist War Effort in the North Midlands 1642–1646

No 67 **The Anglo-Spanish War 1655–1660:** Volume 1: The War in the West Indies

No 68 **For a Parliament Freely Chosen:** The Rebellion of Sir George Booth, 1659

No 69 **The Bavarian Army During the Thirty Years War 1618–1648:** The Backbone of the Catholic League (revised second edition)

No 70 **The Armies and Wars of the Sun King 1643–1715:** Volume 4: The War of the Spanish Succession, Artillery, Engineers and Militias

No 71 **No Armour But Courage:** Colonel Sir George Lisle, 1615–1648 (Paperback reprint)

No 72 **The New Knights:** The Development of Cavalry in Western Europe, 1562–1700

No 73 **Cavalier Capital:** Oxford in the English Civil War 1642–1646 (Paperback reprint)

No 74 **The Anglo-Spanish War 1655–1660:** Volume 2: War in Jamaica

No 75 **The Perfect Militia:** The Stuart Trained Bands of England and Wales 1603–1642

No 76 **Wars and Soldiers in the Early Reign of Louis XIV:** Volume 4 - The Armies of Spain 1659–1688

No 77 **The Battle of Nördlingen 1634:** The Bloody Fight Between Tercios and Brigades

No 78 **Wars and Soldiers in the Early Reign of Louis XIV:** Volume 5 - The Portuguese Army 1659–1690

No 79 **We Came, We Saw, God Conquered:** The Polish-Lithuanian Commonwealth's military effort in the relief of Vienna, 1683

No 80 **Charles X's Wars:** Volume 1 - Armies of the Swedish Deluge, 1655–1660

No 81 **Cromwell's Buffoon:** The Life and Career of the Regicide, Thomas Pride (Paperback reprint)

No 82 **The Colonial Ironsides:** English Expeditions under the Commonwealth and Protectorate, 1650–1660

No 83 **The English Garrison of Tangier:** Charles II's Colonial Venture in the Mediterranean, 1661–1684

No 84 **The Second Battle of Preston, 1715:** The Last Battle on English Soil

No 85 **To Settle the Crown:** Waging Civil War in Shropshire, 1642–1648 (Paperback reprint)

No 86 **A Very Gallant Gentleman:** Colonel Francis Thornhagh (1617–1648) and the Nottinghamshire Horse

No 87 **Charles X's Wars:** Volume 2 - The Wars in the East, 1655–1657

No 88 **The Shōgun's Soldiers:** The Daily Life of Samurai and Soldiers in Edo Period Japan, 1603–1721 Volume 1

No 89 **Campaigns of the Eastern Association:** The Rise of Oliver Cromwell, 1642–1645

No 90 **The Army of Occupation in Ireland 1603–42:** Defending the Protestant Hegemony

No 91 **The Armies and Wars of the Sun King 1643–1715:** Volume 5: Buccaneers and Soldiers in the Americas

No 92 **New Worlds, Old Wars:** The Anglo-American Indian Wars 1607–1678

No 93 **Against the Deluge:** Polish and Lithuanian Armies During the War Against Sweden 1655–1660

No 94 **The Battle of Rocroi:** The Battle, the Myth and the Success of Propaganda

No 95 **The Shōgun's Soldiers:** The Daily Life of Samurai and Soldiers in Edo Period Japan, 1603–1721 Volume 2

No 96 **Science of Arms: the Art of War in the Century of the Soldier 1672–1699:** Volume 1: Preparation for War and the Infantry

No 97 **Charles X's Wars:** Volume 3 - The Danish Wars 1657–1660

No 98 **Wars and Soldiers in the Early Reign of Louis XIV:** Volume 6 - Armies of the Italian States 1660–1690 Part 1

No 99 **Dragoons and Dragoon Operations in the British Civil Wars, 1638–1653**

No 100 **Wars and Soldiers in the Early Reign of Louis XIV:** Volume 6 - Armies of the Italian States 1660–1690 Part 2

No 101 **1648 and All That:** The Scottish Invasions of England, 1648 and 1651: Proceedings of the 2022 Helion and Company 'Century of the Soldier' Conference

No 102 **John Hampden and the Battle of Chalgrove:** The Political and Military Life of Hampden and his Legacy

No 103 **The City Horse:** London's militia cavalry during the English Civil War, 1642–1660

No 104 **The Battle of Lützen 1632:** A Reassessment

No 105 **Monmouth's First Rebellion:** The Later Covenanter Risings, 1660–1685

No 106 **Raw Generals and Green Soldiers:** Catholic Armies in Ireland 1641–1643

SERIES SPECIALS:

No 1 **Charles XII's Karoliners:** Volume 1: The Swedish Infantry & Artillery of the Great Northern War 1700–1721

About the author

Pádraig Lenihan lectures in history at the University of Limerick. His recent publications include *Conquest and Resistance: War in 17th Century Ireland* (2001) and *1690 the Battle of the Boyne* (2003). This is his second book for Helion, the first being *Fluxes, Fevers and Fighting Men: War and Disease in Ancien Regime Europe 1648-1789*.

About the artist

Seán Ó'Brógáin is based in Donegal, Ireland. He studied scientific and natural history illustration at Lancaster University and works for a wide range of international clients. His previous artwork for Helion has been included in *St Ruth's Fatal Gamble: The Battle of Aughrim 1691* and *the Fall of Jacobite Ireland, The King's Irish: The Royalist Anglo-Irish Foot of the English Civil War* and *The Men of Warre: The Clothes, Weapons and Accoutrements of the Scots at War 1460–1600*.